A WORLD OF MANY WORLDS

A WORLD OF MANY WORLDS

Edited by Marisol de la Cadena and Mario Blaser

Duke University Press   Durham and London   2018

© 2018 Duke University Press
All rights reserved
Printed in the United States of America on acid-free paper ∞
Designed by Courtney Leigh Baker
Typeset in Whitman by Westchester Publishing Services

Library of Congress Cataloging-in-Publication Data
Names: Cadena, Marisol de la, editor. | Blaser, Mario, [date] editor.
Title: A world of many worlds /
edited by Marisol de la Cadena and Mario Blaser.
Description: Durham : Duke University Press, 2018. |
Includes bibliographical references and index.
Identifiers: LCCN 2018019512 (print)
LCCN 2018027041 (ebook)
ISBN 9781478004318 (ebook)
ISBN 9781478001362 (hardcover : alk. paper)
ISBN 9781478002956 (pbk. : alk. paper)
Subjects: LCSH: Ethnology. | Indigenous peoples. | Environmentalism.
Classification: LCC GN320 (ebook) | LCC GN320 .W75 2018 (print) | DDC 306—dc23
LC record available at https://lccn.loc.gov/2018019512

COVER ART: *Gyration*, 2016. Acrylic on wood. 22 × 28 inches.
© Paula Overbay, courtesy of the artist.

CONTENTS

ACKNOWLEDGMENTS

This volume is the culmination of the Mellon-Sawyer Seminar "Indigenous Cosmopolitics: Dialogues about the Reconstitution of Worlds." It was a long feast for which Mario, Marisol, Joe, Suzana, and Cristiana and a wonder group of students met weekly throughout the academic year 2012–13, which many of us will never forget. We read great work, dined and wined, and talked vibrantly. Our conversations were dialogues toward the reconstitution of worlds—the title of the seminar that brought us together. The material we talked about was authored by the guests at the seminar, a cast that gave us hope and guts to open up thought to new possibilities for the imagination. In order of arrival, our guests were John Law, Elizabeth Povinelli, Marilyn Strathern, Alberto Corsín Jiménez, Isabelle Stengers, Helen Verran, and Eduardo Viveiros de Castro. Along with them, we invited interlocutors: Arturo Escobar, Mary Pratt, Donna Haraway, Judy Farquhar, Karen Barad, Anna Tsing, Debbora Battaglia, and Marianne Lien contributed their brilliance and generosity. During the two days their visit lasted, they were with the collective that we then all became—we were a cloud, a crowd, a forest, a school with no principal. Thanks to all of you for joining us and for your work—it does help toward a world of many worlds!

Any list we could produce will surely miss some people, but we still want to name you. Personal thanks to Arturo Escobar, our constant co-thinker, and Margaret Wiener, always inspiration. While UC faculty members who accompanied us in this effort have already been mentioned, here they are again with their full names: Joe Dumit, Suzana Sawyer, Cristiana

Giordano, Tim Choy, Caren Kaplan, and Mario Biagioli. Colleagues from elsewhere who spent their sabbatical or postdoctoral placement with us or honored us with a visit were Salvador Schavelzon, Hortensia Muñoz, Tanya Richardson, Cristina Rojas, Astrid Stensrud, Filippo Bertoni, Lesley Green, Astrid Oberbeck Andersen, Andrea Ghelfi, Martina Martignoni, and Elaine Gan.

Non–UC Davis (then) students Claire Poirier, Heather Swanson, Pierre du Plessis, Patricia Alvarez Astacio—your presence made us happy. And our great UCD (then) students Enosh Baker, Juan Camilo Cajigas, Xan Chacko, Jake Culbertson, Nicholas D'Avella, Meghan Donnelly, Duskin Drum, Nate Freiburger, Mariel García Llorens, Stefanie Graeter, Ingrid Lagos, Whitney Larrat-Smith, Kristina Lyons, Sarah McCullough, Laura Meek, Sophie Moore, Julia Morales, Rossio Motta, Kevin O'Connor, Diana Pardo, Rima Praspaliauskiene, Magali Rabasa, and Mayee Wong—your enthusiasm was crucial our collective success. Thanks!

We also want to thank the incredible administrative support of UCD staff, particularly Sande Dyer and Yoke Dellenback; also Jennifer Langdon, then at the UCD Humanities Institute, who helped with all administrative aspects of the proposal. Without her and the encouragement of Caroline Thomas, the proposal would not have gotten to the Andrew W. Mellon Foundation, whose support we gratefully acknowledge.

PLURIVERSE

Proposals for a World of Many Worlds

Mario Blaser and Marisol de la Cadena

Unless there is a global catastrophe—a meteorite impact, a world war or a pandemic—mankind will remain a major environmental force for many millennia. A daunting task lies ahead for scientists and engineers to guide society towards environmentally sustainable management during the era of the Anthropocene. This will require appropriate human behaviour at all scales, and may well involve internationally accepted, large-scale geo-engineering projects, for instance to "optimize" climate. At this stage, however, we are still largely treading on terra incognita.

—PAUL J. CRUTZEN, "Geology of Mankind"

Many words are walked in the world. Many worlds are made. Many worlds make us. There are words and worlds that are lies and injustices. There are words and worlds that are truthful and true. In the world of the powerful there is room only for the big and their helpers. In the world we want, everybody fits. The world we want is a world in which many worlds fit.

—EJÉRCITO ZAPATISTA DE LIBERACIÓN NACIONAL,
"Fourth Declaration of the Lacandón Jungle" (our translation)

This volume works in the tension articulated by these two epigraphs. Accompanying the explosion of political and scholarly discussions about the Anthropocene has been the explosion of protests coming from worlds—usually labeled indigenous—currently threatened by the possibility of immediate destruction by anthropogenic practices. In Latin America—the region with which we, the editors of this volume, are most familiar—political and economic forces that first took hold in the sixteenth century have acquired unprecedented destructive might. They have also become hegemonic among governments, regardless of ideological persuasion to the left or right. The scale and speed of destruction have become a central matter of political contention that has pitted environmentalists against what is currently called extractivism: the accelerated extraction of natural resources to satisfy a global demand for minerals and energy and to provide what national governments consider economic growth.[1] Technologically mighty, extractivism is how the Anthropocene makes itself present in this part of the world: what can be more eloquent of human geological force than the removal of mountains in a time-efficient search for minerals, the damming of large bodies of water to reroute rivers for hydroelectric commercial purposes, the transformation of rain forests into palm oil plantations or cattle grasslands and of deserts into land for industrialized agriculture? Frequently effected through necropolitical alliances between the state and corporations, and said to serve the national common good, these practices create expendable populations in massive proportions. Environmentalists claim that accelerated extraction destroys nature; investors claim that it develops backward regions. We hold that what is currently being destroyed is also other-than-human persons because what extractivist and environmentalist practices enact as nature may be, *also*, other than such. This is one of the things we (the editors) have learned from a mountain in the Andes of Peru that is also a being and from forest animals in Paraguay that are also spirit masters of their world. We have also learned that their destruction, perhaps unlike the destruction of nature, is hard for analysts to grasp. Similarly, making public these kinds of other-than-humans is difficult for those who live with them; translating their destruction into a political issue is often impossible and even disempowering. After all, hegemonic opinion is that nature is—publicly—only nature; to think otherwise, to think that mountains or animals are other-than-human persons is a cultural belief.[2]

We locate this collection in the critical space opened by the tension between the scholarly and political recognition of the ecological crisis that threatens to eradicate life on Earth and the obstinate demands for existence presented by worlds whose disappearance was assumed at the outset of the Anthropocene. The tension is, of course, not new. However, awareness of the possible destruction of life on the planet gives this tension a dynamic specific to the current historical moment: if, before this sense of crisis, "the world of the powerful"—let's call it so, and take it to mean, following the

Zapatista declaration, a world where only one world fits—could disavow the destruction of life that it effected, this is no longer the case. The world of the powerful is now sensitive to the plausibility of its own destruction in a way that may compare, at least in some ways, with the threat imposed on worlds sentenced to disappearance in the name of the common goods of progress, civilization, development, and liberal inclusion. Very few, if any, of the readers of *Nature* can currently deny that the planet is being driven down a perilous path. We all share, as Crutzen says, terra incognita. This is a new condition: now the colonizers are as threatened as the worlds they displaced and destroyed when they took over what they called *terra nullius*. Scientific and economic proposals that would make it possible to survive the moment of planetary crisis are many and diverse. Not infrequently they come from rivals, and at times they involve strange alliances. Proposals range from market-friendly environmentalisms to an end of capitalism as the only path to salvation, and even the composition of the common world through a due process that needs to be devised—who would devise it and how the process would transpire is up for discussion. Across their heterogeneity, proposals share an unsurprising—if discouraging—trait in common: it seems almost impossible to imagine a response to the ecological crisis that does not take the world that is responsible for the plausible destruction of the planet as the exclusive starting point in a conversation about the current condition of the planet.

Many practices allegedly intended to save the planet continue to destroy it. Along with extractivism, such practices manifest the contemporary colonial ontological occupation of territories by what John Law has called the one-world world: a world that has granted itself the right to assimilate all other worlds and, by presenting itself as exclusive, cancels possibilities for what lies beyond its limits.[3] Extractivism continues the practice of terra nullius: it actively creates space for the tangible expansion of the one world by rendering empty the places it occupies and making absent the worlds that make those places. And because central attempts to save the planet are frequently indifferent to those worlds, grassroots protests against extractivism have mushroomed; while they are not exclusively a matter of indigenous concern, groups known as indigenous figure prominently in creative, difficult, and complex partnerships with allies hailing from heterogeneous worlds: nongovernmental organizations, peasants, Afro-descendant groups in Latin America, organic produce growers, small merchants, some workers' unions, university students, liberation theology priests and nuns, feminist lawyers, and, of course, environmentalists. Within these alliances, nature is practiced both as such and not only as such; their goal is to defend the specific ways they make their lives and worlds against extractivist destruction. Their alliance is summoned by what Isabelle Stengers calls "interests in common which are not the same interests," or what we see as the making of an "uncommons": the negotiated coming together of heterogeneous worlds (and their practices) as they strive for what makes each of them be what they are, which is also not without others.[4] We return to the uncommons at the end of this introduction; for now, suffice it to say that built upon a heterogeneity that negotiates for symmetry (if with difficulty), these alliances reveal that the commonality touted in claims about the national common good is an imposition: to be such it requires the destruction of what the state cannot recognize. Instead, acknowledging the uncommons that brings them together—an interest in nature or the environment that acknowledges neither is only such—these alliances may also be capable of refracting the course of the one-world world and proposing, as in the Zapatista declaration, the practice of a world of many worlds, or what we call a pluriverse: heterogeneous worldings coming together as a political ecology of practices, negotiating their difficult being together in heterogeneity. We are inspired by the Zapatista invitation to reworlding possibilities. The moment of the realization of the destruction of the Earth, the current historical moment, can be one when people reconsider the requirement that worlds be destroyed. It can also be one when the conditions for dialogues toward the reconstitution of worlds can be formulated. Thus, we want to pair up the threat posed by the Anthropocene with an opportunity of similar proportion, by taking the present as a moment to reconsider the material-semiotic grammar of *the relation* among worlds that dominates the fabrication of the current historical moment. It is toward that reconsideration that we propose the pluriverse as an analytic tool useful for producing ethnographic compositions capable of conceiving ecologies of practices across heterogeneous(ly) entangled worlds.

Our proposal for the pluriverse as analytic is not only an abstraction: being ethnographic, it emerges from our variously mediated (yet embodied) experiences of worldings that fieldwork confronted us with, and that incited us toward a disposition to be attentive to practices that make worlds even if they do not satisfy our demand (the demand of modern epistemology) to prove their reality (as they do not leave historical evidence, let alone scientific). Examples include human practices with earth beings and with animal spirits that populate forests. Emerging from (and requiring) this disposition, the pluriverse is not a matter of fact or concern but rather an opening toward a possibility that needs care—a "matter of care" as conceptualized by Maria Puig de la Bella Casa.[5]

Presenting the pluriverse as an ethnographic proposal requires a caveat: we think of ethnography as a scholarly genre that conceptually weaves together those sites (and sources) called the theoretical and the empirical so that thereafter they cannot be pulled apart. Practiced in this way, ethnography becomes a concept-making genre—yet ethnographic concepts are idiosyncratically (and perhaps oxymoronically) concrete abstractions. With a disposition toward the pluriverse, ethnographic concepts may also indicate excesses to the theoretical and the empirical—think earth beings or animal spirits that populate the forests once again. Unlike theoretical or philosophical concepts, ethnographic concepts signal their connections to place, for they are not without it. They emerge through the hallmark practice anthropology calls fieldwork. Yet, rather than a means of collecting information, we think of fieldwork as the practice of (and not only at) a crossroads involving the practices of the anthropologist and of those that she works with.[6] At this crossroads, ethnographic concepts are composed with both the separation and the connection that constitute fieldwork practices. Composed ethnographically, these concepts emerge with the awareness that they constitute practices and are, thus, worlding tools. As such, ethnographic concepts lie within the field of political ontology.

We use the term "political ontology" to designate an imaginary for a politics of reality, and a field that stands where political economy and political ecology, formulated with ideas of nature and economic growth, are insufficient (at times even unable) to think antagonisms that, for example, involve things like mountains and forests that emerge as resources through some practices but also as persons through other practices. Where political economy will only accept that, at bottom, such conflicts are about the distribution of resources, political ecology (especially in its post-structuralist version) can only upend the analysis a bit: at best the conflicts are between perspectives on the mountain or the forest, neither of which cease to ultimately be only what they are. In our work, political ontology emerged as a concept at the specific historical moment when anthropocenic practices (such as extractivism) seemed to almightily lean against the plausibility of the pluriverse: in those circumstances, the contention between, for example, practices of intense deforestation and local persons' practices with what we would call forests could be a matter concerning political ontology. Yet political ontology can also underpin the negotiations within the above-mentioned alliances among heterogeneous worlding practices that come together around dissimilar interests in common. Regardless of the analytical condition, political ontology wants to enable political thought and practice beyond the onto-epistemic limits of modern politics and what its practice allows. We capitalize the concept—therefore Political Ontology—to call attention to the specificity of the imaginary that we propose here, namely, the consideration of the pluriverse as a possibility. Political Ontology, as we are using it here, operates on the presumption of divergent worldings constantly coming about through negotiations, enmeshments, crossings, and interruptions. It asks how those practices transpire and with what consequences. Political Ontology thus simultaneously stands for reworking an imaginary of politics (the pluriverse), for a field of study and intervention (the power-charged terrain of entangled worldings and their dynamics), and for a modality of analysis and critique that is permanently concerned with its own effects as a worlding practice.

The rest of this introduction presents the chapters as they engage three thematic axes: concepts as worlding tools, the reworking of politics in terms of the pluriverse, and the Anthropocene as a scenario of politics characterized by an undeclared war.

It Matters What Concepts We Use to Think Concepts

Inasmuch as knowledges are world-making practices, they tend to make the worlds they know. The seeming redundancy of this phrase—which echoes our interpretation of the title of the section, a phrase we borrow from Marilyn Strathern[7]—emphasizes that the knowledge practices we (modern scholars) have at our disposal are, in turn, conditioned to reinstate themselves. A consequence of this feature is that it may perform epistemic and ontological invalidations—or absences—of the possibility of the multiplicity of worlds that the Zapatista declaration calls for. This concern underpins all the chapters in this volume: they show a persistent care for the conceptual grammars through which, on rendering itself and its objects intelligible, scholarly knowledge performs itself. In other words, knowledge is recursive: knowledge reveals itself by making its objects (conceptual or material) through procedures that need to be recognizable (as knowledge) by the community that practices it. What the community of knowers does not recognize as knowledge is displaced along with its reality-making possibilities. As Marilyn Strathern puts it in chapter 1, "knowledge" the concept is a means to knowledge and, in the case of scholarly, modern knowledge, deploying the concept and its requirements, to thus move from means to end (knowledge), may constitute both the subject and object of its practice. Hence the relevance of concepts as a matter of ethnographic concern: as analytic tools—tools used to produce knowledge—they carry a self-duplicating potential that may "explain difference away." The latter is a phrase Helen Verran has made popular to warn about epistemic explanations that may translate difference back to their image and thus cancel the difference. Emerging from the world modern knowledge makes, its concepts and grammars have the capacity to assimilate practices (and also concepts and grammars) that diverge from it. Take, for example, "culture"—"one of the most complicated words in the English language," according to Raymond Williams.[8] He explains that this notion emerged in its modern sense during the late eighteenth and early nineteenth centuries when it was used to differentiate between European and other human groups.[9] Intriguingly, therefore, culture has a history that is itself embedded in the history and imaginary it helped articulate: that of a world populated by heterogeneous human groups. Hence the limits of deploying culture to represent such heterogeneity: explaining through categories that made the difference appear in the first place may amount to explaining the difference through "the same," or difference in terms that are homologous to the self to which difference appears. For example, deploying culture to explain differences that emerge in collectives that do not make themselves with such categories would enact culture and explain away, or block, the possibility of difference as it might emerge if the situation were allowed to display itself without categories awaiting it.[10] There would be knowledge of difference indeed; but that knowledge would be of cultural difference: knowledge enabled and delimited by the practice of the category deployed (culture).

The proposition that modern knowledge co-constitutes subject and object resonates with Alberto Corsín Jiménez's contribution, chapter 2. He proposes "trap" as a concept and ethnographic tool to search the relations that compose and perform knowledge. As a concept, the trap also works as a machine: a gathering of heterogeneously composed relations and conditions required to capture prey that therefore is also of the predator's design. In this sense, the trap works as an interface, proposing that, just as prey and predator are trapped to (and with) each other, the subject and the object of modern knowledge cannot be conceptually (or practically) separated from one another. Recursively making a concept full of relations—trap—to think about concepts (and the relations that make them), the chapter itself illustrates the working of a trap, or a method that releases what it makes or traps and in so doing enables an analytical view of the requirements of modern knowledge. With the notion of a trap, Corsín also signals the importance of the material composition of knowledge: subject to creative originality, its architecture conditions what it catches, but the catch can also surprise the trap maker (within the conditions of the trap we would think).

The systematic recursivity of the chapter is inspired by Roy Wagner's ethnographic analysis of "double encompassment," a condition Wagner illustrates with an analysis of "hospitality as self-guesting": a situation where the conditions of guest and host exist within the same entity. For example, a shaman is guest to the land while, as one of the threads that constitute it, he or she also is the land. Or a soul is guest to a body, which is not without it. These "double captivities" (or "hostings," depending on the situation) are Wagner's ethnographic concepts.[11] As such, they may allow for conceptual transformations of modern epistemic tools while being made by the latter—a double enabling. Corsín Jiménez uses Wagner's doubling as insight to recursively search the relations with which modern knowledge produces itself. In this sense, he writes, "It is in fact one of my central intuitions that modern knowledge is essentially a trap to itself, such that most forms of 'explanation' are guests unaware they are actually being hosted— predators who do not know their own condition as prey."

Chapter 1 is also concerned with knowledge. Strathern anchors her discussion in encounters among worlds that compose themselves, the encounters, and indeed the knowledges and practices brought to them, with heterogeneous tools—including heterogeneous forms of relation. She thus sets out to open up—or look into—the diverse relations (the forms and compositions that make them count as such) that transpire at encounters and even make them possible without becoming the same relation. She uses the term "domain," a notion she has productively deployed in previous works.[12] Domain is both empty (enough) of conceptual meaning and capable of carrying empirical reference to thus allow analysis. Domain may signal spheres of life; for example, we say that the modern world makes itself with the domains of nature and culture and recognizes itself in such division. Encounters (everyday, or extraordinary) across partially connected (and also heterogeneous) worlds may be sustained by conversations that draw from domains in which not all participants in the encounter participate. Continuing with our recent example, not all worlds make themselves with the domains of nature and culture, nor with the epistemic relationship between, say, subject and object that may ensue from it. When such domains are deployed, what transpires and the way it does may not be the same across the worlds that participate in the encounter. Refreshing this conversation—to which she has contributed for a long time[13]—in chapter 1, Marilyn Strathern discusses cases in which the unshared or divergent element is the relation itself. As a means to make knowledge and to organize exchanges, divergence among relations—not only in terms of when they are established or what they connect or disconnect, but in what counts as relation itself—acquires complex saliency in circumstances of knowledge exchanges between, for example, scientists and indigenous ritual practitioners about an event that concerns both, albeit in ways that are not the same.

Divergence is a concept Strathern uses in chapter 1 and with which, in this text, she converses with Isabelle Stengers.[14] Given the specificity of this concept, a brief explanation is necessary. Divergence, as proposed by Stengers, does not refer to difference between people, practices, or cultures conceived as discrete entities that share constitutive properties and therefore can be compared (and thus be similar or different).[15] Rather, divergence constitutes the entities (or practices) as they emerge both in their specificity and with other entities or practices.[16] Strathern foregrounds the knowledge encounters with which she illustrates her arguments as a situation of divergence: for example, an encounter around dead bodies that is both an encounter (a relation) with the kin of one of the groups that participate and with repositories of scientific knowledge. Both groups had an interest in common (knowledge exchange), yet what constituted knowledge (what the dead bodies became as they emerged from relations specific to the groups) was a site of divergence—a disagreement that could not be solved without undoing what each of the groups were in relation to their interest in common: the dead bodies and knowledge exchange.

Significantly, Strathern seems to be saying that the scholarly knowledge practices that make dialogues may include incommensurabilities. Dialogue may be the site of divergence, and thus house an interest in common that is also exceeded by interests that are not the same. Critically, excesses across knowledges (ours and others') and hence not-knowing (as we and they usually know) may be an important condition of dialogues that allow for a form of understanding that does not require sameness, and therefore rather than canceling divergence is constituted by it. It may be important at this point to remind the reader that we are not talking about difference understood as a different (cultural) perspective on dead bodies, the object that both scientific knowers and their cultural others would share yet interpret differently (each from their cultural perspective). Instead, we are talking about the intersecting of understanding and divergence at a partial connection: an encounter of knowledge practices (and entities) as they also continue to exceed each other (in divergence). What constitutes the excess may be obscure to participants in the conversation, yet it would also be constitutive of it. Elements in the dialogue may rest unknown: that may be an awkward condition, yet not a deterrent for conversations across worlds.

Can conditions be created so that heterogeneous knowledge practices (indigenous and nonindigenous, for example) do not encounter each other in a relation of subjects to objects? (Or not only in such relation?) Chapter 1 may suggest such a question; Helen Verran, in chapter 4, may offer grounds to think possible responses. An important assumption of her proposal is that concepts are world-making tools and therefore particular to worlds and their knowers—yet concepts (different from those participants bring with them) can also be made in the here and now of knowledge encounters maintaining the difference between knowers. In situations of knowledge encounters, she explains, there is nothing that everybody knows, for participants are all heterogeneous knowers—yet they need to be aware of such a condition. Doing so requires them to cultivate a specific epistemic demeanor, consisting in the ability to articulate the how and what of their divergent epistemic practices—their knowledges. Bringing crucial attention to the figure of the knower, her proposal is to enable an ethical politics of doing difference together without any participating know-how canceling any other one. This is a politics in which the negotiated agreement through which concepts emerge in the encounter does not cancel differences among knowers; rather, it makes those differences visible as the epistemic then and there from where participants come to the encounter, and which they have to be ready to leave behind (while maintaining awareness of how they go about making them). The encounter thus becomes the opportunity for the creation of concepts different from those every participating knower brought with them.

Verran's proposal is sustained empirically: ideas for the process were produced by participants in a project to create the Garma Maths Curriculum—an entity emerging in conversations between modern math and Yolngu Aboriginal ways of measuring and counting (that were not a practice of mathematics). Promoted by the liberal Australian state in the 1980s, it was taken up by Aboriginal and white Australians interested in doing difference together. Using Strathern's terms, the Garma Maths Curriculum would be one with no subject knowledge creating its object knowledge. The process required from participants in the encounter, first, to not know as they would know as either a modern thinker or a Yolngu thinker; and, second, to compose with what emerged to them unmediated by their knowledges. Verran characterizes the first requirement as "bad will," cultivating a feeling of alertness with respect to one's own habits of knowledge so as to be able to reject the temptation, always present, to propose one's common sense to think difference. Exercising bad will, the knower is able to do both—recognize the demands of her knowledge and refuse to implement them; in so doing, she may acquire the capacity to attend to what emerges in the here and now of the space opened by the shifting of the two conditions, with and without the requirements. This is the stage for the practice of the second requirement, which Verran calls "good faith": a commitment to articulate analysis with the conditions that constitute the here and now of the encounter itself with participants emerging self-different, not only what they were, while remaining aware of their there and then as well. When difference is done together, none of the heterogeneous knower participants becomes the other, yet they do not remain only what they were either.

This mode of participation requires working at the site of divergence, where the coincidence among participants does not absorb their being who they are. This may create the conditions for a decolonial practice where modern thinkers—herself, the readers, us—may be caught (as Verran was) in analytical and experiential incongruous discomfort (for example, both criticizing and understanding the requirements of Yolngu practices, or of mathematics) that is not only such, for they also make sense: they work in different registers, may talk to each other, and offer space to work toward making mutual differences emerge. The incongruous discomfort creates a welcome disjuncture—one that does not make the usual sense and where difference can be made together. This is, Verran says, a cosmopolitical practice: the working together of divergent cosmologies where knowers (and not just her entities or concepts) dissolve themselves (are able to give up and maintain their there and then) in the practice of the here and now of a knowledge encounter that produces a know-how that becomes through the encounter and includes what was there before, yet it also changes it.

Cosmopolitics Meets Political Ontology

Cosmopolitics is a concept that we originally borrowed from Isabelle Stengers.[17] She originally proposed it with the intent of opening modern politics to the possibility of divergence among collectives composed of humans and nonhumans that, following her (Greek-inspired) definition of politics, agreed to gather around a concern. Members of these collectives all recognized the importance of the concern and could also disagree about it precisely because they could recognize its importance. Among the events inspiring Stengers's cosmopolitics was the European anti-GMO movement bringing together young urbanites, farmers, and biologists from the Continent along with African and Indian peasants—all with their own specific reasons to resist GMOs. The movement made all these groups interdependent: the anti-GMO collective expressed an interest in common that was not the same interest. It was underpinned by the divergence among the groups that composed the collective.

In chapter 3, Stengers explains that the demands posed by Political Ontology exceed her original conception. We agree: we used Political Ontology to suggest a politics among heterogeneous worlds and called this a cosmopolitics, a notion whereby cosmos is always an emergent condition resulting from disagreements among divergent worlding practices participating in the discussion. Thus, we borrowed cosmopolitics from Stengers and gave the term an inflection of our own.[18] Grounded in ethnographic situations, for us cosmopolitics was a tool to think about disputes (we can also call them gatherings) that concerned and included participants whose presence was not recognized by all who participated in the gatherings. As mentioned, our paradigmatic ethnographic examples involved a mountain that is also an earth being and forest animals that are also spirit masters of their world. We called them other-than-humans (instead of nonhumans) to emphasize that, while actors, they did not share the epistemic or on-tological status of laboratory things.[19] We also proposed that these other-than-humans participated in political gatherings (usually convoked in connection with their potential destruction) both as existents (but not nature or humans) and as beliefs (about nature). The dispute about what these other-than-humans were, which depended on the relations that enacted them, composed a complex negotiation that included cultural tolerance (or intolerance) of "indigenous beliefs" and ontological politics (through enactments of the entities in question and the denial of their being—other than beliefs).

Engaging our ethnographic setting, Stengers suggests that tolerance may protect what she calls "those that know" (for example, "that other-than-humans are beliefs about nature") from a frightening prospect: that of having to consider that those practices and entities they deem unreal (and destined for extinction) could present themselves with the power to create a situation where ontological clashes would have to be anticipated everywhere without offering guarantees for the preservation of that which makes "those that know" who they are. She calls this prospect the "chal-lenge of animism": it is frightening because it unsettles what she calls the modern command "to not regress" to a supposed earlier stage when "we" were unable to discern reality from belief. This command, she says, makes us (those that know) who we are: those that move forward protected against past illusions. Rejecting what we consider regression, we form a collective that disdains others that we also tolerate as we wait for their disappearance, or actively destroy them when driven by intolerance. The fright that animism produces is not irrelevant; it may level the terrain, for "when ontological politics demands that we take seriously the existence and power of other-than-human beings, it is we who cry: do not demand that we do that when we ourselves are concerned, or you will destroy us" (Stengers, this volume.) Hence the possibility of animism threatens those that were not previously threatened with extinction; the prospect that what makes them be could be taken away from them frightens them. This op-portunity is not to be lost, and accordingly, animism should be reclaimed. This, Stengers clarifies, does not mean that the reality of other-than-human beings needs to be proven. Doing so would imply translating practices with those entities into the sphere that distinguishes "those who know" from "those who believe." Instead, reclaiming animism might translate, among other things, into recovering that which we (those who know) have been expropriated from and regenerating the practices that the expropriation has destroyed.[20]

To draw an image of what she means by "expropriation," Stengers uses the figure of the testator, the character who tested (the reality of) what alchemists presented to a prince as gold. Like a prince would do with his testator, we have delegated to a routinized debunking habit (for example, a proclivity to demand epistemic or historical evidence) the charge of protecting us from what cannot demonstrate its "real" existence. Snickering is a manifestation of that debunking habit; even the possibility of questioning such a habit is met with a smirk. Escaping the compulsion to debunk as nonexistent that which we (those who know) cannot recognize (which could have as concomitant sequel its destruction, either immediate or tolerantly deferred) requires that we face our fear of animism so as to betray it and thus recompose ourselves as the situation demands. Recomposing does not mean making ourselves larger or more comprehensive by adding the practices that make other-than-humans to the practices with which "those who know" make nature—mountains or animals—to follow our example. That would make us all the same and cancel the divergences among heterogeneity that make us who we are. Recomposing ourselves means disowning our testator's habit so as to recover the capacity that Stengers calls "the pragmatic art of immanent attention." This she describes as "an empirical practice of 'realization'" ("realization" is Whitehead's term) and "an art of diagnosis, which our addiction for 'the truth that defeats illusion' has too often despised as too weak and uncertain." Translating Stengers to our goal in this volume: nurtured by what Helen Verran calls "bad will"—the practice of a deliberate abjuration to the transcendence of the "then and there" that makes us who "we" are—immanent attention could include the ability to attend to presences that are or can be but do not meet the requirements of modern knowledge and therefore cannot be proven in its terms.

The Anthropocene as an Opportunity
for Pluriversal Worldings

The phenomena bagged under the term Anthropocene disrupt the nature/culture divide that had made the world one. Seemingly, then, Anthropocene houses a paradox. On the one hand, by revealing the historicity of the nature/culture divide, it opens a crack through which modern knowers can consider the possibility of collectives that do not make themselves through such a divide, and in turn these collectives can make a bid to emerge into a public space that effectively excluded them until now. On the other hand, modern knowers know about this event through an epistemic regime that rests on the divide under question. In this context, it is worth asking how the commitment to the one world occurs in practice.

Chapter 5 sheds some light on how the one-world commitment works. John Law and Marianne Lien's contribution is a detailed rendering of how nature (and culture) is done along with salmon in Norway. By attending to the practices that make a nature-culture entity (salmon), their chapter complicates the now well-known argument that modern knowledge represents culture as multiple and nature as singular, coherent, and stable. Following the practices that make both wild and farmed salmon (as well as the distinctions between them), they describe how, rather than singular, these practices make a nature that is multiple, noncoherent, and ongoing. And yet, they say, the assumption of a single nature holds. They surmise that at least in part this is because each practice of nature assumes and enacts a single world, a unified space-time container where the multiplicities of practices occur. In this way, chapter 5 suggests that not even awareness of the notion of nature as done by humans (or culture) undoes the assumption of a one-world world.

Analogously, we suggest that to open up the possibility of a world where many worlds fit, it is not enough for the Anthropocene to disrupt the nature and culture divide that makes the world one. Rather, the practices that render the Anthropocene visible—as well as the proposals for survival—must also disrupt such a divide. As a matter of planetary concern, the Anthropocene requires analyses and proposals that would reveal the inner workings of the one-world world so as to prevent their destructive capacity—including when they work as tolerance to what is not itself. This is an overriding concern in chapter 6, by Eduardo Viveiros de Castro and Déborah Danowski. They take issue with Chakrabarty's argument that the Anthropocene could only be met by the human species, which would emerge as subject only after the realization by all of humanity of its common doomed destiny as implied by the Anthropocene.[21] In other words, differences would stand in the way of self-preservation of the species and, paradoxically, could only be overcome, if at all, by the threat of common demise. To this proposal Viveiros de Castro and Danowski respond that the problem is not one of the human species fighting internally along lines of self-destruction or self-preservation and therefore needing unity. Instead, they say that while there are two camps in conflict, culprits and victims, the dividing line that forms the camps is not simply internal to *Homo sapiens*. Forming the camps are entire assemblages of humans and nonhumans (think of organisms such as transgenic soy whose very existence depends on that complex assemblage we call industrial capitalism). Thus, they argue, while it is very hard to trace the lines between one camp and the other (most humans and nonhumans enrolled are victims and culprits at once), it is important not to lose sight of the difference between assemblages that are thoroughly invested in the practices that generate the Anthropocene and those that are more or less forcefully dragged along. The authors identify the former as Humans; they call the latter Terrans.

Who are the Terrans? Viveiros de Castro and Danowski do not have a definite answer to this question; however, they do have a sense that Terrans are not a molar body, a Deleuzian whole that is self-similar in spite of its variations. They also reject the idea that a big-scale problem must be given a big-scale solution. Rather, they ask if it is not precisely a reduction of scales that the Anthropocene calls for. What they call the people of Pachamama, those myriad worlds who, since the conquest of the Americas, have been encroached on and damaged, could be an example of the Terrans. Distinguishing between Humans and Terrans allows an engagement with the current fate of the planet that takes stock of the colonial destruction of worlds as the destruction that the culprits of the Anthropocene imposed on its victims. The peculiarity of this destruction is that, waged in the name of progress (or under the command not to regress, as Stengers would say), it has never been recognized as such. Paradoxically, the end of the world as we know it may mean the end of its being made through destruction: facing destruction at an unprecedented rate, the collectives that colonialism—in its earliest and latest versions—doomed to extinction emerge to publicly denounce the principles of their destruction, which may coincide with the assumptions that made a one-world world.

Could the moment of the Anthropocene bring to the fore the possibility of the pluriverse? Could it offer the opportunity for a condition to emerge that, instead of destruction, thrives on the encounter of heterogeneous worldings, taking place alongside each other with their divergent here(s) and now(s), and therefore makes of their taking place a negotiation of their going on together in divergence? Can the Anthropocene be the scenario of both the end of the world (as hegemonically conceived and practiced) and the inauguration of what Helen Verran calls "a cosmopolitics as the politics of collectively doing cosmologies together and separately"? That the latter phrase was inspired by Verran's work with her Yolngu colleagues makes for a hopeful answer.

A Speculative Opening, Not a Conclusion

Almost fifty years ago, Pierre Clastres suggested that the limitations of anthropology were a consequence of its habit of following the road mapped by its own world. He deemed that road "the easiest road," one that could be "followed blindly." Away from the limits of anthropology's own world and on a different road, he proposed "taking seriously" the men and women inhabiting what he conceptualized as "primitive societies . . . from every viewpoint," even from those that negated those of "the Western world." "It is imperative to accept . . . that negation does not signify nothingness; that when the mirror does not reflect our own likeness it does not prove there is nothing."[22] Currently, the limitations facing anthropology are not felt by the discipline only. They are experienced beyond anthropology as a result of the upheaval of the crisis facing the planet expressed in the word Anthropocene, allegedly the "most influential concept in environmental studies over the past decade."[23] The crisis this word (and cognates) brings to the conceptual fore may also offer some critical opportunity to slow down thought and take time to consider the possibility of nature that is not only such like the mountains and forest animals that have inspired our works and this discussion. We echo Clastres and translate his ideas to our proposal: the absence of our image does not reflect nothingness. Our proposal takes the opportunity of the current planetary crisis to invite anthropology to reckon with the idea that much of what the discipline deemed cultural beliefs might be *not only* such. This invitation may be difficult to accept. Many will deem it irresponsible, warn us of its dangers, and turn around shaking their heads in irritation.

Our proposal affects modern disciplines and their forms of knowledge. It questions the power granted to their capacity to distribute the real-real (or the natural-real) from the cultural-real as well as the benevolent authority with which they permit the latter (not infrequently as a lesser presence.) We consider all these—the division that distributes realities as well as the combination of power and benevolence that sustains it—as historical events. We then suggest that such capacity might be limited to the province of the division that those disciplines and their knowledges require;

not meeting those requirements (or "absence of their likeness," Clastres would say) may indicate an excess to such division, not the emptiness of nonexistence, and not only the workings of culture. In such cases, rather than concluding that there is nothing to talk about, conversations about what *is* might take place in a political field—political ontology—where modern knowledges may or may not present themselves as an exclusive decision-making field or result in one.

The proposal does destabilize a hegemonic state of affairs; the irritation of those so destabilized is to be expected—even understandable. But the proposal is not irresponsible. Instead, it alters the conditions of the response, which would now include the obligation to consider (rather than denying) the possibility (of being) of that which does not reflect the image of the hegemonic order of things. Considering that the power of modern disciplines and their knowledges to cancel the possibility of what emerges beyond their grasp was a historical event (the result of a coloniality that needs not be such), our proposal offers those disciplines the possibility to use their creative might differently: without the undisputable certainty of superiority, and accepting that rather than resting on colonial world-making, their prevalence could be achieved in constant negotiation with worlding practices that might not—or might not only—reflect them.

Our proposal also opens space to rethink what a political circumstance might be and how it might become. To partake in political gatherings, or to be considered a political matter, entities (or, perhaps, events and relations) would not require, like current practices of politics demand, to (re)present themselves deploying historical (or scientific) evidence of existence. They would instead be required to present themselves with what makes them be— in all their heterogeneity. Our proposal is an invitation to think that instead of the sameness that recognition supposes, politics might not start from, nor resolve in ontologically homogeneous grounds. Rather, the grounds of adversarial dispute or of allied agreement would be what we call uncommons.

And this is our last point: we propose uncommons as counterpoint to the common good and to enclosures, and, as important, to slow down the commons (including its progressive versions.) While usually deployed across adversarial political positions, all three concepts converge in that they require a common form of relation, one that (like labor or property) connects humans and nature conceived as ontologically distinct and detached from each other. Any of these three concepts—including the commons in its progressive version—may cancel the possibility of worldings that diverge from the ontological divisions and relational forms they require. Repeating that "it is important what concepts think concepts," and to avoid cancelling divergence, we propose the uncommons as the heterogeneous grounds where negotiations take place toward a commons that would be a continuous achievement, an event whose vocation is not to be final because it remembers that the uncommons is its constant starting point.

NOTES

1. Eduardo Gudynas, "El Nuevo Extractivismo Progresista," *El Observador del OBIE* 8 (2010): 1–10; Anthony Bebbington, "Political Ecologies of Resource Extraction: Agendas Pendientes," ERLACS 100 (2015): 85–98; Fabiana Li, *Unearthing Conflict: Corporate Mining, Activism, and Expertise in Peru* (Durham, NC: Duke University Press, 2015); Maristella Svampa, "Commodities Consensus: Neoextractivism and Enclosure of the Commons in Latin America," *South Atlantic Quarterly* 114, no. 1 (2015): 65–82.

2. Mario Blaser, "The Threat of the Yrmo: The Political Ontology of a Sustainable Hunting Program," *American Anthropologist* 111, no. 1 (2009): 10–20; Mario Blaser, "Notes Towards a Political Ontology of 'Environmental' Conflicts," in *Contested Ecologies: Nature and Knowledge*, ed. Lesley Green, 13–27 (Cape Town: HSRC Press, 2013); Marisol de la Cadena, "Indigenous Cosmopolitics in the Andes: Conceptual Reflections beyond 'Politics,'" *Cultural Anthropology* 25, no. 2 (2010): 334–70; Marisol de la Cadena, *Earth Beings: Ecologies of Practice across Andean Worlds* (Durham, NC: Duke University Press, 2015).

3. John Law, "What's Wrong with a One-World World?," *Distinktion: Scandinavian Journal of Social Theory* 16, no. 1 (2015): 126–39. On the idea of ontological occupation, see Arturo Escobar, *Autonomía y Diseño: La Realización de lo comunal* (Popayan, Colombia: Editorial de la Universidad del Cauca, 2016).

4. See Isabelle Stengers, "Introductory Notes on an Ecology of Practices," *Cultural Studies Review* 1, no. 1 (2005):183–96; and Isabelle Stengers, "Comparison as a Matter of Concern," *Common Knowledge* 17, no. 1 (2011): 60.

5. Maria Puig de la Bellacasa, "Matters of Care in Technoscience: Assembling Neglected Things," *Social Studies of Science* 41, no. 1 (2011): 85–106; Maria Puig de la Bellacasa, *Matters of Care: Speculative Ethics in More Than Human Worlds* (Minneapolis: University of Minnesota Press, 2017).

6. As a practice of/at the crossroads of practices, fieldwork is a site of many sites, localized and also nomadic; it includes sites away from the ethnographer's office but does not end there.

7. Marilyn Strathern, *Reproducing the Future: Essays on Anthropology, Kinship and the New Reproductive Technologies* (Manchester: University of Manchester Press, 1992).

8. Raymond Williams, *Keywords: A Vocabulary of Culture and Society*, rev. ed. (Oxford: Oxford University Press, 1983), 87.

9. Williams, *Keywords*, 88–93.

10. "Difference" here is a placeholder, an empty signifier for what would emerge in the absence of culture as world-making category.

11. Roy Wagner, "'Luck in the Double Focus': Ritualized Hospitality in Melanesia," *Journal of the Royal Anthropological Institute* 18, no. S1 (2012): S161–S174.

12. Marilyn Strathern, *The Gender of the Gift: Problems with Women and Problems with Society in Melanesia* (Berkeley: University of California Press, 1988).

13. Marilyn Strathern, "No Nature, No Culture: The Hagen Case," in *Nature, Culture and Gender*, ed. Carol P. MacCormack and Marilyn Strathern, 174–222 (Cambridge: Cambridge University Press, 1980).

14. Marilyn Strathern uses "divergence" in previous texts as well—perhaps not in conversation with Stengers. See Marilyn Strathern, *Kinship, Law, and the Unexpected: Relatives Are Always a Surprise* (Cambridge: Cambridge University Press, 2005), 7; see also Stengers, "Introductory Notes on an Ecology of Practices."

15. Those differences, the relation that makes them, and their explanation would be within the same domain.

16. Importantly, divergence is a tool to think what we have called "interests in common that are not the same interest." Stengers, "Comparison as a Matter of Concern."

17. Stengers, "Introductory Notes on an Ecology of Practices." See also de la Cadena, "Indigenous Cosmopolitics in the Andes."

18. See Stengers, "Introductory Notes on an Ecology of Practices."

19. See de la Cadena, "Indigenous Cosmopolitics in the Andes"; de la Cadena, *Earth Beings*; Blaser, "The Threat of the Yrmo"; Blaser, "Notes Towards a Political Ontology of 'Environmental' Conflicts."

20. Here, we are paraphrasing Stengers.

21. Dipesh Chakrabarty, "The Climate of History: Four Theses," *Critical Inquiry* 35, no. 2 (2009): 197–222.

22. Pierre Clastres, *Society against the State*, rev. ed. (New York: Zone, 2007), 20.

23. Jason Moore, "Introduction: Anthropocene or Capitalocene? Nature, History, and the Crisis of Capitalism," in *Anthropocene or Capitalocene: Nature, History and the Crisis of Capitalism*, ed. Jason Moore, 1–11 (Oakland, CA: PM Press, 2016), 2.

BIBLIOGRAPHY

Bebbington, Anthony. "Political Ecologies of Resource Extraction: Agendas Pendientes." ERLACS 100 (2015): 85–98.

Blaser, Mario. "Is Another Cosmopolitics Possible?" *Cultural Anthropology* 31, no. 4 (2016): 545–70.

Blaser, Mario. "Notes Towards a Political Ontology of 'Environmental' Conflicts." In *Contested Ecologies: Nature and Knowledge*, edited by Lesley Green, 13–27. Cape Town: HSRC Press, 2013.

Blaser, Mario. "The Threat of the Yrmo: The Political Ontology of a Sustainable Hunting Program." *American Anthropologist* 111, no. 1 (2009): 10–20.

Chakrabarty, Dipesh. "The Climate of History: Four Theses." *Critical Inquiry* 35, no. 2 (2009): 197–222.

Clastres, Pierre. *Society against the State*. Rev. ed. New York: Zone, 2007.

Crutzen, Paul J. "Geology of Mankind." *Nature* 415, no. 23 (2002): 23.

de la Cadena, Marisol. *Earth Beings: Ecologies of Practice across Andean Worlds*. Durham, NC: Duke University Press, 2015.

de la Cadena, Marisol. "Indigenous Cosmopolitics in the Andes: Conceptual Reflections beyond 'Politics.'" *Cultural Anthropology* 25, no. 2 (2010): 334–70.

de la Cadena, Marisol. "Uncommoning Nature." *e-Flux: Apocalypsis*. August 22, 2015. http://supercommunity.e-flux.com/authors/marisol-de-la-cadena/.

Ejército Zapatista de Liberación Nacional. "Cuarta Declaración de la Selva Lacandona" [Fourth declaration of the Lacandón jungle]. January 1, 1996. http://enlacezapatista .ezln.org.mx/1996/01/01/cuarta-declaracion-de-la-selva-lacandona/.

Escobar, Arturo. *Autonomía y Diseño: La Realización de lo comunal*. Popayan, Colombia: Editorial de la Universidad del Cauca, 2016.

Gudynas, Eduardo. "El Nuevo Extractivismo Progresista." *El Observador del OBIE* 8 (2010): 1–10.

Law, John. "What's Wrong with a One-World World?" *Distinktion: Scandinavian Journal of Social Theory* 16, no. 1 (2015): 126–39.

Li, Fabiana. *Unearthing Conflict: Corporate Mining, Activism, and Expertise in Peru*. Durham, NC: Duke University Press, 2015.

Moore, Jason. "Introduction: Anthropocene or Capitalocene? Nature, History, and the Crisis of Capitalism." In *Anthropocene or Capitalocene: Nature, History and the Crisis of Capitalism*, edited by Jason Moore, 1–11. Oakland, CA: PM Press, 2016.

Puig de la Bellacasa, Maria. *Matters of Care: Speculative Ethics in More Than Human Worlds*. Minneapolis: University of Minnesota Press, 2017.

Puig de la Bellacasa, Maria. "Matters of Care in Technoscience: Assembling Neglected Things." *Social Studies of Science* 41, no. 1 (2011): 85–106.

Stengers, Isabelle. "Comparison as a Matter of Concern." *Common Knowledge* 17, no. 1 (2011): 48–63.

Stengers, Isabelle. "Introductory Notes on an Ecology of Practices." *Cultural Studies Review* 1, no. 1 (2005): 183–96.

Strathern, Marilyn. *The Gender of the Gift: Problems with Women and Problems with Society in Melanesia*. Berkeley: University of California Press, 1988.

Strathern, Marilyn. *Kinship, Law, and the Unexpected: Relatives Are Always a Surprise*. Cambridge: Cambridge University Press, 2005.

Strathern, Marilyn. "No Nature, No Culture: The Hagen Case." In *Nature, Culture and Gender*, edited by Carol P. MacCormack and Marilyn Strathern, 174–222. Cambridge: Cambridge University Press, 1980.

Strathern, Marilyn. *Reproducing the Future: Essays on Anthropology, Kinship and the New Reproductive Technologies*. Manchester: University of Manchester Press, 1992.

Svampa, Maristella. "Commodities Consensus: Neoextractivism and Enclosure of the Commons in Latin America." *South Atlantic Quarterly* 114, no. 1 (2015): 65–82.

Verran, Helen. "A Postcolonial Moment in Science Studies: Alternative Firing Regimes of Environmental Scientists and Aboriginal Landowners." *Social Studies of Science* 32, nos. 5/6 (2002): 729–62.

Wagner, Roy. "'Luck in the Double Focus': Ritualized Hospitality in Melanesia." *Journal of the Royal Anthropological Institute* 18, no. s1 (2012): s161–s174.

Williams, Raymond. *Keywords: A Vocabulary of Culture and Society*. Rev. ed. Oxford: Oxford University Press, 1983.

ONE

OPENING UP RELATIONS

Marilyn Strathern

What might be interesting about the idea that the concept of "knowledge" is itself often a means to knowledge? I refer both to the duplication of terms and to what English speakers might understand when knowledge is evoked like this. For it becomes the kind of concept that can seemingly occupy both an object position and a subject position in relation to itself. Without doing violence to sense or logic, some other concepts appear to do this too, and a term just deployed (relation) provides an example. As far as the marking is concerned, there is nothing unusual about it: to demarcate "knowledge" is to be explicit about or reflective on knowledge making, in the anthropologists' case this no doubt including an awareness of the situatedness of their studies. What is interesting in the apparent equivalence between them is that subject and object may also, to the contrary, differentiate domains or relative positions, taxonomic or otherwise. Thus it is equally usual to differentiate the subject (e.g., a concept of "knowledge" as a means) from the object (e.g., a concept of whatever is under investigation and is being made known). There is an issue here for anthropological description.

The duplication of terms can be interpreted as hyperdefinitive or delimiting. If one imagined its context as a world full of concepts, each occupying its own domain, the several parts of a whole, allowing of course for overlapping in places, then the boundaries of individual concepts might become a focus of attention. It could become crucial to distinguish "knowledge" from "information," thereby emphasizing what is knowledge-like about knowledge. The same is true of distinguishing, say, state from society, collective from individual, which, as Luhmann observed, became prevalent in (nineteenth-century) European social theory.[1] But then the same character of duplication was seemingly present in his reanalysis of Western modernity, an analysis that allowed no whole and no parts. Instead of domains (of a whole), he spoke of environments: functional differentiation creates autopoetic, self-reproducing systems, each distinctively differentiated from an environment that can only be its own (a system in this formula cannot share an environment with another). These are not domains or divisions of the same whole; rather, systems intersect in terms of their functionality, and he talked in an unremarked way of relations between economics and politics or between politics and education.[2] Such systems and subsystems apprehend themselves through self-reference: organizations must show an organized world how organized they are; educational establishments meet educational needs, and so on. And so too an observer might say that self-consciousness about "knowledge" is a tool for knowledge making.

"Supplanting" (Luhmann's notion) the imaginary of parts and wholes was offered at that moment in twentieth-century social science as a redescription, a radical displacement of other theorizings through "a recasting of the general framework within which systems are perceived and analyzed."[3] Insofar as recastings of this kind appear to upturn old worlds in making new worlds visible, and there are of course no end of them in volumes of Euro-American criticism and reflection, there is some interest here for the imagining of cosmopolitics.[4] Luhmann's quite specific focus was how one might describe society, but I do not take that issue any further. Rather, what prompted this recall of his work was the phenomenon of concept duplication that is not quite duplication (a difference is intended), as reflected in the doubling of terms. For such a practice seemingly finds a niche in either descriptive mode, whether in an evocation or a denial of wholes. It snakes between what one might otherwise have regarded as worlds apart.

This chapter's contribution to the present volume lies in its address to what de la Cadena calls the subject-object mode of relationality that flows from thinking in terms of domains, above all from those flowing from the nature-culture divide.[5] I apply it to how we make things known. For when it comes to knowledge making knowledge, it is as though subject and object cocreate one another. The question is whether we can sneak on the back of this into other kinds of world making altogether. The starting point is a salient anthropological assumption that the descriptive task includes making relations known, so that relations appear as an object of knowledge.

Opening Up

Paradoxically, perhaps, duplication often opens things up a bit. I have mentioned the common habit of expressing the location of the observer (pointing self-consciously to a subject position) through doubling the terms of analysis, dividing a semantic domain into two, as when a writer uses terms with and without emphasis. If this resolves the apparent tautology of "knowledge" as a means to knowledge, through separating the knowing subject from the objects of knowing, it is interesting how equivocal anthropologists often are. There is no end to the number of epistemic objects that they produce, while at the moment of production becoming at the same time wary of or apologetic for the terms in their hands. The awareness they have of how concepts have come into being in effect, and sometimes literally, puts quotation marks around the terms themselves—"group," "ethnicity," "economics," "Melanesian," whatever. However, this rather mundane practice can open up as well as close off problems implied by thinking in terms of domains.

De la Cadena shows this in the concept of culture as an anthropological object.[6] Even if in dialogue a term is apparently shared, anthropologists know that objects of knowledge for the ethnographer may have little correspondence in the vernacular under study. She pushes us to consider the truism cosmologically. It is not that in deploying the concept of culture the ethnographer and her interlocutors evoke different semantic domains; there are no domains. That is, and I am translating the point de la Cadena expounds, what look like semantic domains are not divisions of the same whole. Rather, what intersect at unpredictable junctures are worlds, each of which (an observer might say) recognizes its own environment. One way of thinking about numerous efforts at description in relation to those with whom anthropologists work is to appreciate that the resultant pluriverse cannot in any simple manner occupy an object position in their work (any more than they can occupy a simple subject position). It is as though anthropologists could imagine engaging in knowledge practices that would make something other than "[more] knowledge."

As a critique in the old-fashioned sense, this chapter indicates certain creative moments, as well as impasses, into which Euro-American anthropological discourse can lead. Maybe in these lies the promise of intersections, contributions to the constitution of a pluriverse of which such a discourse is only partly part. My cue comes from another Melanesianist. Crook refers to the Euro-American habit "of eliding the solidity of a social relationship with the solidity of knowledge—and then taking one as a measure of the other. . . . In making an equivalence between the qualities of knowledge and the relational conduit, Anthropology reveals its own crucial metaphor [namely, 'relations'] of knowledge."[7] In this view, relations and knowledge double each other: an apparent epistemic object (relations) appears inseparable from processes of knowledge making. We have been here before. In lieu of the impossibility of taking their separation seriously, it may indeed be helpful to open up this double.[8] Knowledge relations emerge as the subject-object of my narrative.

Knowledge

Demands from the South Pacific

Activating relations of sharing or exchange between holders of knowledge is often proposed as a toning down of subject-object relations between persons. Thus knowledge exchange was an idiom through which Pacific Islanders—in an academic setting—voiced their claims on research workers. The way they did it has been creative, not least for its illumination of what could have been a moment of impasse.

The European Consortium for Pacific Studies (ECOPAS) is a network of university and research institutions in Fiji, Papua New Guinea, France, the Netherlands, Norway, and the UK, under the aegis of the European Commission. With a focus on climate change, the hope is for scholarly collaboration in developing long-term strategies for social science and humanities research on the Pacific. Its origins lay in a previous moment,[9] when a round table of Pacific Island academics had urged their colleagues "to recognize the responsibilities to Oceanic peoples, to the Academy and to Civil Society that come with the exchange of expert knowledge." Their listeners were researchers who had carried out fieldwork in or otherwise knew the region, the predominant discipline being (sociocultural) anthropology. Pacific Island scholars were expressing frustration that, for all the apparent exchanges there had been, there were still unmet obligations on the researchers' side. Quite simply, it was said, they wanted academics to act. The formation of ECOPAS was a direct political response. In international bureaucratese, "knowledge exchange" has routinely replaced the old phrase "knowledge transfer"; it was not a Pacific Island neologism, although these Pacific Islanders seem to have given it a special emphasis. They drew attention to the need to remedy what so often seemed a one-way flow of information. Not voiced at that moment but in the background on both sides lay a question that has been asked many times before: What was to count as knowledge?[10]

In the multiple layerings of such an occasion, each party was also aware of the background of the other. Pacific Island scholars spoke of responsibilities to the academy as much as European scholars acknowledged those persons who had been party to their research in the field. Everyone was acting in a particular register. But was there also a "divergence" of registers, to use Stengers's term?[11] If so, perhaps it was hidden in the very appeal from the Pacific Islanders to which the European scholars responded. Researchers had to acknowledge the obligations activated by their (social) relations with people in the Pacific. This was the common language. Admittedly (in this representation of Islanders' demands) Europeans needed to be told what Islanders took for granted, but the former were open to their relational obligations and glad no doubt that interpersonal relationships with the Island scholars and academics they knew could be a sign of relations with many others. A successful exchange would be the beginning, not the end, of future interchange. There was almost a cosmological force to this: world restitution—recognizing a world where one has to act on one's debts—was a step toward world reconstitution.[12]

Now Haraway made it clear a long time ago that issues do not have to attach to whole persons—that is not the relevant mathematic (me plus my culture); to the contrary, issues divide people in different ways. When in the 1980s she famously argued for "politics and epistemologies of location, positioning, and situating, where partiality and not universality is the condition for being heard," the answer she gave to what can count as knowledge turned crucially on recognizing the agency of the world and objects of knowledge as actors. "Situated knowledges require that the object of knowledge be pictured as an actor and agent, not a screen or a ground or a resource."[13] Let me give a half-turn to this phrasing, from the "objects" Haraway had in mind practices and procedures as objects of knowledge too. For we might use her phrase of the means of knowledge, insofar as practices of knowledge making also have effects. Situatedness was never simply an issue of identifying preexisting interests but of appreciating the coconstitution of interests as they emerge in interchanges of all kinds. In these, the form or technique of knowing, the means to knowledge, is surely an actor as well. For example, the way in which knowledge is regarded as available to acquisition or conservation is among the effects that the "knowledge" has, giving it a particular purchase on people's deliberations. This kind of actor is there in the very idea that knowledge might be exchanged.

There was, I think, a divergence of registers, although it was not between Pacific Islanders and Europeans, many as might have been the differences through which each could describe the other. In fact, the Pacific Islanders' reproach at once brought to light and resolved a potential impasse. This was the divergence instantiated, and concealed, at the moment of agreement between them. The agreement was over a means to knowledge: acknowledging relations. Yet what Pacific Islanders might take as prior to and underlying any exchange or interchange (what they took for granted), their European counterparts might well imagine as having to be put creatively in place (in their needing to be told). That difference is cosmological, a divergence in what people take relations to be.[14] So what counts as relations? That's the question that makes relations something of an unknown actor. It is an interesting question, I think, for cosmo- or pluriversal politics.[15] For in Euro-American thought, relations are what keeps the world and all our worlds comprehensible.

The world that the politics of research addresses is made demonstrable through epistemic relations: cause and effect, covariation, taxonomic hierarchies, evaluation, comparison. Relations are also a means for comprehending a world thought of as connections between persons, however fractious, and however we describe values, collectivities, institutions, alliances, intimacies, and so on. Pushed to it, an observer might observe, most scholars would take the ontological position that relational descriptions of the world are made possible by its inherently relational properties. Denial therefore becomes arresting. Thus when Stengers admonishes that divergence "is not relational[,] it is constitutive," "relational" here refers to domains of knowledge imagined as connected through exchanges or interchanges between practices or across boundaries.[16] This is the world as it appears much of the time, so that, in bureaucratese, boundaries delimit different kinds of expert knowledge, and the need to create or produce those kinds of relations is constantly stressed. By contrast, divergence (Stengers says) is not "between" practices—a practice does not define itself in terms of its divergence from others, for each "produces itself." Insofar as divergence is constitutive, then, it allows no domaining; practices appearing juxtaposed to one another are not divisions of the same world, do not occupy the same environment. Her "ecology of practices" introduces a different kind of relation: "I use ecology, as a transversal category, to help define relational heterogeneity . . . situations that relate heterogeneous protagonists."[17] The supposition at which we have arrived, that the question as to what counts as knowledge is going to be intimately bound up with the question as to what counts as relations, becomes descriptively challenging.

A Debate about Knowledge

How might differences that are not divisions of the same social world appear? There are many examples in the anthropological corpus, and I take one from more than a decade ago, an ostensible debate about knowledge that afforded a context where restitution was literally taken as a (partial) reconstitution of social life.

When the UK Working Group on Human Remains in Museum Collections was preparing its report, it heard representations from both scientific experts and indigenous peoples, particular interest being generated by Australian Aboriginal activists.[18] Its remit was to draw up guidelines to assist UK legislation for the tenure and repatriation of human remains—from skeletons to samples of tissue and hair—held in museums. Scientific or research interest in such materials was justified by the medical and evolutionary information the remains were capable of yielding, including their relationship to other collections. It was feared that knowledge would be lost with repatriation, knowledge that only experts could extract and relate to other sources of information. Statements from interested people in Australia, as well as in New Zealand and North America, were put side by side the research view. The Australian Aboriginal depositions talked about something quite different: kinship. This was fairly easy for an anthropologist to understand in relational terms. Whether it was a matter of Aborigines being related to their ancestors while the scientists were not, or of the relations being different, either way their relationships rendered the Aborigines (kinsfolk) different kinds of people from those with research interests (strangers). We may add that, to the Aborigines, there was nothing more they needed by way of information about themselves in order to press their claims; entitlement was proved through narrative, dance, and song. That kind of knowledge could only be effective when deployed by those with the right to use it: such effectiveness could not be transferred or enhanced through acquiring someone else's "knowledge." (You are not a descendant of someone else's ancestor.) Enhanced knowledge was of course the only card that the researchers held.

The UK Working Group bent over backward to be open to cultural sensitivities (recognizing cultures as each occupying its own domain). It did so, albeit with compassion and respect, on the basis of certain expectations about expert knowledge. Its premise was that knowledge is something that people habitually convert into information in their communications with one another, so when people say things about themselves they are imparting information. Should demands compete, the form of interchange can be moderated, as though positions defended or promulgated were positions in a debate. Debate, in this Euro-American view, fruitfully opens up information about the nature of the world. Sharing and exchanging information go hand in hand (ideally reinforce each other) and together are widely regarded as one route to reaching agreement. The Working Group's politics was articulated in its anticipation of such an agreement: cross-cultural understanding was the idiom in which it apprehended its task, and cultural difference—implying respect for cultural boundaries—could be managed like any other difference of viewpoint. Indeed, the report itself, constructed out of diverse discussions, statements, and face-to-face representations, created the sense of a confrontation between two sides each with its viewpoint or perspective.[19] Either side might attempt to persuade the other to see the force of the argument being put forward; a compromise or balance of viewpoints would inform the Working Group's recommendations. In other words, the discussion on the Working Group's side ultimately framed these as perspectives that could be compared.

The politics of the activists taking the claimants' position evoked what we can now call another environment. This was one from which debate itself looked alien. Difference between the two sides could not be reduced to a difference of viewpoint, nor to the idea that through information sharing they (indigenous people) would appreciate the context from which the scientists were operating, and shift their own viewpoint accordingly. Informing the Working Group in turn of the context from which they were operating would not offer the basis of a compromise agreement from their side either. Some of the opposition was expressed in terms of the repeated refusal to acknowledge that their ancestors were scientific specimens. There was, in other words, no agreement about the knowledge at stake.

Scientists (and others taking the researchers' position) suggested that if repatriation were inevitable, then in return for handing over material, they could extract information from it first, with the understanding that such information would be as available to the claimants as to anyone. Indeed, the Working Group had fancied a kind of exchange (not its term). On the one hand, in the group's view, claimants might allow UK museums who repatriated remains to retain portions of the materials for (say) future DNA investigation. On the other hand, in the same view, while taking back all the remains, claimants might nonetheless be willing to make arrangements that would perpetuate their accessibility to scientific inquiry. In either case there would in effect be an exchange of knowledge, since in return for what the claimants knew about their ancestors would come knowledge that only scientific methods could obtain. To some claimants, both offers of exchange were offensive.[20] There was no agreement about the relations at stake. Spokespersons for indigenous claimants regarded the confrontation between them and what they took to be the museums' or researchers' entrenched view not in terms of knowing at all; if anything, it was in terms of being, specifically how the two parties existed with the remains/ancestors.

It would be too simple to say that the difference was between the kinds of relational potential the researchers saw (conceptual or epistemic relations, gaining more knowledge about the samples) and relations between persons (interpersonal or social relations, as between ancestors and descendants). Because at this point I must pause. Whether by combining or differentiating between them, holding together epistemic and interpersonal relations is a double characteristic of the anthropologist's Euro-American repertoire.[21] Even within the interpersonal register, if it seems that kinship relations were being contrasted with strangers' relations to the remains/ancestors, that relational model is my gloss too. Their words sounded like this: "We went to the Natural History Museum [in London] to see our ancestors and we were told that we cannot see them. For us it is like going to see somebody in hospital. To us the people in museums are not dead, they are living"; "It is our direct ancestors that are being experimented on"; "How can research possibly compare? We're tired of other people interpreting us to ourselves."[22] It was not that scientists and researchers could not also take a relational perspective of the interpersonal kind; of course they could. Yet that is exactly what it would be: a relation that was simultaneously a relation between perspectives (as understood in the English vernacular), that is, an interpersonal or social relation between

different parties that was simultaneously a conceptual or epistemic relation between viewpoints. In this view, putting oneself in another person's
position would entail also an enactment of a relation between different
domains of knowledge.[23] Yet if Aboriginal representatives (say) regarded
themselves as different kinds of people than researchers, their being could
not be posed in terms of such a relation. The very idea that one might put
oneself in the other's shoes comes close to being nonsense. This is the point
on which Verran's work with Australian Aborigines has been forcefully
taken up by Law.[24] Referring to the worlds belonging to stories of—about,
through, with, in—landscapes, he wrote that "we [Euro-Americans] are
not a part of these worlds. . . . We do not exist to those worlds. Just as they
do not exist to us."[25] The conflict is not always evident precisely because it
is cosmological—the difference is too vast to see.

Continuing the Debate

In what sense was this also true for the Pacific Island scholars? Theirs was
an academic and research-interested view, and they deliberately cast their
claims in terms of knowledge. What they expressed was that for all the
interchanges there had been between themselves (*sensu latu*) and waves
of overseas researchers, there was still a deficit; however, it was one that
could be made up through focusing on knowledge. As one of its work pack-
ages, ECOPAS was to endorse knowledge exchange. As we have just seen,
compromising on the demands of repatriation, the UK museum researchers
would have been only too happy if this had been an outcome for them too.
So what was at issue in just such a demand being instigated by a group of
Pacific Islanders?

Members of the ECOPAS consortium would be the first to observe that
the formula of knowledge exchange could be no more than a provisional
starting point for future interactions, including future relationships.[26]
The common language, it will be recalled, was that researchers had to acknowledge the obligations activated by their (interpersonal) relations with
people in the Pacific. The question it raised was what was to count as relations. It would not be surprising if the European researchers read this
appeal as an ethical position that gave some kind of moral authority to stimulating flows of knowledge. The ethics would be consonant with the kind of
importance Euro-Americans give to interpersonal relations, as we saw in
the Working Group's attitude, a domain of right acting that would offer a

legitimate basis upon which to acquire things from others.[27] (The domain might even be bureaucratized as good practice.) The question is whether such an understanding would have been commensurate with all of the connotations that the Pacific Islanders might have accorded the acknowledgment of relations. If not, in what sense might the understandings have been in conflict?

An ethnographer's sketch from one part of Papua New Guinea gives some hints. Leach describes how the people of Reite (Madang Province) value knowledge in the form of narratives, potent stories that have an effect on the landscape as they do on persons. They are not marked out as an intellectual activity. "Differences are between kinds of people, with different control over knowledge, not between intellectual and other forms of activity."[28] People would only talk of knowledge that they themselves owned, an owner remaining liable for the effects of anything passed on to another. "Expressing knowledge amounts to claiming inclusion in the relationships (including those to land and spirits) that generated the knowledge. One cannot 'know' something without it being a part of one's make-up, and as such, something that connects one to others."[29] Leach suggests that in this kind of transmission between persons we are witnessing something analogous to what English speakers would call "kinship." It is a kinship rooted in a place; land underwrites the social relationships it nurtures, and knowledge inheres in particular landscapes. "If kinship is about the production of persons, [then] relations focused on, and made possible by, the emergence of knowledge are the basis of kinship."[30] Knowledge, and not bits of biological material, is the substance that links people in close relations, and thus a means of those relations coming into being.[31]

That sharing knowledge makes kinship in turn inflects the meaning of exchanging it. In Reite, regular exchange is not of knowledge itself but of its products: the wealth and food that a place produces. These are given to people from other places, primarily in-laws and maternal kin, as in competitive displays that acknowledge the debt of their nurturing contributions. So there are two kinds of relations here. Affinal kin are related in a manner quite distinct from what binds people of a single place together. Affinal ties give evidence of, are the effects of, the potency and efficacy of knowledge; nonetheless, affines enjoy the products of knowledge without controlling its source, for that continues to belong to those of the place it comes from.[32] Such ideas about attachment and detachment are pertinent to the concept of knowledge exchange.

Leach reflects on a contrast with two deep-seated Euro-American assumptions: first, that knowledge can be detached from those who produce
it and can be circulated or exchanged without reference to them; second,
that its effect is dependent not on such persons (interpersonal relations),
but on the correctness of its correlation with apparently independently
occurring phenomena (epistemic relations).[33] The two assumptions can
take on a political cast when the work of detachment is concealed in an
apprehension of knowledge as (free-floating) items of information, as typi-
fied in some arguments defending museum retention of remains.[34] Leach
enacted an example. In the spirit of knowledge exchange, the ethnographer
coauthored a book on local plants with Nombo, himself from Reite, juxta-
posing descriptions in Tok Pisin (neo-Melanesian pidgin) and English with
Reite plant names.[35] Yet it seemed less the presence of foreign knowledge
or the exposure of indigenous knowledge to outsiders than the presentation of the plants that was to lead to questions. When it was launched at a
university in Papua New Guinea, there was intense interest in reattaching
the specimen photographs to the Reite author, a conflictual moment in
a cosmological sense: where exactly had the plants come from, in what
place were they growing, and was Nombo responsible for their use in his
village?[36] The politics of attachment—and that is partly what restitution or
the ECOPAS interest in the exchange of knowledge was about—shows up
the politics of detachment. For the view of Nombo's Papua New Guinean
interlocutors could not diverge further from the notion of knowledge dis-
tilled in a (detachable) representation of the world. Nombo himself talked
of "knowledge as remembering, as acting, as thinking on an experience or
moment of transmission between persons. It is clear what he describes is
acting in and on [interpersonal] relations."[37]

Reite people would concur that diverse local knowledges cannot be ac-
commodated as different viewpoints on a single world. Indeed, the commensurability that the concept of knowledge apparently offers, and thus the
basis of agreement or exchange, runs up against different evaluations when
that single world is taken for granted by Euro-American researchers as a
reference point for reality. Only some knowledge will be recognized as
such and accorded status in explanations of phenomena (the rest is erro-
neous belief, inappropriate personification, and so forth).[38] This gives an
unmistakably political dimension to the Euro-American insistence that the
concept of "knowledge" itself is a means to knowledge, precisely insofar as
what is concealed in this doubling is that only certain kinds of knowledge

make knowledge. Hence comes the suggestion of following "another route, and . . . think[ing] about transformations and effects around a recognition that things are or could be knowledge. . . . [So] the impetus to redefine things as knowledge or knowledge producing is exactly the process we should be interrogating."[39]

If anthropologists have many times before witnessed the social conditions that give rise to this kind of insight, and to the kind of conflicts that uncover incommensurability, openness to knowledge exchange does not get us out of the impasse that was so striking in the museum claims case. But it does suggest possibilities of interaction in which commensuration (after Povinelli) might be deliberately practiced.[40] In an English-speaking interchange, Pacific Islanders pointedly evoked one of anthropology's favorite analytics, relations. There is of course nothing bland or soothing about this term in and of itself, and Pacific Island and European academics alike have resources at their backs in their own (internal) arguments (for the sake of argument) about relations, and in the conflicts they routinely encounter among themselves, for fashioning objects of exchange.

Relations

Other People's Unknowns

Recalling de la Cadena's observations on the concept of culture, let me introduce some of its adventures in the hands of Carneiro da Cunha.[41] Her concern is the way anthropologists slide in and out of usages doing quite different jobs. Lightly inflecting a primary distinction between "culture" (in quotation marks) and culture, she describes how "culture" travels the world, often imported to profound political effect into people's delineation of themselves. At the same time, this explicit "culture" coexists with an implicit culture. The latter is evident as a matter of endemic internal logic, even though its name (culture) is one outsiders bestowed. The coexistence of the two concepts, between which public discourse—indigenous or metropolitan—forever weaves in and out, gives rise to misunderstandings, she says, over the nature of knowledge. Her distinction opens things up through a creative doubling of the terms of analysis, each term pointing to another version of itself. Carneiro da Cunha's principal concern is not just with degrees of self-consciousness; it is with a contrast between the public interethnic logic of "culture," with its (relational) adages about sharing, "a collective regime imposed on what was previously a network of differential rights,"[42] and the internal logic of culture, precisely that differentiated network, which has room for all kinds of divisions within.[43]

Carneiro da Cunha pairs "culture" and culture, then, much as I have referred to "knowledge" and knowledge. This gives an opportunity to move from the kinds of encounters that mobilize gross categories such as Pacific Islanders and Europeans to what work as (internal) differentiations local to each. To transfer Leach's question of knowledge to relations, should the anthropologist be looking at the effects of recognizing relations? Recognizing relations entails knowing how they are known, and with the device of inflection, I propose to talk of "relations" and relations. The case in hand concerns differences between certain kinds of doubt, not dissimilar to that which arises whenever we question how we know what we know, but not explicitly handled as a matter of knowledge. One issue will be how radical the relational difference is, and whether we might detect internal (cosmological) divergence.

A pioneering ethnographer of the Papua New Guinea Highlands, Reay once described the display of aggression that men of a Kuma (Middle Wahgi) clan would mount in the course of a fertility-promoting Pig Ceremonial.[44] Their dance with spears, a stylized brandishing of weapons against unseen enemies, directed aggression outside. At the same time, such ceremonies were also occasions on which people attacked one another within the clan community. These were more like games or sporting contests; the protagonists would be rival subclans or, spectacularly, men versus women. A mock battle that Reay witnessed in 1955 began with men and women grouping at opposite ends of a ceremonial ground, stinging nettles in their hands, rushing forward to brush the skin of their opponents, then retreating to hurl soft ash and lumps of mud from a distance. Apropos Carneiro da Cunha's divisions internal to culture, difference was thus enacted in different ways. Aggression, mediated by weapons and decorations, was displayed against traditional enemies, normally quite remote, always to be attacked, and certainly not present on this occasion. Between men and women, familiar to one another, body contact was much closer to being unmediated: nettles, ash, and mud created bodily intimacy. In versions played between boys of different subclans, the prescribed method of kicking often degenerated into fisticuffs and hair pulling. Reay contrasts the "two types of ritual conflict." In the games, "the drama lies in the conflict itself," while in the stylized war display drama is supplied by the ornamentation and dance movements.[45] For the "spear dance dramatizes readiness for conflict rather than conflict itself."[46] When it happened, warfare resulted in deaths, whereas the games would stop at the first serious injury. I intervene in this account to suggest that we take dramatizing readiness and dramatizing conflict as efforts on the part of Kuma people to make certain relations known; they emerge as of two kinds.

"Relations": the assertion of clan solidarity in the spear dance tested the strength of preexisting "relations," as in the categorical designation of traditional enmity; sustaining such antagonism was said to be a condition of the clansmen's own increase and future strength.[47] In this, the dance had something of a divinatory effect in its impact on themselves. The conviction of the performance comes close to Holbraad's "infinition" (an "inventive definition") in Cuban divination, a categorical announcement that will provide a newly conceived baseline for future action, inaugurating new meaning.[48] With that future in mind, dramatizing aggression took the categorical knowledge of preexisting "relations" as a newly enacted premise for the fertility to come. Reenactment was required, or the world would not be thereby renewed. Otherwise put, "relations" with the enemy already existed; it was the clan of men (the dancers) that had to be remade.[49]

Relations: although the nettle games had rules, Kuma men and women acted out a state of affairs that had no resolution—confrontation simply ended when the participants stopped. The "relation" between men and women was remade in their absolute separation on this occasion; division between the sexes was categorical. However, what was also brought into being, this time an unremarked relation, was the delineation of a conflict whose outcome was, by contrast, unpredictable. Setting into motion conflict between the sexes, this relation subverted the certainty of the categories— it left wide open how "men" and "women" would appear in the course of (re)enactment. I would interpret this as an existential indeterminacy as to what kinds of creatures were joined in this relation. No one knew quite how people would behave, and thus what they would show of themselves. This entailed less a new premise for action than an experimental probing of what, in this particular situation, the effects of interchange might be. Hovering over the men and women, one could say, was a question about how their relating would reveal what men and women were.

Both interchanges were premised on doubts as to the outcome of relations. The difference was between the remaking of explicit preexisting "relations" as a premise for acting, where uncertainty was about the effectiveness of the clan's claims to the conventional properties of strength and fertility, and uncovering previously implicit relations, where something more like indeterminacy attached to the very properties people would evince (how they would appear as gendered beings). In other words, "relations" bring into new positions of stability the properties of the terms to the "relation," uncertainty resting in what the "relation" can accomplish in connecting them, while relations seem indeterminate as to the existential state of the terms themselves. In the latter, the relation is evident (in conflict), but people do not necessarily know where it will lead them, precisely insofar as the terms (the properties of phenomena) will be the outcome or effect of such relational movement.

To ask how we know "relations"/relations is to ask about concepts that may contain within themselves a generative unknowing. The unknowing is (in the examples here) seemingly of different kinds. Now Reay wanted to bound the concept of "conflict" by calling these "ritual" conflicts. To answer the question about how radical the differentiations are in terms of the conflict between clans or between men and women, whether the conditions that produce these actors reach a point of divergence, is to take the difference between them to task. For the clans also duplicate one another in their efforts, and there are senses in which males and females are versions of each other. Nonetheless, maybe we can see something approaching divergence, not between the parties in each case but between the two types of conflict. The degree of confrontation in either instance is shadowed or outlined in the conventional limits on people's behavior, yet to very distinct effect. So the dynamic of doubt, the states of not-knowing, have consequences that go off in quite different directions. The one tips into overt reinforcements of solidarity and enmity; the other draws back into possibilities for private intimacy that have been implicit all along.

A Pacific Island scholar might well comment on the artificiality of this analytical exercise, at least if what appears to the reader is a domaining of the two enactments of doubt. By analogy with a criticism put forward by Moutu, who undertook ethnographic work with the Iatmul, from the Sepik River area of Papua New Guinea, it is the noncomparability of these conflicts that should take our attention.[50] (It is as though each is its own line of divergence.) The English-language device I have been using ("relations" and relations) is misleading if it only implies commensurability between the two; I hope enough has been said to show the pair works equally well for incommensurables.

Moutu's argument is worth attention on its own terms. It takes the form of disagreement concerning the double that has already made its appearance several times—what has been presented as a double is in fact elements of life that have no parity with each other. "Contra Strathern, I argue that what distinguishes 'relationships' ontologically from the epistemological forms of relational practices—such as connection, association, resemblance, comparison, etc.—is necessity and transcendence, which give 'relationships' the character of an infinite being."[51] He wishes to get away from an obsession with anthropology's epistemological understanding of relationality; instead, what an ethnographer needs in a place such as Iatmul is an ontological theory of relationships. As a shorthand, we may say such relationships implicate persons, but that designation in turn covers a range of phenomena. For Moutu, the Iatmul archetype of a person embodies a pair of brothers who are life and death to one another.[52] As he would formulate it, the ontology of brotherhood exists as an internal necessity that leads to an orientation toward a certain kind of becoming: one brother is always becoming the other brother.

The reference to brothers echoes Viveiros de Castro's oft-quoted comparison of paradigmatic or canonical relations between certain indigenous peoples of Amazonia and Brazilians, along with other Western peoples, from a Euro-Christian background. For the latter, "brotherhood is in itself the general form of relation," where the Amazonian form would be the affinity of brothers-in-law.[53] While brothers-in-law are linked by the difference that divides them, "brotherhood" speaks to partners in a relation being connected through what unites them, insofar as each is "in the same relation to a third term."[54] However, this kind of brotherhood is not at all what Moutu was describing for the Melanesian Iatmul. There, elder is divided from younger—indeed, at its most radical, life is the elder brother and death the younger (death is always becoming life and vice versa), a conceptualization that applies to both men and women. Iatmul brothers are more like Amazonian brothers-in-law than they are like Euro-Christian brothers, whose pairing or doubling may reinforce a common identity. This invites one to look again at that (Euro-American) identity. Leaving the third term aside, two entities or beings can simply appear connected through the similarity of one to the other. Where the canonical form of the relation is that of brotherhood, this is as true epistemically as interpersonally: terms linked by a relation of similarity. Yet exactly when it comes to (relations between) relations and their terms, I might as well write of terms linked by a relation of difference. We know that for Euro-American thinkers what is linked as subject and object in this case is reversible. Conventionally, "term" and "relation" may become folded into each other, individual terms either occupying the position of preexisting, independent entities to be related or else rendered distinct and individuated as an outcome of relations. Pacific Islanders dealing with the English language, like their ethnographers, may well find this kind of conceptual capacity an intellectual resource. However, Moutu provides us with something else, and not just a criticism of holding two kinds of relations commensurable, or, for that matter (insofar as it is further implied), incommensurable.

The Iatmul orientation toward certain kinds of becoming shows the anthropologist relationships in an unconventional form. Always becoming is another kind of differentiation, where being in one state anticipates being in the other. The other is not simply a later stage of growth or development in evolutionary time but closer to an alternative, an alter made episodically present. The apparently radical divide between elder and younger lies in the very conversion of the one into the other, and thus in the reversibility of phenomena. As a consequence, the degree of difference is underlain by a further kind of not-knowing, by an anticipation that something is other than what it appears to be or, more appositely, than what it is now. More so perhaps than in the Kuma conflicts, there is a sense in which such transformational maneuvers sit on the boundaries of possibility for an indigenous cosmopolitics. They might or might not lend themselves to nonrelational positionings, including but not confined to the connotations I understand Stengers's "nonrelational" to imply.[55]

Moutu's crisp distinction between epistemic relations and ontologically grounded relationships forces the question, in respect of those epistemic relations, of what we make of knowledge. In describing the Kuma conflicts as though they were concerned with how relations are made known, I was both drawing (a particular sort of) anthropological knowledge from them and drawing attention to how anthropologists arrive at such "knowledge." At large, one might be tempted to suggest that for modern Euro-Americans—whether they live in a world of domains or divergences—relating is at once necessary to and transcendent of knowledge making. There is no knowledge that does not relate "relations." Yet just as one can deploy the concept of relation in talking of the nonrelational, these widespread understandings can also break out of their own apparent limitations. I conclude with two instances, the one inspired by a Spanish philosopher and the other by an American biologist and feminist critic.

Nonrelational Forms of Knowledge

In describing the reversibility of the Iatmul elder/younger pair, I have already drawn on Corsín Jiménez's article with Willerslev, which attends precisely to a distinction that is radical in its anticipation of alternative yet copresent states of affairs.[56]

Corsín Jiménez and Willerslev offer "an indigenous re-description of the Euro-American concept of the relation."[57] It does not resemble a relation, and the vocabulary they use is oppositional (hence redescription): imagine a nonrelational shape. Such a presence accompanies Yukaghir hunters of Siberia, in the form of a shadow force, an immaterial twin that appears simultaneously with the perceived person. All physical entities have this "hidden side"; this means that things "are never just themselves, but always something else as well."[58] The economic relations of "sharing" and the economic relations of (hierarchical) "exchange" shadow each other in this sense. So there is at once a radical difference between hunters' relations, now with their kin and now with their Russian sponsors (their source of fuel and ammunition), and the possibility of each kind of interaction becoming the other, a reversibility especially apparent in somewhat parallel relations with spirits. Thus an elk hunter himself is always on two missions, visible and invisible: the hunter is able to seduce the elk because his shadow spirit has already seduced the elk's spirit. The hunter's shadow spirit, it is said, "moves in and out of these two hunts, turning the visible and the invisible inside out, and recasting the shadows of both worlds as it . . . sneaks between their limits."[59] Given that every being casts such a shadow, Corsín Jiménez and Willerslev perceive it (the shadow) working like the general category of "concept." However, its conviction rests not on a relational definition but on a specific effect, as one might say Reite knowledge is known through its effects: the effect here is its capacity for self-displacement. In other words, one recognizes (something analogous to) a concept not because one can lay out the relation of one entity with other entities but from the way the concept creates its own space for expression. Basically, then, this shadow points to an idea of entity or being that is also always something else. The shadow is not so much an autonomous or self-referencing image as an alternative of the same shape or outline as the being in question—yet not it. As they promised, this is not a description of the Euro-American concept of relation but a redescription in Yukaghir terms.

The redescription was inspired by a Euro-American philosopher taking up an unconventional argument about the idea of a concept at its limits. Corsín Jiménez and Willerslev look to the work of the notable Spanish thinker Trías, who characterized traditional philosophy as delimitative, outlining the conditions under which a concept has a purchase, rather than seeing how concepts work by pursuing them to their limits, which are the limits of their world.[60] (A philosophy of the shadow is not just a Siberian conceit.) As we have seen, the paradigmatic Euro-American form of the relation (brotherhood) takes a delimitative shape. Between the different Yukaghir possibilities, an anticipated reversibility sustains relatively stable pairings of states of being/becoming. Yet such reversibility is nonrelational in that there is no explicit connection between these states, as for example comparison would provide; only an existential given, with one position being occupied rather than another. However, what might be imagined as an even less comparable divergence, as between Yukaghir and Euro-American reasonings, momentarily affords an intersection. It comes out of the energy that the authors derive from this 1980s work of Trías on concepts, and out of their controlled equivocation with respect to Yukaghir ideas, that is, the explicit analogy they make between the shadow (form) and the (concept of) relation. While these Siberians describe a thing by evoking its outline in the shadow it casts, the analogy with relation lies in the very convention by which Euro-Americans might articulate connections (and might even wish to see reversibility itself in this light) in comparing any one thing to other entities.

What is in the anthropologist's hands is, as always, their descriptive ambition. Corsín Jiménez and Willerslev have in effect accomplished a dialogue with the Siberian material. From out of different relational descriptions of their own world, from diverse Euro-American ideas of a concept to an idea of it as displaceable by the Yukaghir shadow, the anthropologists have found an intersection with the nonrelational conceptualizations Yukaghir have created. I turn now to a strategic example within Euro-American discourse, another displacement of a kind.

I refer to Haraway's astonishingly prescient "A Cyborg Manifesto," which we might describe as the shadow of a world taken (conceptually) to its limits.[61] This is the familiar world of entities that are imagined relationally, as parts of a whole, with innumerable programs to erase contradiction and seek virtue in unification. It is the single world of domains, contexts, and perspectival viewpoints that Luhmann reanalyzed in terms of multiple autopoetic systems. But, as I see it, through different modalities of relations Haraway effects something closer to a Yukaghir redescription. Thus she presents her principal actor, the cyborg, as an image or a myth, refusing to match its reality with the realism of social analysis (though there is much social analysis in the manifesto). Cyborgs dissolve the domaining sustained by dualisms, boundaries, and the politics of domination, including the domination of women, alongside all those "constituted as others."[62] Cyborgs do not do so through reinstating sisterhood; that would be a form of brotherhood in the Euro-American sense. They do not point to the perfection of relational interconnectedness; that would reinvent a communion that overcomes dualisms and aspires to connect up all the divisions of a one world.[63] Connections and relations are doing something quite different in this piece.

The cyborg was summoned at a specific political moment in scientific-feminist history to capture, among other things, the then-emergent feedback loops of communication technopolitics and the already-apparent effects of the microchip revolution. It is this very situatedness that seems, looking back on it, so evocative now. It is as though Haraway had taken Luhmann's complex systems and subsystems, each creating their own environments, but refused them—and the power of myth is to allow such refusals—autopoesis. Self-reference loses its force when the cyborg self "is a kind of a disassembled and reassembled, postmodern collective and personal self."[64] To the contrary, because their reproduction is already mixed, then systems are already made up of other systems. More crucially than that, however, cyborgs do not, after all, reproduce—they regenerate. As a text, "A Cyborg Manifesto" is at once an ironic comment on organicism as a misplaced image of holism and a foreshadowing of the profoundly already-related skeins of symbiosis on which Haraway has since written.[65] Contacts involving beings that continue to diverge can be imagined as intersections, or connecting events, just as cyborgs are "needy for connection."[66] We might also say, then, that far from relating discrete domains of life, or simply activating the inevitable relation a system has with its environment, the cyborg's relations are constitutive. It is all relation in that sense. Haraway subsequently observed, "The technical and the political are like the abstract and the concrete, the foreground and the background, the text and the context . . . questions of pattern, not of ontological difference. The terms pass into each other; they are shifting sedimentations of the one fundamental thing about the world—relationality."[67]

What was Haraway's trick with relations, and why have the cyborgs follow the Spanish-Siberian shadow? It is here that I would want to draw on anthropological knowledge making, and by that I mean its contact with or intersection with indigenous worlds of (for the sake of argument) knowledge. Let me make the conclusion to revisiting the 1980s cyborg also a conclusion more generally.

THE HAPPENSTANCES NOTED here have taken place in the best of times and the worst of times, to good outcomes and ill, with expectations raised or dashed. Different languages of description can only snake—sneak— their way through. As far as knowledge relations are concerned, if there is conflict in agreement (to dramatize creative hopes for knowledge exchange), there can also be exchange in disagreement (to dramatize creative hopes for scholarly criticism). Through instances momentarily foregrounded for reflection, I have tried to indicate some of the many ways, different or divergent, in which relations are a means to knowledge. None of them matches completely onto the others, although they are here strung together to bring out certain continuities in people's aspirations and how their self-descriptions position them. These distinct ways (hopefully) touch one another. In this narrative I have had the cyborg touch the Yukaghir hunter. For the hunter's relations give us a way of imagining the cyborg's relations, yet are not them (for example, Haraway's world is not hinged with a reversible alternative). What I take here from the manifesto is that it was not sufficient to imagine that cyborgs were in conflict with or in disagreement with the world they redescribed. Instead of setting out a relation to that world, they displaced it. Residing as its shadow, where cyborgs lived was at once not that world and more like it than the world understood of itself. In short, cyborgs were able to effect displacement precisely because they were already in existence. These are the contours of a nonrelational shape.

It was a knowing move, a touching point, on the part of the Pacific Island scholars to hold out relations—not forgetting the sense of Moutu's relationships—to their Euro-American counterparts. When anthropologists make "relations" through relations they are caught up in how they recognize, and thus in the means of knowing, the one through the other;

they can imagine knowledge as an object of relation making quite as much as relations as an object of knowledge making. In the course of the chapter, however, we have also encountered moments best grasped as generative not-knowing, and moments of generative not-relating too. In the writing of texts, to recall the question of what anyone takes relations to be, it is a descriptive (knowledge-based) decision as to whether other possibilities are best made present as relational or nonrelational phenomena. The politics caught up in the decision will likely weight the matter one way or the other.

ACKNOWLEDGMENTS

My appreciation of the invitation to participate in the Sawyer Seminar, and of the work of Marisol de la Cadena and Mario Blaser, should be evident. Departments at UC Davis and UC Santa Cruz collaborated to make my participation possible, intellectually as well as through other means, and this chapter comes from presentations at both campuses. Donna Haraway was my stalwart, generous, and sharply insightful interlocutor on each occasion; indeed what is rewritten here stems from the stimulus of her questioning, which pushed an argument considerably beyond its original confines. Above all, this comes with warm thanks to colleagues and friends (old and new) who enriched the occasions by their comments.

NOTES

1. Niklas Luhmann, *Essays on Self-Reference* (New York: Columbia University Press, 1990), 129–31.

2. Niklas Luhmann, *The Differentiation of Society*, trans. Stephen Holmes and Charles Larmore (New York: Columbia University Press, 1982), 81.

3. Luhmann, *The Differentiation of Society*, 229.

4. In Luhmann's work, what is accessible specifically to the observer may be concealed from other actors. "Modern society does not admit that its self-description faces a problem of tautology or paradox." Luhmann, *Essays on Self-Reference*, 127.

5. Marisol de la Cadena, "Indigenous Cosmopolitics: Dialogues about the Reconstitution of Worlds," proposal for John E. Sawyer Seminar, 2012, http://sawyerseminar .ucdavis.edu/files/2012/01/Sawyer_Seminar_Proposal.pdf.

6. Marisol de la Cadena, "Indigenous Cosmopolitics in the Andes: Conceptual Reflections beyond 'Politics,'" *Cultural Anthropology* 25, no. 2 (2010): 350–51.

7. Tony Crook, *Exchanging Skin: Anthropological Knowledge, Secrecy and Bolivip, Papua New Guinea* (Oxford: Oxford University Press, 2007), 10. This led him to experiment with an ethnographic account that did not overtly depend on the explication of social relations. "We might begin to imagine the semantic paradox of a social anthropology not mediated by 'social relationships.' . . . Angkaiyakmin have language neither for social relationships nor for the relationality anthropologists work with to 'put things

in context' and to produce descriptions, analyses and interpretations. Participation of persons and things in each other is conceived without an idiom of 'relationality' . . . and is instead simply assumed." Crook, *Exchanging Skin*, 28.

8. See Marilyn Strathern, *Kinship, Law and the Unexpected: Relatives Are Always a Surprise* (Cambridge: Cambridge University Press, 2005), 91. "We have been here before" refers to the fact that these are old issues in epistemology, at the same time made present to great effect in contemporary writings by diverse colleagues, including other contributors to this volume.

9. At the 2008 biennial conference of the European Society for Oceanists (ESfO), brought up as a theme for the 2010 conference; the quotation that follows is in the words of the 2010 conference organizers. Since then, ECOPAS has been formally asked to advise the European Parliament on development strategy in the Pacific. See ESfO, "Theme," *ESfO 2010: Exchanging Knowledge in Oceania*, University of St. Andrews, 2009–10, https://www.st-andrews.ac.uk/esfo2010/.

10. See for example James Leach and Richard Davis, "Recognising and Translating Knowledge: Navigating the Political, Epistemological, Legal and Ontological," *Anthropological Forum* 22, no. 3 (2012): 211. Over the last twenty-five years, oceanist anthropologists have been concerned with knowledge exchanges in fields such as intellectual property rights, cultural property, heritage, and repatriation, and all those situations where development aspirations have drawn on "indigenous knowledge."

11. Isabelle Stengers, "Comparison as a Matter of Concern," *Common Knowledge* 17, no. 1 (2011): 59.

12. Here by means of a reconstitution of the international scholarly community that would contain diverse reasons for acknowledging debt and obligation.

13. Donna Haraway, "Situated Knowledges: The Science Question in Feminism and the Privilege of Partial Perspective," in *Simians, Cyborgs, and Women: The Reinvention of Nature* (1988; repr., London: Free Association, 1991), 195, 198.

14. Roy Wagner, *The Invention of Culture* (Englewood Cliffs, NJ: Prentice-Hall, 1975).

15. De la Cadena, "Indigenous Cosmopolitics," 361–62.

16. Stengers, "Comparison as a Matter of Concern," 59.

17. Stengers, "Comparison as a Matter of Concern."

18. DCMS, *The Report of the Working Group on Human Remains* (London: Department for Culture, Media and Sport, UK Government, 2003). I was a member of the Working Group, an independent advisory committee that reported to the then Department for Culture, Media and Sport (DCMS); I confine my remarks, which draw on descriptions given elsewhere, to the published report. See, for example, Marilyn Strathern, "Can One Rely on Knowledge?," in *Evidence, Ethics and Experiment: The Anthropology and History of Medical Research in Africa*, ed. P. Wenzel Geissler and Catherine Molyneux, 57–75 (Oxford: Berghahn, 2011).

19. The beginning of the report talks of "an irreconcilable conflict between 'scientists' and 'indigenous people'" and of "polarized views," which meant that consensus would be difficult although it would be the group's achievement to show that some was possible. The last chapter before the recommendations is called "Resolving the Conflict." This polarization meant, among other things, that the voices of indigenous

scientists were taken as some kind of compromise position between opposed camps. DCMS, *The Report of the Working Group on Human Remains*, 29.

20. "Incidentally, having read the offensive language used by the museum submission we must say it is little wonder there is an increasing lack of sympathy for scientific research of us as a people. We are not animals to be described as 'pure' or 'spoiled' by intermarriage." Reply by the Tasmanian Aboriginal Centre to a collective letter from diverse museums in the UK quoted in DCMS, *The Report of the Working Group on Human Remains*, 43.

21. Strathern, *Kinship, Law and the Unexpected*, 7.

22. DCMS, *The Report of the Working Group on Human Remains*, 55, emphasis omitted.

23. An instance of Euro-American perspectivalism, after Law (to differentiate it from Amazonian perspectivism). This is not to say that on other occasions claimants' representatives could not handle this form of perspectivalism, but the political moment in this specific situation came from elsewhere. John Law, *After Method: Mess in Social Science Research* (London: Routledge, 2004).

24. See Helen Verran, "Re-imagining Land Ownership in Australia," *Postcolonial Studies* 1 (1998): 237–54.

25. Law, *After Method*, 135, emphasis omitted.

26. Its very basis was a tacit understanding (on both sides) that what was to count as knowledge could not be assumed, hence the need for an informed network. It is probably not necessary to add that ECOPAS's anthropologists have themselves articulated just such conflicts (see following), even if not under this name.

27. Notably, through their consent. The Working Group was much bothered, in relation to the Australian remains especially, about the brutal methods of extraction by which skeletal material ended up in museum collections; the other side of this was museums' concerns about the legitimacy of their holdings insofar as this was protected by the domain of UK law.

28. James Leach, "Knowledge as Kinship: Mutable Essence and the Significance of Transmission on the Rai Coast of Papua New Guinea," in *Kinship and Beyond: The Genealogical Model Reconsidered*, ed. Sandra Bamford and James Leach, 175–92 (Oxford: Berghahn, 2009), 181. So knowledge is not being treated as a matter of expertise that distinguishes people, because (to paraphrase Viveiros de Castro) basically everyone has the same kind of knowledge, that is, their own knowledge. It is the relative power and position of people, their relationships and state of being, that distinguish them. Eduardo Viveiros de Castro, "And," speech presented at Anthropology and Science, the 5th Decennial Conference of the Association of Social Anthropologists of Great Britain and Commonwealth, in *Manchester Papers in Social Anthropology* 7 (Manchester: Department of Social Anthropology, 2003).

29. Leach, "Knowledge as Kinship," 182.

30. Leach, "Knowledge as Kinship," 184.

31. See Sandra Bamford, "'Family Trees' among the Kamea of Papua New Guinea: A Non-genealogical Approach to Imagining Relatedness," in *Kinship and Beyond: The Genealogical Model Reconsidered*, ed. Sandra Bamford and James Leach, 159–74 (Oxford: Berghahn, 2009).

32. A kinship calculus sets up the possibility of seeing things from another's viewpoint (my relation to you and yours to mine). Exchange may similarly articulate the distinction between owners (of a place) and users (of its products), each of whom, as donor or recipient, also anticipates subsequently occupying the position of recipient or donor.

33. James Leach, "Leaving the Magic Out: Knowledge and Effect in Different Places," *Anthropological Forum* 22, no. 3 (2012): 255.

34. Euro-Americans have long acknowledged that what is assumed here also requires work to achieve: detachment has to be created, just as labor is detached from human life as a commodity, or people involved in all kinds of relations are turned into economistically minded marketeers, not to speak of the indifference of bureaucrats or the nonchalance of surgeons.

35. Porer Nombo and James Leach, *Reite Plants: An Ethnobotanical Study in Tok Pisin and English* (Canberra: Australian National University E Press, 2010).

36. This puts it too simply. Nombo had been meticulous to include only plants for which he could trace the route through which he knew them—namely, diverse people and places; moreover, he had deliberately left out the special formulas ("magic") that made knowledge locally efficacious, and was quizzed on this.

37. Leach, "Leaving the Magic Out," 264.

38. To rehearse an all too familiar point. For a recent analysis, see Bonifacio on the fate of Paraguayan shamans, and the insights drawn from Blaser (for example, who gets to say what "organization" is?). Valentina Bonifacio, "Building Up the Collective: A Critical Assessment of the Relationship between Indigenous Organisations and International Cooperation in the Paraguayan Chaco," *Social Anthropology* 21, no. 4 (2013): 510–22; Mario Blaser, *Storytelling Globalization from the Chaco and Beyond* (Durham, NC: Duke University Press, 2010).

39. Leach and Davis, "Recognising and Translating Knowledge," 211, 218.

40. Elizabeth Povinelli, "Radical Worlds: The Anthropology of Incommensurability and Inconceivability," *Annual Review of Anthropology* 30 (2001): 319–34.

41. Manuela Carneiro da Cunha, *"Culture" and Culture: Traditional Knowledge and Intellectual Rights* (Chicago: Prickly Paradigm, 2009). Some of the following was initially aired at a symposium convened by Manuela Carneiro da Cunha as a tribute to *La Pensée Sauvage*, at the Collège de France, 2012. I am grateful for the impetus of the occasion.

42. It is a world divided into ethnic or cultural domains that entails what she calls interethnic logic, "a way of organizing a relationship to other logics." (The rights she mentions are rights to indigenous knowledge.) Carneiro da Cunha, *"Culture" and Culture*, 69.

43. Carneiro da Cunha, *"Culture" and Culture*, 80–81.

44. Marie Reay, *The Kuma: Freedom and Conformity in the New Guinea Highlands* (Carlton, Australia: Melbourne University Press, 1959); Marie Reay, "Two Kinds of Ritual Conflict," *Oceania* 29 (1959): 290–96.

45. Reay, "Two Kinds of Ritual Conflict," 295.

46. Reay, "Two Kinds of Ritual Conflict," 291.

47. The relationship with perpetually hostile clans contrasted with that which they enjoyed with more friendly "temporary enemies," who could also be allies and marriage partners and would be among the spectators. Reay, "Two Kinds of Ritual Conflict," 290.

48. Martin Holbraad, *Truth in Motion: The Recursive Anthropology of Cuban Divination* (Chicago: University of Chicago Press, 2012), 220.

49. The properties of the world to which infinitions refer are already given, but have to be pulled into a basis for action. The Kuma clan asserting itself against its traditional enemies reinvents the meaning of the clan with these clan members at this time for that purpose in their minds—not as it was at the last ceremonial. The performance would become a baseline for the subsequent recognition of future flourishing, a judgment necessarily retrospective: the Pig Ceremonial has made the clan prosper.

50. Andrew Moutu, *Names Are Thicker Than Blood: Kinship and Ownership amongst the Iatmul* (Oxford: Oxford University Press, 2013).

51. Moutu, *Names Are Thicker Than Blood*, 202. Moutu's observation extends out from the often-argued proposition that Melanesians, including the Papua New Guineans he is talking about, take relationships as the implicit ground of being, the contrast being with the Euro-American impetus to see making relations and relationships as a matter of human agency. He draws on certain (Euro-American) philosophical arguments in the course of offering his own. Moutu, *Names Are Thicker Than Blood*, 199.

52. This is not the place to consider what counts as a person in Iatmul. Iatmul have thousands of proper names for things, features, events, phenomena of all kinds, and these names come in pairs, elder and younger brother; they have always existed, and are taken as a matter of necessity.

53. Eduardo Viveiros de Castro, "Perspectival Anthropology and the Method of Controlled Equivocation," *Tipití* 2, no. 1 (2004): 18.

54. Viveiros de Castro, "Perspectival Anthropology and the Method of Controlled Equivocation," emphasis omitted.

55. To avoid misunderstanding through cross-contamination with other debates, it should be categorically stated that "nonrelational" has nothing to do with resurrecting the individuality of phenomena. Indeed, in what ensues I go further than Stengers (for whom I doubt the negative was particularly significant in this context) and pose nonrelational as a kind of counterpart to the relational.

56. Alberto Corsín Jiménez and Rane Willerslev, "'An Anthropological Concept of the Concept': Reversibility among the Siberian Yukaghirs," *JRAI*, n.s., 13 (2007): 527–44.

57. Corsín Jiménez and Willerslev, "'An Anthropological Concept of the Concept,'" 537.

58. Corsín Jiménez and Willerslev, "'An Anthropological Concept of the Concept,'" 528.

59. Corsín Jiménez and Willerslev, "'An Anthropological Concept of the Concept,'" 536. The source of the metaphor (sneaking) used at the beginning.

60. Corsín Jiménez and Willerslev, "'An Anthropological Concept of the Concept,'" 537–38.

61. Donna Haraway, "A Cyborg Manifesto: Science, Technology, and Socialist-Feminism in the Late Twentieth Century," in *Simians, Cyborgs, and Women: The Reinvention of Nature* (1985; repr., London: Free Association, 1991).

62. Haraway, "A Cyborg Manifesto," 177.

63. Haraway, "A Cyborg Manifesto," 176. For the cybernetic organism, machine-organism relationships ("relations") are obsolete (178).

64. Haraway, "A Cyborg Manifesto," 163. This needs opening up further; the "self" in "self-reference" behaves in complicated ways, as when "systems produce the elements that they interrelate by the elements that they interrelate," or when "self-simplifying devices . . . make it possible to use the system as a premise of its own operation." Autopoesis (in a communication system) is summed up as "to continue to communicate." Luhmann, *Essays on Self-Reference*, 145, 167, 14.

65. Donna Haraway, *The Companion Species Manifesto: Dogs, People, and Significant Otherness* (Chicago: Prickly Paradigm, 2003).

66. Stengers, "Comparison as a Matter of Concern," 60. "Symbiosis means that . . . beings are related by common interests, but *common* does not mean having the same interest in common, only that the diverging interests now need each other"; such "connections" break indifference but bring no encompassing unity (60–61). Haraway, "A Cyborg Manifesto," 151.

67. Donna Haraway, "Modest_Witness@Second_Millennium.FemaleMan©_meets Oncomouse™," in *Modest_Witness@Second_Millennium.FemaleMan©_Meets Oncomouse™: Feminism and Technoscience* (New York: Routledge, 1997), 37.

BIBLIOGRAPHY

Bamford, Sandra. "'Family Trees' among the Kamea of Papua New Guinea: A Non-genealogical Approach to Imagining Relatedness." In *Kinship and Beyond: The Genealogical Model Reconsidered*, edited by Sandra Bamford and James Leach, 159–74. Oxford: Berghahn, 2009.

Blaser, Mario. *Storytelling Globalization from the Chaco and Beyond*. Durham, NC: Duke University Press, 2010.

Bonifacio, Valentina. "Building Up the Collective: A Critical Assessment of the Relationship between Indigenous Organisations and International Cooperation in the Paraguayan Chaco." *Social Anthropology* 21, no. 4 (2013): 510–22.

Carneiro da Cunha, Manuela. *"Culture" and Culture: Traditional Knowledge and Intellectual Rights*. Chicago: Prickly Paradigm, 2009.

Corsín Jiménez, Alberto, and Rane Willerslev. "'An Anthropological Concept of the Concept': Reversibility among the Siberian Yukaghirs." *JRAI*, n.s., 13 (2007): 527–44.

Crook, Tony. *Exchanging Skin: Anthropological Knowledge, Secrecy and Bolivip, Papua New Guinea*. Oxford: Oxford University Press, 2007.

DCMS. *The Report of the Working Group on Human Remains*. London: Department for Culture, Media and Sport, UK Government, 2003.

de la Cadena, Marisol. "Indigenous Cosmopolitics: Dialogues about the Reconstitution of Worlds." Proposal for John E. Sawyer Seminar, UC Davis, California, 2012. http://sawyerseminar.ucdavis.edu/files/2012/01/Sawyer_Seminar_Proposal.pdf.

de la Cadena, Marisol. "Indigenous Cosmopolitics in the Andes: Conceptual Reflections beyond 'Politics.'" *Cultural Anthropology* 25, no. 2 (2010): 334–70.

ESfO. "Theme." *ESfO 2010: Exchanging Knowledge in Oceania*, University of St. Andrews, 2009–10. https://www.st-andrews.ac.uk/esfo2010/.

Haraway, Donna. *The Companion Species Manifesto: Dogs, People, and Significant Otherness*. Chicago: Prickly Paradigm, 2003.

Haraway, Donna. "A Cyborg Manifesto: Science, Technology, and Socialist-Feminism in the Late Twentieth Century." In *Simians, Cyborgs, and Women: The Reinvention of Nature*. 1985. Reprint, London: Free Association, 1991.

Haraway, Donna. "Modest_Witness@Second_Millennium.FemaleMan©_meets Oncomouse™." In *Modest_Witness@Second_Millennium.FemaleMan©_Meets Oncomouse™: Feminism and Technoscience*. New York: Routledge, 1997.

Haraway, Donna. "Situated Knowledges: The Science Question in Feminism and the Privilege of Partial Perspective." In *Simians, Cyborgs, and Women: The Reinvention of Nature*. 1985. Reprint, London: Free Association, 1991.

Holbraad, Martin. *Truth in Motion: The Recursive Anthropology of Cuban Divination*. Chicago: University of Chicago Press, 2012.

Law, John. *After Method: Mess in Social Science Research*. London: Routledge, 2004.

Leach, James. "Knowledge as Kinship: Mutable Essence and the Significance of Transmission on the Rai Coast of Papua New Guinea." In *Kinship and Beyond: The Genealogical Model Reconsidered*, edited by Sandra Bamford and James Leach, 175–92. Oxford: Berghahn, 2009.

Leach, James. "Leaving the Magic Out: Knowledge and Effect in Different Places. *Anthropological Forum* 22, no. 3 (2012): 251–70.

Leach, James, and Richard Davis. "Recognising and Translating Knowledge: Navigating the Political, Epistemological, Legal and Ontological." *Anthropological Forum* 22, no. 3 (2012): 209–23.

Luhmann, Niklas. *The Differentiation of Society*. Translated by Stephen Holmes and Charles Larmore. New York: Columbia University Press, 1982.

Luhmann, Niklas. *Essays on Self-Reference*. New York: Columbia University Press, 1990.

Moutu, Andrew. *Names Are Thicker Than Blood: Kinship and Ownership amongst the Iatmul*. Oxford: Oxford University Press, 2013.

Nombo, Porer, and James Leach. *Reite Plants: An Ethnobotanical Study in Tok Pisin and English*. Canberra: Australian National University E Press, 2010.

Povinelli, Elizabeth. "Radical Worlds: The Anthropology of Incommensurability and Inconceivability." *Annual Review of Anthropology* 30 (2001): 319–34.

Reay, Marie. *The Kuma: Freedom and Conformity in the New Guinea Highlands*. Carlton, Australia: Melbourne University Press, 1959.

Reay, Marie. "Two Kinds of Ritual Conflict." *Oceania* 29 (1959): 290–96.

Stengers, Isabelle. "Comparison as a Matter of Concern." *Common Knowledge* 17, no. 1 (2011): 48–63.

Strathern, Marilyn. "Can One Rely on Knowledge?" In *Evidence, Ethics and Experiment: The Anthropology and History of Medical Research in Africa*, edited by P. Wenzel Geissler and Catherine Molyneux, 57–75. Oxford: Berghahn, 2011.

Strathern, Marilyn. *Kinship, Law and the Unexpected: Relatives Are Always a Surprise.* Cambridge: Cambridge University Press, 2005.

Verran, Helen. "Re-imagining Land Ownership in Australia." *Postcolonial Studies* 1 (1998): 237–54.

Verran, Helen. "Transferring Strategies of Land Management: Indigenous Land Owners and Environmental Scientists." In *Research in Science and Technology Studies,* vol. 13: *Knowledge and Technology Transfer,* edited by Marianne de Laet, 158–81. New York: JAI Press, 2002.

Viveiros de Castro, Eduardo. "And." Speech presented at Anthropology and Science, the 5th Decennial Conference of the Association of Social Anthropologists of Great Britain and Commonwealth. In *Manchester Papers in Social Anthropology* 7. Manchester: Department of Social Anthropology, 2003.

Viveiros de Castro, Eduardo. "Perspectival Anthropology and the Method of Controlled Equivocation." *Tipití* 2, no. 1 (2004): 3–22.

Wagner, Roy. *The Invention of Culture.* Englewood Cliffs, NJ: Prentice-Hall, 1975.

TWO

SPIDERWEB ANTHROPOLOGIES

Ecologies, Infrastructures, Entanglements

Alberto Corsín Jiménez

Ecologies, infrastructures, entanglements. Anthropology and social studies of science (STS) have found some unsuspected common groundings in the relational, emergent, and self-organizational affordances of these three conceptual systems. Vibrant yet fragile, interactive and responsive while simultaneously resilient and solicitous, the earthy and muddled and tenacious engagements afforded by ecologies, infrastructures, and entanglements have brought new sources of analytical vitality and valence to social theory.[1] These are languages of description that conjure worlds of material and biotic interdependencies, human and nonhuman agencies weaving themselves into and around filaments of energy, matter, history, and decay. Worlds that hold on; worlds that creep up. Spider worlds and spiderwebs calling for spiderweb anthropologies.

In this chapter I want to introduce the figure of the spiderweb as a heuristic to help us think our current predicament of expulsion, ruin, and precarity. The spiderweb, I want to suggest, offers an apposite metaphor for a world that holds itself in precarious balance, that tenses itself with violence and catastrophe but also grace and beauty, and that calls out and silhouettes promissory worlds of entanglements. However, what draws me to the metaphoric seduction of the spiderweb, I must add, is one specific trait: its semblance and vocation as a trap. Spiderwebs are traps. It is their materiality as traps, their condition as material and epistemic interfaces between worlds, that helps us capture new openings for the work of imagination and description today.

I am interested in the work that traps can do for description, in the trap as a method for description. The spiderweb offers a beautiful example of how this method works: the spiderweb entangles the worlds of prey and predator and in so doing outlines and crystallizes the infrastructure of their ecologies. The spiderweb trap is an ecology, but it is also an entanglement, and it is also an infrastructure. I shall return to each one of these registers in more detail shortly.

The method of description that the spiderweb trap sets in motion is a specific type of recursive operation: think of the spider's spinning of the web, eating part of it daily to recuperate some of the energy expended in spinning. The operation of recursion works therefore as a source environment for future descriptions and an environmental palette itself. We may think of it as a technique of double environmentalization: weaving worlds into existence at the same time as it recaptures existing worlds. Describing worlds and worlding descriptions. Worlds that hold on, worlds that creep up. Such recursive self-spinning is also, inevitably, my method. So let me move on by rewinding, and start by providing some ethnographic background to the notion of double environmentalization.

Double Environmentalizations

Among the Tibeto-Burman Nuosu people of the Greater Cool Mountains of Sichuan Province, China, the soul of a living person is said to inhabit the outer surface of the human body in the form of a "soul-spider."[2] Although the body of a Nuosu person "hosts" the soul-spider, who otherwise "leads a vulnerably exposed existence, since it may 'fall off' of its owner's body and 'become lost' when its owner is frightened, ill, or stumbles while walking," we may similarly speak of the soul-spider as "hosting" the person, for the latter's well-being largely depends on his or her remaining attached to the soul-spider and the cloud of web filaments that it spins on the body.[3] These filaments often ambush and capture things that circulate in the surrounds of the body, whose corresponding expansions or contractions may be thought of as body enhancements or depletions responding to its "guesting" on the soul-spider's web. Katherine Swancutt, whose Nuasu ethnography I follow here, describes thus the Nuasu "web of hospitality" wherein body and soul trap each other as part of a larger "spider-slave complex," where hosts and guests employ "intimate trickery" more generally to gain leverage and advantage vis-à-vis one another in a form of "double-captivity."[4]

The notion of double captivity is one that Swancutt draws building on Roy Wagner's image of the "double agent" of hospitality, a "grifter" model of sociability where the complex play of suspicion and trust energizes the social game.[5] Elsewhere Wagner has spoken more widely of the "double encompassment" that characterizes all forms of symbolic agency.[6] An example is his description of "land shamanism" among the Daribi people of Mount Karimi.[7] Here a *hoa-bidi*, "soul-person" or "die-person," upon being denied proper ritual burial, "expersonates" herself by taking over the land and becoming the territory.[8] This brings about a formidable transformation in the internal circulation of human and nonhuman capacities: the soul-person's knowledge of the land, "his wayfinding abilities . . . become the way itself"; "he acquires the ability to estrange the self-orientation body-images (a navigational necessity for all motile creatures) of game animals and birds from their rightful owners and deliver them to living hunters in their dreams at night."[9] The world thus terraforms to the hoa-bidi's dispositions and will. In this capacity he can for example take the souls of hunters hostage by effectively deploying his charmed landscape to lure them into a world of abundance.

The risk of depredation and depletion that the territory-shifting strategies of the "place-soul" posits to the Daribi can only be redressed through the *habu* ritual, a ceremonial communion that requites the omitted burial feast denied to the die-person.[10] The funerary ritual stages a relation where the Daribi and the land shaman play guest and host to each other, and where the lurking tensions of double encompassment are finally maximized and blown out: in habu the exchange of encompassments is encompassed yet one more time, when "the people of the community . . . are [themselves] feasted as *guests of the land*."[11] We may therefore think of this maximal form of encompassment as a specific expression of the spider-slave complex, one, however, where the environment (the land) traps all—where the double encompassment is now outhosted by a double environmentalization.

Although neither Swancutt nor Wagner say as much, I would like to suggest that the maximal description toward which their ethnographies of double captivity tend—the process of double environmentalization—may be thought of as the ethnographic spinning of a spiderweb, where environments trap people and where people trap environments, and where the very notion of trapping is subjected to continuous examination and trial, such that in its spinning—in its recursions—description is allowed to become a method that traps doubles: now predator, now prey; now host, now guest; now community, now territory; now environments that environmentalize themselves.

Sticky entanglements, terraforming ecologies, material deceits and tensions: the spiderweb trap advances as method by capturing and environmentalizing every new description. Such a method, however, is not exclusive to Nuoso or Daribi anthropology. As intimated in my opening paragraphs, I want to make a more general claim here about the trap as a method of description for social theory today. I want to put forward an argument—fragile and "temptative" as the metaphor itself—that the form of recursion that traps set in motion has in fact been central to the sustenance and fueling of the modern episteme.[12] In their modesty, in their material humbleness, in their accessorial role to the allegedly more important operations of thinking or conceptualization, traps have however persistently captured and furnished multiple worlds for us.

Part of my excursus here, then, will be to gesture to some of the ways in which certain classical epistemes of the modern condition—epistemology, experimentation, ecology, information—have trapped themselves out. I do not mean this in a negative sense. One must not be judgmental about the effects that entrapments bring forth. Traps are predatory, but they are also productive. They trick and trade on worlds to be. Thus, rather than boldly struggling to escape the traps of modern knowledge, what follows is an attempt at spiderwebbing our way with them. I want to clear a space from where we might see how anthropological description traps itself out—an outline of how far the trap may go to revitalize anthropological comparison.

I spin the rest of my argument around three ethnographic-cum-historical vignettes: on seventeenth-century trompe l'oeil painting, experimental designs in science, and the media-ethological and environmental intelligences of informational capitalism. Although the narrative has a temporal sequence to it (from the seventeenth century to our times), the argument is as far from linearity and progression as it can get. As noted above, it is one of my central intuitions that modern knowledge is essentially a trap to itself, such that most forms of explanation are guests unaware they are actually being hosted—predators who do not know their own condition as prey. There are some respects in which the arguments I make at the end of the chapter are therefore hosts to the arguments I make earlier on. It is part of my game here to convey a sense for a mode of argumentation that doubles—that traps and environmentalizes—itself throughout. In this guise I venture a modality of anthropological description that aims to make the modern production of knowledge face up to the conditions of its own predation.[13]

The Trap of Entanglements

Let me introduce you to *The Reverse of a Framed Painting* (see figure 2.1), a painting by seventeenth-century Dutch artist Cornelius Gijsbrechts. Gijsbrechts was relatively well known in his time as a painter of still lifes. In fact, as far as we know, he only painted still lifes.

Despite having a certain reputation while alive, his oeuvre gradually fell into oblivion. Recently, however, some art historians have returned to it, and in particular to this one painting. For Victor Stoichita, for instance, *The Reverse of a Framed Painting* signals no less than the closure of a historical epoch.[14] The painting marks the culmination of that tradition of baroque art that inaugurated the conditions for metapictorial reflection. This was a time when the most cunning of artists (Diego Velázquez, Johannes Vermeer) experimented with visual registers, robbing spectators of the presumed privilege of representational awareness and thrusting this back into the interiority of the paintings themselves. Let me explain.

Take a look at Gijsbrechts's painting. What gets represented here is quite literally the reverse of a framed painting. Stoichita and other commentators have noted that in its original setting the painting likely would have been placed on the floor, leaning against a wall. Imagine someone walking into the room where the painting lies. They see a wooden frame, held together by six frail nails. The stretcher holds a canvas, and a label with a number on it (36) has been pegged to the back of the canvas, in all likelihood indicating that the work is one in a series of many, or part of a collection. So, as Hanneke Grootenboer has put it, "If we follow our inclination to turn this canvas around in order to see what is represented on its front side, its shock effect would reside less in the deception, and more in the discovery that there is nothing there to see. Nothing, except for the same image, back as front."[15]

In a previous analysis of this painting, I suggested that Gijsbrechts's work may be seen as signaling not just the birth of painting as a nonrepresentational activity—for the painting does not stand for anything; it actually, quite literally, stands for itself: it is a self-standing object.[16] But as I said, it is not just the birth of nonrepresentational painting that we encounter

FIGURE 2.1. Cornelius Gijsbrechts, *The Reverse of a Framed Painting*, 1670.

here. The painting may also be seen to endow this flipping compulsion—this need to reverse the canvas, back to front, and back again—with an epistemic status of sorts.

The Reverse of a Framed Painting (Gijsbrechts's work) and the reverse of a framed painting (of any painting) both index the same presentation of the world (the reverse of a framed painting), but they do so from, respectively, an epistemological and an ontological point of view; or, let us say, a human and an object-centered point of view. Whereas *The Reverse of a Framed Painting* is the view we hold of the picture as viewers, that is, a view that obtains through the act of eliciting the painting as object, the reverse side of a canvas, on the other hand, elicits not an epistemological point of view, but an ontological position: an object (the wooden stretcher) that no longer requires the epistemological elicitation of a viewer to come into existence.

However, I would like to stress that this dazzling display of double relations (between representation:presentation; human:object; epistemology: ontology) is only temporarily held stable through the flipping itself. The painting and the canvas appear mixed up and entangled, part of one confusing and blurred epistemic register, only because we can flip the frame around. The flipping makes the entanglement visible as an epistemic operation. The relations double as relations—they become visible to themselves—through the act of flipping. Oscillating between a human-centered and an object-centered point of view, between an epistemological and an onto-logical location, the trompe l'oeil's very reversible structure emerges as the only possible comfort zone for stabilizing the turbulence and confusion of all such double movements. It is the painting's reversibility that holds all such reversions meaningful. It is reversibility itself that rises therefore to the status of epistemic operator.

It is worth stressing that the reversibility effect is itself the outcome of a trap, in this case, the aesthetic trap of the trompe l'oeil. It is the trompe l'oeil that tricks reversibility into existence. The trap "traps out"—it simultaneously captures and liberates—an epistemic effect.

Now I am no historian of art, so I am a little out of my depth here. I should note, however, that the tricks of the trompe l'oeil respond to a symbolic economy of production. The masters of seventeenth-century baroque art (Velázquez, Vermeer, Rembrandt, Pieter Saenredam) sought to complexify, if not directly undermine, the traditional system of symbolic representations of the art world of their time. Up until the seventeenth century, artists aimed to have their works enter an established symbolic economy of pictorial and allegorical cross-references. The meaning of a painting was established through its emplacement in a larger historical economy of images.

The paintings of collectors' cabinets that proliferated in the seventeenth century capture the paroxysm of this economy, such that the best a painting could do was to aspire to its own inclusion in the system of images that it represented. Willem van Haecht's rendering of van der Geest's pictorial gallery is a well-known example (see figure 2.2). This is the economy of representation that the masters of baroque art hoped to escape and undermine.

The tricks of the trompe l'oeil were therefore as much illusionistic as economic. Their iconoclasm was as much aesthetic as sociological. The traps were aimed at bringing into existence novel conceptions of authorship, new economic relations of patronage and artistic enterprise, new techniques and styles of craftsmanship, a modality of participatory spectatorship, and even a material and aesthetic basis for (political) consciousness and (relational) cogitation, as well as, of course, a wholesale new visual culture.[17] This is why I say that the trapping was epistemic.

FIGURE 2.2. Willem van Haecht, *The Gallery of Cornelis van der Geest*, c. 1628.

I have one last comment about Gijsbrechts's wonderful painting. Think of the painting in its original trapping position: lying on the floor, perhaps leaning against a wall. In this position, the painting has abandoned its pictorial qualities. It calls for its recognition, not as a painting, but as an object. It hopes to look just like any other piece of furniture: a wooden stretcher that solicits it being turned around and placed in a proper setting and position. We need to find a place for this painting. First, however, we need to pick up the frame, carry it, hang it somewhere. As an object, then, the painting no longer solicits our gaze. Rather, it mobilizes our whole body in an immersive environmentalization. This is the work of interior design and decoration, which is both an aesthetic and material project. The painting, in other words, enfolds the pictorial moment in the atmospherics of objecthood. It becomes an object by trapping its own environment, us included. It describes a world by worlding its own description.

This is as far as my first trap takes us. Somewhere in the seventeenth century a group of artists discover in the trompe l'oeil an epistemic operator for doubling—for entangling—the descriptive affordances of worlds. The trompe l'oeil tricks and trades in possible worlds. These worlds are neither visible nor invisible, neither wholly perspectival and geometrical nor classical and mimetic. Rather, they are worlds captured in the turbulence of double relations, worlds that crack in between perspectives—quite literally, by cracking perspectivalism itself open. Seventeenth-century trompe l'oeil and anamorphic paintings function thus as traps that thrust our bodies before our eyes. They enrapture the body and leave the gaze behind. They are also in this sense worlds that come with environments attached.

Traps for Ecologies . . .

Let me keep in view this image of a form of trapping that comes with environments attached—of environments that entrap themselves. To do so I shall rely on the work of anthropologist Ann Kelly, who has for some time now been studying a type of experimental hut that is used for entomological research in southeastern Tanzania.[18] Experimental huts are in fact a classic tool of entomological science. First designed in the 1940s by British researchers in Kenya, they have since been used to monitor the flight patterns of malaria-carrying mosquitoes.

The huts are built emulating vernacular architectural models and are erected in the periphery of villages. The architecture, notes Kelly, "serves a dual purpose: to isolate 'natural' mosquito behaviour on the one hand and to represent 'typical' village conditions on the other."[19]

The commitment to build the huts following local architectural designs (mud surfaces, thatched roofs, detachable windows, etc.) responds to an experimental exigency to model and "keep the interspecies [human-mosquito] encounter intimate."[20] There are a number of reasons why this is so, not least because transmission vectors and epidemiological dynamics vary widely according to local circumstances. For example, by having one, two, and up to ten volunteers sleeping overnight in a hut, early experimenters revealed the effect of body mass on malaria transmission. Later experiments also showed that pregnant women were predisposed to malaria infection because of mosquito olfaction.[21] The spatial and sociological architecture of the huts thus conditions the type of data collected under their roof.

The huts are therefore conceived as "experimental architectures" equipped with an array of "techniques of capture."[22] I do not think it does much violence to Kelly's ethnography to describe the huts as epistemic traps: experimental-cum-environmental traps, for mosquitoes, of course, but also for tracking epidemiological data.[23] I use the term "epistemic" here advertently, because it is actually central to Kelly's project to show that as experimental architectures the huts' functionality depends precisely on taking stock of their "built-in uncertainty."[24] The uncertainty is crucial to their experimental design. As she puts it, "The provisional character of these experiments works to situate their claims. The huts' aesthetic—their detachable traps, open eaves, wire baffles, automotive coils, sheets and meshes—interrupts the causal linearity of proof. Instead, these rooms provide a momentary resting place to observe and record the site-specific details of man–mosquito interaction. Their experimental framework allows for evidentiary expansion from model to home, but the wiggle room between the two suggests that these extensions are subject to revision and adjustment."[25]

We could say therefore that the huts' materiality functions as a sort of interface between environmental and social relations. The huts capture the environmental dynamics of mosquitoes in epidemiological terms, that is, their movement across time-space; but the huts are also designed to suspend momentarily—to function as "momentary resting places," as Kelly puts it—human-mosquito relations. So in a sense the huts are indeed ecological traps. They are not unlike spiderwebs: infrastructural space-time interventions in a cultural ecology that open up a space of différance where the agentival capacities of mosquitoes, local villagers, entomologists, thatched roofs, or public health research are temporarily suspended so that their relations can be reassembled anew.

. . . And Ecologies That Trap

The image of an experimental arrangement as a trap of sorts is actually a common epistemological trope (and ploy) in twentieth-century science. In his historical epistemology of the development of twentieth-century molecular biology, Hans-Jörg Rheinberger has described, for example, the implicit rules of scientific experimentation as constituting "a kind of experimental spider's web: the web must be meshed in such a way that unknown and unexpected prey is likely to be caught. The web must 'see' what the spider actually is unable to foresee with its unaided senses."[26]

Of course, the image of the spiderweb as a trap for epistemic things has traversed twentieth-century scientific thought ever since it was most eloquently deployed by Jacob von Uexküll in his investigations into animal environments.[27] The spiderweb is a central—and arguably one of the most important—images in Uexküll's book. It is regularly resorted to in the book as an analogy or trope for other forms of environmentalization. For example, when Uexküll describes how animals transform their homes into territories, he compares the structured tunnel systems built by moles to a spiderweb.[28] When he explains the developmental rules that give form to the bat's echolocational radar, he similarly draws on the spider's web to make the point that "neither of them is only meant for one, physically present subject, but for all animals of the same structure."[29]

But the spiderweb plays more than an exemplary role in Uexküll's text, for, as he puts it, "one can recognize the reign of Nature's plans in the weaving of a spider's web."[30] Thus, the web stands for the self-elicitation of Nature's designs. It is a cipher that holds within the intricacies of Nature's meaning. Indeed, it is "the interpretation of the spider's web"—a dedicated epigraph in the book—that supplies Uexküll the "primal image" with which to build his biosemiotic metaphysics.[31] As he famously put it, the "spider's web represents a meaning utilizer of the carrier of meaning 'prey' in the spider's environment."[32] The spider and the fly, in other words, mirror each other in the ecological interface of the web. And the "meaning" of nature—the meaning of the web, in this case—is but its surface tension: it "surfaces" in the tension that "counterpoints" the spider's and the fly's environmental relations: "The spider's web is configured in a fly-like way, because the spider is also fly-like. To be fly-like means that the spider has taken up certain elements of the fly in its constitution. . . . The fly-likeness of the spider means that it has taken up certain motifs of the fly melody in its bodily composition. . . . The theory of meaning culminates in the uncovering of this connection."[33]

The spiderweb is for Uexküll, then, the symbol of an onto-ecology. It is the trap that entangles ecology in its self-determining vocation. Nature is a trap and ecology is its infrastructure. And the spiderweb is the interface that mediates their entanglement.

I would like to dwell for a moment on this view of the spiderweb as an artifactualization of ecological relations: where the mutual describability of spider-fly relations is trapped in the form of an ecological infrastructure, or, said somewhat differently, where the spiderweb provides the infrastructure for the double capture (in the terms used earlier on) of ecology and description. I am interested in what kind of work this mutual describability is seen to do.

One of the few anthropologists who has taken the trap seriously as an anthropological problem is Alfred Gell.[34] Gell approached the question of trapping indirectly, for he was actually examining how and what makes an artwork artistic in the first place. Famously, Gell suggested that artworks functioned as traps, in that they successfully retained complexes of social relations within the vicinity of their environmental influence.[35] In this sense, Gell suggested, traps are little different from, say, Marcel Duchamp's readymades, for they both index forms of surrogate agency and model the world as a human-environmental entanglement. A trap, noted Gell,

> is a model as well as an implement. . . . The arrow trap is particularly clearly a model of its creator, because it has to substitute for him; a surrogate hunter, it does its owner's hunting for him. It is, in fact, an automaton or robot, whose design epitomizes the design of its maker. . . . It is equipped with a rudimentary sensory transducer (the cord, sensitive to the animal's touch). This afferent nervous system brings information to the automaton's central processor (the trigger mechanism, a switch, the basis of all information-processing devices) which activates the efferent system, releasing the energy stored in the bow, which propels the arrows, which produce action-at-a-distance (the victim's death). This is not just a model of a person . . . but a "working" model of a person.[36]

But traps do not just model their creators; they model their targets too. Hunters manufacture traps to emulate a prey's environs. "Traps are lethal parodies of the animal's *Umwelt*," says Gell.[37]

The parody, in Gell's unparalleled witty formulation, is not unlike what Uexküll described as the "contrapuntal" spider-fly likeness. It is the sensorium of a mutual describability between spider and fly worlds. It is lethal, however, because it traps the likeness and makes it deadly visible. The trap artifactualizes the parody. It extricates the mutual describability of spider-fly entanglements as infrastructure—as an interface.

You may have noted the use above that Gell makes of cybernetic images in his description of the trap's environmental circuitry. Although he speaks of the trap as an "automaton or robot," he is in fact describing a sensory and nervous system. The trap, for Gell, is a media and information-processing device. It is an interface, a binary switch code, that alternately contains and releases energy/information. However, it is still, ultimately, a trap: that is, an artifact modeled on, and that functions as a vehicle or conduit for, exo-environmental relations. The trap may be an infrastructure for carrying information, but it is the infrastructure (of ecological relations) that matters.[38]

So this is as far as my second trap takes us. If the trompe l'oeil trap was used by seventeenth-century baroque artists to make doubled worlds visible, perhaps it is fair to say that some strands of twentieth-century experimental thought have found the aesthetics of trapping useful as a tool for making ecologies visible. Or, said somewhat differently, that ecological thought has itself been trapped out: that it has been bodied forth as an infrastructure through which ecological entanglements become visible. Moreover, captured in the figure of the environment as trap, there also seems to be the notion of information as a trapping impulse, as something that jumps outside or ahead of itself.

Media Ecologies: Sentient Intelligences

When I employed the phrase "mutual describability" of spider-fly likenesses above, I was in fact echoing a description that digital art and media theorist Matthew Fuller has made of Uexküll's spiderweb. Fuller comes to the spiderweb in an exercise to rethink the spatial and medial qualities of architectural structures: "In that 'a subtle portrait of the fly' is drawn in the web of the spider, this is also a system that evinces proper medial qualities of integration and communication, whilst at the same time promising the dissolution of the domains previously internal to that which is drawn into communication. Sensual extension, capture and the precise delineation of space in a spontaneous, tirelessly reworked and cunningly arranged net is crucial to the medial trope of dispersal."[39] Architecture, proposes Fuller, works just like spider's webs do. While much recent media and systems theory has blossomed on the idea of the "mutual describability of media, information and space in terms of flow," for Fuller, the crucial question remains not how ecologies of information thrive on flows, but how they develop intrinsic capacities—how the flows are brought to a halt.[40] Building on the ecological trope, he notes that "space is, in certain ways and to differing degrees, species-specific. Each landscape reveals affordances and dangers that, like the web to the fly, are significant only to certain sensorial natures, intelligences and capacities."[41] Space, Fuller seems to suggest, is a trap that, if properly laid out, may result in the release of fecund intellectual energies.

When it comes to imagining and developing such spider-architectures, Fuller proposes that we attend to designing spatialities capable of becoming at once interfaces and placeholders for very different "kinds of intelligence."[42] I quote at length:

> Firstly, one of the most urgent means of developing such an approach is by engendering a sensitivity to the urban in which multiple kinds of intelligence, including those of non-human species and their spatial practices in all their fundamental alienness to humans, have a significant place. . . . Secondly, to recognize that in the generative development of spatialities that intensify intelligence, specialization takes place. . . . Cities can be characterized as a concentrated process of the gathering, enfolding and dispersal of such spaces. In becoming strange themselves through such specialization and congruence, they create mutant fitness landscapes for forms of intelligence to interpret, cohabit, or to disperse from.[43]

What we have here, then, is a proposition where the spider architecture is imagined no longer as simply a surface tensor of ecological relations, the infrastructure enabling/enabled by mutual describabilities, but as a lively episteme in its own right. The spider architecture functions as a web of intelligences—"mutant fitness landscapes for forms of intelligence," as Fuller puts it.

Fuller's interest in environmental intelligences forms part of a field of scholarship that aims to reorient ecological thinking outside the realm of linguistic and symbolic representation and toward a conception of relationality based on the intensive assembling of affects, capacities, and energetics.[44] Thus, drawing on the novel sensor and network capacities of digital media and relations, Fuller has elsewhere spoken of the rise of new "media ecologies," while Jussi Parikka has imagined an "insect" theory of media, where insect worlds provide an imago for "media as a milieu of intensive capabilities, an ethology."[45] These ethological media worlds are called into life as habitats of tensional and ephemeral "palpations," which "like the vortices of . . . whirlpools . . . simply vanish when the special geometry of constraints that sustains it disappears."[46] Perhaps unsurprisingly, spiderwebs have provided a common point of reference for this "entrapment" (my term) of theory as vitalistic ethology.

Urban theory has likewise been inflected by these spider ecologies. Nigel Thrift has referred, for example, to the irruption of ubiquitous computing technologies in the urban fabric as deploying novel "expressive infrastructures" that "thicken space" and cloak our surroundings with the atmospheric pressures and intensities of "some of the characteristics of weather."[47] Mark Shepard speaks of "informatic weather systems" whose invisible (digital) winds and currents steep our surroundings deep with new relational affordances and affects, shaping emotional and intensive landscapes of data in action.[48] An example is the work of new media artist and theorist Natalie Jeremijenko, who has experimented with the use of open-source digital sensors to measure water quality and aquatic life in the East River and Bronx River in New York. Known as *Amphibious Architecture*, the aquatic sensor interface aims to employ the technological affordances of ubiquitous computing to expand the ontological register of "interaction partners for environmental governance."[49] Nigel Thrift goes as far as positing that the multiplication of such ontological registers demands on the part of the social sciences the "re-examination of the notion of the environment," as well as the development of the "atmospheric means of understanding what is in the world and how to control it."[50]

In the final part of this essay, I want to explore the idea of ecological and ambient intelligences. If the trompe l'oeil and the spiderweb were the epistemic traps that made, respectively, double and onto-ecological worlds possible, I wonder whether there might be any purchase in looking for the traps of ambient and informational intelligences today.

To this effect, I present ethnographic work that, along with my colleague Adolfo Estalella, we have been carrying out since 2011 with Basurama and Zuloark, two guerrilla and open-source architectural collectives in Madrid. These collectives are widely recognized in Spanish and Latin American artistic and architectural circuits for being at the vanguard of what a MOMA exhibition (where work by Zuloark was showcased) has dubbed "tactical urbanism": experiments with architectural form and media that respond to the challenges of uneven urban growth in the "global South."[51] What makes the approach developed by Basurama and Zuloark distinctive in this context is their development of open-source, auto-constructive strategies for negotiating such urban challenges.[52]

A good example of the work that Basurama and Zuloark do is a series of workshops that they organized between 2011 and 2014 called Handmade Urbanism. The aim of the workshops is to invite participants to implode

the grandiloquence of urban designs by making their own urban equipment. They call this practice "brico-urbanism." Brico-urbanism is all about
designing and making objects. But, as they put it, "brico-urbanism workshops are not industrial design workshops. They are rather laboratories on
the urban condition. For urbanism today is made from things [el urban-
ismo se hace desde las cosas]."[53]

The objects made at a Handmade Urbanism are all assembled by re-
cycling trash or abandoned materials. To this effect, in the early days of a
workshop, participants engage in a "trash safari" around the local neighborhood in a hunt for wood planks, plastics, and other types of materials
that might prove useful in future design and construction sessions. These
safaris go out to the city at night and offer participants an opportunity to
engage with the otherwise invisible materiality of the city's residual waste-
lands. In homage to the Situationists' urban deambulations, the term *dérive*
is applied to these drifting walkabouts around a neighborhood, which in
Situationist fashion are also therefore somewhat aimed at recuperating the
psychogeography of neighborly life that lies outside the circuits of capital.[54]

The Situationist reference gestures to a larger concern of Basurama
and Zuloark, namely, that the pieces of furniture become boundary objects
for the communities they work with. For both collectives, the furniture
must materialize the community of relations wherein it is to be emplaced.
Thus, they go to great lengths to source their building materials locally, to
have local craftsmen and technicians join the project, and to document
as much as possible the socioeconomic context that has led the community to express a need for a particular piece of furniture. But their projects
are also heavily invested in an exploration of the languages and grammar
of architectural and sociological form and media. The objects created at a
workshop do not have a stable (technical, graphic, media, diagrammatic)
representation. As open-source designs, they are continuously subjected
to ontological scrutiny and intervention: open to modulations and reap-
propriations, to new renderings and redeployments, to retrofitting and reas-
sembling, in different territories, communities, (software) languages, files,
formats, and materialities.

Thus, the pieces of furniture developed at these workshops do not just
point to the "atmospheric" intercessions of new environmental intelligences, as Nigel Thrift has put it.[55] The ontological challenge here does not
respond to an awakening to novel sensorial and network capacities. These
are not so much ecologies in flux, responding to the intensive affordances

of weather-like streams of digital currents and emotional data, as ecologies in beta, whose landscapes would seem to echo rather Roy Wagner's description of Daribi land shamanism: landscapes that can both host and hold hostage, but also terraform and reorient the capacities of human and nonhuman persons—environments that are neither subjected to agency nor the holders of agency themselves, but rather sources for opening (open-sourcing) the very epistemics of agency.

Ecologies in Beta

Sometime in the winter of 2012, Adolfo and I sat down with Basurama and Zuloark to explore the "conceptual furniture" animating the crossover between their open-source and autoconstructive approaches to urbanism and the recent Madrid Occupy developments (locally known as May 15, 15M movement). We had all been involved in various capacities in the protests and shared a dissatisfaction with their widespread theorization as "digital revolutions" or new "commons-oriented" social movements.[56] We were intrigued instead by the analogies between architectural autoconstruction and the material affordances of urban assembling.[57] We found in the notion of *amueblamiento* (furnishing) a promising point of departure for exploring how the assemblies refurnished and autoconstructed the political landscape of the city. If the urban condition was terraforming anew under the aegis of the Occupy spirit, we were provoked to reimagine it instead as a *terre mueble*—a furnishing of the territory.[58] We called the project *15Muebles*, fifteen pieces of furniture, a playful homage to the 15M movement.

The furnishing of the territory, as we have come to understand it, does not amount simply to a constructionist and material intervention in the urban condition. The *muebles* are not (just) items of urban equipment. Rather, they are signs of an ecology in beta. Their political entity, too, must be thought as being in beta, which rather than "unfinished" or "partial" should be read in this context as meaning in "productive suspension." To better explain what the political ontology of "in beta" amounts to, let me turn to the history of one of the most fascinating pieces of furniture we have encountered to date.

In July 2012, Madrid's City Hall set in motion a consultation exercise for a new strategic plan for its cultural industries sector. The consultation process received severe criticism for availing itself of a commons and social innovation rhetoric and yet failing to open up to serious debate. In response,

City Hall asked Medialab-Prado (a new media and digital lab part of municipal government) to organize a call for citizen panels whose proceedings might inform the final consultation document. News of 15Muebles had reached the Medialab, who approached us inquiring whether we would be interested in organizing one such panel on gestión ciudadana de lo público, citizen-led initiatives for public resources.

We were kindly surprised by the invitation and agreed to organize it. We sent out a call to a very wide spectrum of community-led initiatives in Madrid: squatted social centers, urban community gardens (which were illegal in Madrid at the time), architectural collectives, neighborhood associations, and cultural centers. At the meeting, different collectives narrated their own experiences in taking over (legally or illegally) the management of public spaces and resources. We talked about how the initiatives funded themselves and sought sustainability over time, about the management of infrastructure (electricity, water, toilets), and about the difficulties of finding suitable interlocutors inside City Hall.

The encounter was on the whole rated a success. It was felt by many that the occasion to have various collectives share their experiences was a rare one and ought to be repeated. We met again in a fortnight's time, and then again two weeks later. By mid-November the encounters had consolidated and were widely known as La Mesa—the citizens' roundtable.

Roughly at the same time, Basurama and Zuloark were invited by City Hall to design its stand at the National Environmental Conference that was taking place in Madrid later in the month. The stand was built reusing wood from historical city benches, and Basurama and Zuloark stipulated that the materials used in its construction would be dismantled and made available to be reused by marginal communities in Madrid's periurban districts following the conference's closure. The stand re-created an urban community garden, whose plants were transplanted from existing (illegal) community garden projects in the city. Each plant symbolized a community project and had a label attached explaining the initiative. Moreover, the stand was described in the label welcoming its visitors as a "space of collective creativity, built with an evocative character, and with the aim to promote a diversity of perspectives and reflections."

When I first saw the stand, it took me a while to get my head around it (see figure 2.3). It was a beautiful and indeed evocative piece of furniture. It literally blossomed amid the tedious commercial and corporate landscape of electricity and gas company, even NGO, stands. Further, it

FIGURE 2.3. La Mesa meets City Hall at the National Environmental Conference.
Photo by the author.

made me wonder what exactly City Hall had seen in the stand to assume all the connotations of its symbolic infrastructure—with all those references and nods to urban community gardens, squatted social centers, or guerrilla architectural collectives. As it turns out, although much of the stand's publicity had the inflections proper to the empty rhetoric of political ventriloquism, the preparations leading to its construction anticipated and rehearsed a number of future developments.

The commission of the stand to Basurama and Zuloark had in fact been facilitated by a couple of City Hall employees who were members of various community projects in Madrid and who had been attending the meetings of La Mesa since its inception. These people had taken upon themselves the task of trying to open up a political space within City Hall—tenuous and fragile as it certainly was—that would make the construction of such a stand feasible.

More importantly, coinciding with the ongoing celebrations of La Mesa, these City Hall employees suggested to some of their colleagues that the stand could perhaps be a good place to rehearse an informal meeting with some of the radical collectives responsible for building the stand, as well as others whose spirit was "evoked" by the stand's celebratory blurb when speaking of "space[s] of collective creativity."

The suggestion to hold a meeting between radical collectives and City Hall representatives was accepted. A message was sent out to members of La Mesa that some representatives from Hall were keen to meet us in order to initiate a conversation about our diverse interests and stakes over the management of public spaces. The meeting was scheduled to take place at City Hall's stand at the National Environmental Conference, although it was strategically removed from the conference's program so as to, as the Hall's delegates put it, "not to draw too much political attention."

The meeting was by all accounts a success. The members of City Hall all insisted on making clear that their presence there was in a personal capacity—they were not on official City Hall business, and their words were not to be taken as representing City Hall views. Nonetheless, they all agreed that their presence was a reaction to a failure on the part of Hall to understand "new models of urban governance." There was a shared perception that we all had a great deal to learn from each other.

The meeting closed with a decision to set up a permanent *mesa de aprendizaje* (learning roundtable) that would meet periodically with a view to identifying questions of urban governance of interest to both City Hall

delegates and the collectives. By December 2013, the roundtable had succeeded in establishing a regular calendar of meetings.

The success, however, had not brought about an institutionalization
or stabilization of La Mesa's political strategies. Much to the contrary, the
furniture kept refurbishing itself. Thus, over time members of La Mesa
multiplied and contracted, with people appearing and disappearing, and
sometimes reappearing again when La Mesa diverged into specialized task
forces, which included groups on digital cartographies of collective action,
a book club, or a task force on Madrid's General Urban Plan. We experimented with the format of our meetings: where we met (at cultural centers,
in bars, at the Spanish National Research Council), but also with how we
conducted a meeting. We took turns taking minutes, which we called *rela-
torías* (storytelling), and which sometimes read like ethnographic accounts,
while at other times they looked like architectural sketches. Sometimes the
remit of our activities seemed defined and taken over by the concerns of
architects (who were overrepresented at La Mesa, which became a concern
in itself), while on some occasions it was the voice of cultural agents or of
urban gardening communities that assumed the wisdom of political praxis.
Sometimes, even, it was the anthropologists whom everyone turned to for
inspiration.

After our first meeting with delegates from City Hall at the National
Environmental Conference, Manuel, a member of Zuloark, noted that this
truly marked an unprecedented development in the configuration of urban
public space in Madrid. "It is unheard of," he said, "of City Hall wanting
to establish some kind of dialogue with radical collectives like us." Others
tried to caution his words, noting that City Hall had in fact taken good
precautions to erase our meeting from the conference's program, or that
the whole rhetoric of social innovation and creative collaboration was
but the latest of fads in the arts of political persuasion. "Sure," he retorted,
"but here we are: seated around a gigantic piece of furniture, playing a
game of seduction with them."

The images of furniture and seduction that Manuel drew on invoke a
specific media ecology. As a member of one of the collectives in charge of
designing the conference's stand, he was no doubt well aware of the extent
to which playing the game of seduction had required, first and foremost,
constructing seduction's furniture. City Hall's stand at the conference was
unlike any other. Spectacular, organic, vegetative, it refused to play into the
corporate aesthetic of environmental correctness and performed instead

a game of estrangement, of allurement and surprise. The stand was a true exemplar of brico-urbanism: built using recycled and transplanted materials, itself but a temporary holder for these materials' future destination of community projects in some of Madrid's marginal areas.

What sort of object was the stand, then: a garden, a table, a political vitrine, a development project, a commentary on environments in scale? The stand indeed made the environment visible like no other at the conference, yet it did so through a complex play of political cross-references and games of scale. The stand's "host"—City Hall—had been in some ways taken "hostage" by the radical collectives. Yet this was not simply a question of who was a more faithful representative of environmental concerns. There was no politics of representation at stake, for there was no environment proper to be found anywhere at the stand. If one wished to see in the transplantation of urban community gardens a co-optation by City Hall of the gardens' success, such that the gardens were guests at the stand, it is no less true that the radical collectives were ultimately out-hosting Hall by taking the stand outside the conference to marginal communities in the city: they were moving the stand out to another environment. Likewise, the rhetoric around social innovation rested uneasily next to the floral imagery of squatted social centers. As an open-source and auto-constructive piece of furniture, then, the stand was neither host nor guest to classical environmental politics.

When asked about the design of the stand, members of Basurama and Zuloark would describe it as a "prototype." The term had gained currency among radical collectives in Madrid over the previous five years. The stand, as they saw it, was the first of many future assemblages of its kind: it would be disassembled and reassembled, following the same or similar designs, using original and new materials, bringing together some of the same people and makers but also new communities. The stand was neither one of a kind nor an instance of many different kinds. It was a version, an ongoing draft: a political program "more than many and less than one."[59] In this sense, perhaps one ought to approach the stand as a particular instance of double captivity—hosts and guests mutually trapped in an unstable game—yet one that manages also to out-trap itself: for the stand somehow managed to trap the environment, yet it also open-sourced it by making available and redeploying its material capacities, tending these out for ongoing re-descriptions, or, in the language of open-source projects, by keeping all descriptions in beta.

Conclusion

La Mesa's work has managed to invest its political interventions with a particular kind of epistemic recognition, even if this recognition can only very tentatively be described in terms of suspension or prototyping. A type of actor unheard of in municipal but also radical politics, La Mesa's strangeness succeeded in carving an epistemic space for itself amid Madrid's political landscape—a space that I have referred to as an ecology in beta.

Perhaps it is not unreasonable to think of this beta status as a trapping impulse, yet one whose trick lies in jumping ahead of itself. In this vein, the furniture seems less intent on trying to trap an ecology, the way spiderwebs do, than on trying to trap its own capacity for redescription. It aims less for mutual describability as for describability itself. I am reminded here of Roy Wagner's uncanny description of human knowledge as "a predator that learned to stalk its own image . . . like the false nonpresence that the cat pounces out of."[60] The cat's quietness, now predator, now prey, inhabits that state of suspension, that beta state, where it is description itself that is at stake.

The states of suspension I have introduced in this chapter lay out a tentative argument for thinking of the trap as a method of description. There are of course many different kinds of traps, and it has certainly not been my intention to subsume these under one overarching heuristic. Thus, while I have drawn my argument from the specific evocative powers of the spiderweb trap, I hope to have shown that if trapping may indeed prove a productive anthropological technology, it is so because it has so many different ways of generating "suspension without releasing the hold of context," as Debbora Battaglia has put it.[61] Traps carry context and let it go—although the different techniques of capture, containment, and release will of course inflect how an episteme is seen to be doing any work to start with.

Traps capture, caution, and captivate; they provoke wonder, suspension, and elicitation. Traps can make the world spin slowly, at least for those who are awaiting rescue, or they can accelerate our impatience, if prey never shows up. Some traps, even, are falsely triggered by a whisper or a hiss and jump off ahead of themselves. Sometimes, predator and prey collapse under the catastrophic pressure of an exterior force. Traps have spatial, temporal, and ontological effects.

In this vein, the three qualities of the spiderweb trap that I have described have allowed me to center a number of questions. The aesthetic trap of the trompe l'oeil allowed us to see how epistemology and ontology are doubly encompassed by a notion of entanglements that is itself unstable. In the trompe l'oeil, relations double themselves and open up the relation to novel forms of description. One way in which they do this, we have seen, is by self-encompassing relationality into an environment of sorts.

Traps are also well-known ecological infrastructures: think of them as the interior design of an Umwelt. They extricate from Nature its interfaces, the infrastructure of its mutual describabilities. And in this capacity they would seem to place the project of onto-ecology once again in the hands of description.

Last, traps embody the interiorizing and exteriorizing recursions that accompany the location of an environment. The prototypes of urban furniture work just in this fashion: they help assemble and furnish the conditions for social seduction. Pouncing out from the shadows of their nonpresence, the muebles prototype their own repredation. They are trying to fascinate and seduce a community into existence. To trap it out.

A trap for entanglements, then, and a trap for ecologies. And a trap for description's own reappearances. Three traps many.

ACKNOWLEDGMENTS

I am most grateful to Marisol de la Cadena for inviting me to the Indigenous Cosmopolitics seminar series that first got me thinking about the description of traps and the traps of description, in/for/between epistemologies and ontologies. At UC Davis I had the privilege of finding in Karen Barad a most generous and insightful interlocutor. Conversations sparked by the warmth and hospitality of my seminar attendants, including Marisol, Mario Blaser, Joseph Dumit, Timothy Choy, and Mario Biagioli, have proved invaluable sources of inspiration. Debbora Battaglia and Marilyn Strathern read early versions of the chapter, and it is to their ongoing support and encouragement that I owe its (perhaps rather) flippant—trompe l'oeil—articulation. Adolfo Estalella and Tomás Sánchez Criado kindly invited me to present a second version of the essay at the online seminar Culturas Tecnocientíficas. I am thankful for the invitation, as well as for the enthusiastic engagement of all participants, especially Blanca Callén, Ana Delgado, Rebeca Ibañez, and Isaac Marrero-Guillamón for their written comments. Adolfo's ethnographic fellowship in our investigation of Madrid's pluriverse is a continuous source of inspiration.

1. On ecologies, see, for example, Eben Kirksey, *Emergent Ecologies* (Durham, NC: Duke University Press, 2015); Eduardo Kohn, *How Forests Think: Toward an Anthropology beyond the Human* (Berkeley: University of California Press, 2013). On infrastructures, see Stephen Graham and Colin McFarlane, *Infrastructural Lives: Urban Infrastructure in Context* (London: Routledge, 2014); Brian Larkin, "The Politics and Poetics of Infrastructure," *Annual Review of Anthropology* 42, no. 1 (2013): 327–43. On entanglements, see Karen Barad, *Meeting the Universe Halfway: Quantum Physics and the Entanglement of Matter and Meaning* (Durham, NC: Duke University Press, 2007); Anna Lowenhaupt Tsing, *The Mushroom at the End of the World: On the Possibility of Life in Capitalist Ruins* (Princeton, NJ: Princeton University Press, 2015). I shall address each of these literatures in more depth as the argument unfolds.

2. Katherine Swancutt, "The Captive Guest: Spider Webs of Hospitality among the Nuosu of Southwest China," *Journal of the Royal Anthropological Institute* 18 (2012): S103–S116.

3. Swancutt, "The Captive Guest," S105.

4. Swancutt, "The Captive Guest," S108.

5. Roy Wagner, "'Luck in the Double Focus': Ritualized Hospitality in Melanesia," *Journal of the Royal Anthropological Institute* 18 (2012): S168.

6. Roy Wagner, *An Anthropology of the Subject: Holographic Worldview in New Guinea and Its Meaning and Significance for the World of Anthropology* (Berkeley: University of California Press, 2001).

7. Wagner, "'Luck in the Double Focus.'"

8. Wagner, "'Luck in the Double Focus,'" S163.

9. Wagner, "'Luck in the Double Focus,'" S163

10. Wagner, "'Luck in the Double Focus.'"

11. Wagner, "'Luck in the Double Focus.'" S164, emphasis in original.

12. For a description of how traps have prefigured the work of analysis in modern science and social theory, see Alberto Corsín Jiménez, *An Anthropological Trompe L'oeil for a Common World: An Essay on the Economy of Knowledge* (Oxford: Berghahn, 2013).

13. Eduardo Viveiros de Castro, *A Inconstância da Alma Selvagem, e Outros Ensaios de Antropologia* (São Paulo: Cosac Naify, 2002), 15.

14. Victor I. Stoichita, *The Self-Aware Image: An Insight into Early Modern Meta-Painting* (Cambridge: Cambridge University Press, 1997).

15. Hanneke Grootenboer, *The Rhetoric of Perspective: Realism and Illusionism in Seventeenth-Century Dutch Still-Life Painting* (Chicago: University of Chicago Press, 2005), 59.

16. Corsín Jiménez, *An Anthropological Trompe L'oeil for a Common World.* And in this sense perhaps one of the most pertinent images for what Roy Wagner famously termed "symbols that stand for themselves." Roy Wagner, *Symbols That Stand for Themselves* (Chicago: University of Chicago Press, 1986).

17. See Svetlana Alpers, *Rembrandt's Enterprise: The Studio and the Market* (Chicago: University of Chicago Press, 1995); Bryan Jay Wolf, *Vermeer and the Invention of Seeing* (Chicago: University of Chicago Press, 2001).

18. Ann Kelly, "Entomological Extensions: Model Huts and Fieldworks," in *Recasting Anthropological Knowledge: Inspiration and Social Science*, ed. Jeanette Edwards and Maja Petrović-Šteger, 70–87 (Cambridge: Cambridge University Press, 2011).

19. Kelly, "Entomological Extensions," 70.

20. Kelly, "Entomological Extensions," 75.

21. Kelly, "Entomological Extensions," 74.

22. Kelly, "Entomological Extensions," 75.

23. The huts, writes Kelly, mix "genres of experimentation and environmental management." Kelly, "Entomological Extensions," 71fn.

24. Kelly, "Entomological Extensions," 78.

25. Kelly, "Entomological Extensions," 78.

26. Hans-Jörg Rheinberger, *Toward a History of Epistemic Things: Synthesizing Proteins in the Test Tube* (Stanford, CA: Stanford University Press, 1997), 78.

27. Jakob von Uexküll, *A Foray into the Worlds of Animals and Humans: With a Theory of Meaning*, trans. Joseph D. Oneil (Minneapolis: University of Minnesota Press, 2010). It is perhaps worth pointing out, as Giorgio Agamben reminds us, that Uexküll's investigations were "contemporary with quantum physics and the artistic avant-gardes." Giorgio Agamben, *The Open: Man and Animal* (Stanford: Stanford University Press, 2004), 39.

28. Uexküll, *A Foray into the Worlds of Animals and Humans*, 103.

29. Uexküll, *A Foray into the Worlds of Animals and Humans*, 167.

30. Uexküll, *A Foray into the Worlds of Animals and Humans*, 92.

31. "The web," he writes, cannot "be a representation of a physical fly, but rather, it represents the *primal image* of the fly, which is physically not at all present." Uexküll, *A Foray into the Worlds of Animals and Humans*, 159, emphasis in original.

32. Uexküll, *A Foray into the Worlds of Animals and Humans*, 158.

33. Uexküll, *A Foray into the Worlds of Animals and Humans*, 190–91.

34. Alfred Gell, "Vogel's Net: Traps as Artworks and Artworks as Traps," in *The Art of Anthropology: Essays and Diagrams*, ed. Eric Hirsch, Monographs on Social Anthropology 67, 187–214 (London: Athlone, 1999).

35. Gell, "Vogel's Net." See also Alfred Gell, *Art and Agency: An Anthropological Theory* (Oxford: Clarendon, 1998).

36. Gell, "Vogel's Net," 201.

37. Gell, "Vogel's Net."

38. Compare Sahlins's description of traps as tools in *Stone Age Economics*: "A technology is not comprehended by its physical properties alone. In use, tools are brought into specific relationships with their users. On the largest view, this relationship and not the tool itself is the determinate historic quality of a technology. No purely physical difference between the traps of certain spiders and those of certain (human) hunters, or between the bee's hive and the Bantu's, is historically as meaningful as the difference in the instrument-user relation." Marshall Sahlins, *Stone Age Economics* (London:

Tavistock, 1972), 79. Whereas for Sahlins the cultural significance of the technology trap shows in the relation between the instrument and its user, for Gell technology can only be understood if one attends to the "enchantment" (entrapment, entanglement) of their relations. Alfred Gell, "The Technology of Enchantment and the Enchantment of Technology," in *The Art of Anthropology: Essays and Diagrams*, ed. Eric Hirsch, Monographs on Social Anthropology 67, 159–86 (London: Athlone, 1999). In other words, rather than the trap being a social technology, it is the technology that should be considered, first and foremost, a trap.

39. Matthew Fuller, "Boxes towards Bananas: Spatial Dispersal, Intelligent Cities and Animal Structures," in *Sentient City: Ubiquitous Computing, Architecture, and the Future of Urban Space*, ed. Mark Shepard, 173–81 (Cambridge, MA: MIT Press, 2011), 176.

40. Fuller, "Boxes towards Bananas."

41. Fuller, "Boxes towards Bananas," 177.

42. Fuller, "Boxes towards Bananas," 181.

43. Fuller, "Boxes towards Bananas," 181.

44. For example, see Barad, *Meeting the Universe Halfway*; Kohn, *How Forests Think*.

45. Matthew Fuller, *Media Ecologies: Materialist Energies in Art and Technoculture* (Cambridge, MA: MIT Press, 2005); Jussi Parikka, *Insect Media: An Archaeology of Animals and Technology* (Minneapolis: University of Minnesota Press, 2010), xx.

46. Kohn, *How Forests Think*, 20.

47. Nigel Thrift, "The Insubstantial Pageant: Producing an Untoward Land," *Cultural Geographies* 19, no. 2 (February 2012): 4, 17, 15.

48. Mark Shepard, "Toward the Sentient City," in *Sentient City: Ubiquitous Computing, Architecture, and the Future of Urban Space*, ed. Mark Shepard, 16–37 (Cambridge, MA: MIT Press, 2011), 18.

49. David Benjamin, Soo-In Yang, and Natalie Jeremijenko, "New Interaction Partners for Environmental Governance: Amphibious Architecture," in *Sentient City: Ubiquitous Computing, Architecture, and the Future of Urban Space*, ed. Mark Shepard, 48–63 (Cambridge, MA: MIT Press, 2011).

50. Thrift, "The Insubstantial Pageant," 8, 4.

51. See AbdouMaliq Simone, "People as Infrastructure: Intersecting Fragments in Johannesburg," *Public Culture* 16, no. 3 (2004): 407–29; Faranak Miraftab, "Insurgent Planning: Situating Radical Planning in the Global South," *Planning Theory* 8, no. 1 (2009): 32–50.

52. Alberto Corsín Jiménez, "The Right to Infrastructure: A Prototype for Open-Source Urbanism," *Environment and Planning D: Society and Space* 32, no. 2 (2014): 342–62.

53. Manuel Pascual, Zuloark Collective, personal communication (2014).

54. McKenzie Wark, *50 Years of Recuperation of the Situationist International* (New York: Princeton Architectural Press, 2008).

55. Thrift, "The Insubstantial Pageant," 4.

56. Alberto Corsín Jiménez and Adolfo Estalella, "The Atmospheric Person: Value, Experiment, and 'Making Neighbors' in Madrid's Popular Assemblies," HAU: *Journal of Ethnographic Theory* 3, no. 2 (2013): 119–39; Alberto Corsín Jiménez and Adolfo

Estalella, "Assembling Neighbors: The City as Hardware, Method, and 'a Very Messy Kind of Archive,'" *Common Knowledge* 20, no. 1 (2014): 150–71.

57. Alberto Corsín Jiménez, "Auto-Construction Redux: The City as Method," *Cultural Anthropology* 32, no. 3 (2017): 450–78.

58. Bernard Cache, *Earth Moves: The Furnishing of Territories*, trans. Anne Boyman (Cambridge, MA: MIT Press, 1995).

59. Corsín Jiménez, *An Anthropological Trompe L'oeil for a Common World*.

60. Wagner, *An Anthropology of the Subject*, 63.

61. Battaglia is describing the "exo-suprises" that cosmonauts encounter when confronting zero gravity. They are captured or arrested by the nongravity of space. Debbora Battaglia, "Coming in at an Unusual Angle: Exo-Surprise and the Fieldworking Cosmonaut," *Anthropological Quarterly* 85, no. 4 (2012): 1094.

BIBLIOGRAPHY

Agamben, Giorgio. *The Open: Man and Animal*. Stanford, CA: Stanford University Press, 2004.

Alpers, Svetlana. *Rembrandt's Enterprise: The Studio and the Market*. Chicago: University of Chicago Press, 1995.

Barad, Karen. *Meeting the Universe Halfway: Quantum Physics and the Entanglement of Matter and Meaning*. Durham, NC: Duke University Press, 2007.

Battaglia, Debbora. "Coming in at an Unusual Angle: Exo-Surprise and the Fieldworking Cosmonaut." *Anthropological Quarterly* 85, no. 4 (2012): 1089–1106.

Benjamin, David, Soo-In Yang, and Natalie Jeremijenko. "New Interaction Partners for Environmental Governance: Amphibious Architecture." In *Sentient City: Ubiquitous Computing, Architecture, and the Future of Urban Space*, edited by Mark Shepard, 48–63. Cambridge, MA: MIT Press, 2011.

Cache, Bernard. *Earth Moves: The Furnishing of Territories*. Translated by Anne Boyman. Cambridge, MA: MIT Press, 1995.

Corsín Jiménez, Alberto. *An Anthropological Trompe L'oeil for a Common World: An Essay on the Economy of Knowledge*. Oxford: Berghahn, 2013.

Corsín Jiménez, Alberto. "The Right to Infrastructure: A Prototype for Open-Source Urbanism." *Environment and Planning D: Society and Space* 32, no. 2 (2014): 342–62.

Corsín Jiménez, Alberto. "Auto-Construction Redux: The City as Method." *Cultural Anthropology* 32, no. 3 (2017): 450–78.

Corsín Jiménez, Alberto, and Adolfo Estalella. "Assembling Neighbors: The City as Hardware, Method, and 'a Very Messy Kind of Archive.'" *Common Knowledge* 20, no. 1 (2014): 150–71.

Corsín Jiménez, Alberto, and Adolfo Estalella. "The Atmospheric Person: Value, Experiment, and 'Making Neighbors' in Madrid's Popular Assemblies." *HAU: Journal of Ethnographic Theory* 3, no. 2 (2013): 119–39.

Fuller, Matthew. "Boxes towards Bananas: Spatial Dispersal, Intelligent Cities and Animal Structures." In *Sentient City: Ubiquitous Computing, Architecture, and* the *Future of Urban Space*, edited by Mark Shepard, 173–81. Cambridge, MA: MIT Press, 2011.

Fuller, Matthew. *Media Ecologies: Materialist Energies in Art and Technoculture.* Cambridge, MA: MIT Press, 2005.

Gell, Alfred. *Art and Agency: An Anthropological Theory.* Oxford: Clarendon, 1998.

Gell, Alfred. "The Technology of Enchantment and the Enchantment of Technology." In *The Art of Anthropology: Essays and Diagrams*, edited by Eric Hirsch, 159–86. Monographs on Social Anthropology 67. London: Athlone, 1999.

Gell, Alfred. "Vogel's Net: Traps as Artworks and Artworks as Traps." In *The Art of Anthropology: Essays and Diagrams*, edited by Eric Hirsch, 187–214. Monographs on Social Anthropology 67. London: Athlone, 1999.

Graham, Stephen, and Colin McFarlane. *Infrastructural Lives: Urban Infrastructure in Context.* London: Routledge, 2014.

Grootenboer, Hanneke. *The Rhetoric of Perspective: Realism and Illusionism in Seventeenth-Century Dutch Still-Life Painting.* Chicago: University of Chicago Press, 2005.

Kelly, Ann. "Entomological Extensions: Model Huts and Fieldworks." In *Recasting Anthropological Knowledge: Inspiration and Social Science*, edited by Jeanette Edwards and Maja Petrović-Šteger, 70–87. Cambridge: Cambridge University Press, 2011.

Kirksey, Eben. *Emergent Ecologies.* Durham, NC: Duke University Press, 2015.

Kohn, Eduardo. *How Forests Think: Toward an Anthropology beyond the Human.* Berkeley: University of California Press, 2013.

Larkin, Brian. "The Politics and Poetics of Infrastructure." *Annual Review of Anthropology* 42, no. 1 (2013): 327–43.

Miraftab, Faranak. "Insurgent Planning: Situating Radical Planning in the Global South." *Planning Theory* 8, no. 1 (2009): 32–50.

Parikka, Jussi. *Insect Media: An Archaeology of Animals and Technology.* Minneapolis: University of Minnesota Press, 2010.

Rheinberger, Hans-Jörg. *Toward a History of Epistemic Things: Synthesizing Proteins in the Test Tube.* Stanford, CA: Stanford University Press, 1997.

Sahlins, Marshall. *Stone Age Economics.* London: Tavistock, 1972.

Shepard, Mark. "Toward the Sentient City." In *Sentient City: Ubiquitous Computing, Architecture, and the Future of Urban Space*, edited by Mark Shepard, 16–37. Cambridge, MA: MIT Press, 2011.

Simone, AbdouMaliq. "People as Infrastructure: Intersecting Fragments in Johannesburg." *Public Culture* 16, no. 3 (2004): 407–29.

Stoichita, Victor I. *The Self-Aware Image: An Insight into Early Modern Meta-Painting.* Cambridge: Cambridge University Press, 1997.

Swancutt, Katherine. "The Captive Guest: Spider Webs of Hospitality among the Nuosu of Southwest China." *Journal of the Royal Anthropological Institute* 18 (2012): S103–S116.

Thrift, Nigel. "The Insubstantial Pageant: Producing an Untoward Land." *Cultural Geographies* 19, no. 2 (February 2012): 141–68.

Tsing, Anna Lowenhaupt. *The Mushroom at the End of the World: On the Possibility of Life in Capitalist Ruins.* Princeton, NJ: Princeton University Press, 2015.

Uexküll, Jakob von. *A Foray into the Worlds of Animals and Humans: With a Theory of Meaning*. Translated by Joseph D. Oneil. Minneapolis: University of Minnesota Press, 2010.

Viveiros de Castro, Eduardo. *A Inconstância da Alma Selvagem, e Outros Ensaios de Antropologia*. São Paulo: Cosac Naify, 2002.

Wagner, Roy. *An Anthropology of the Subject: Holographic Worldview in New Guinea and Its Meaning and Significance for the World of Anthropology*. Berkeley: University of California Press, 2001.

Wagner, Roy. "'Luck in the Double Focus': Ritualized Hospitality in Melanesia." *Journal of the Royal Anthropological Institute* 18 (2012): S161–S174.

Wagner, Roy. *Symbols That Stand for Themselves*. Chicago: University of Chicago Press, 1986.

Wark, McKenzie. *50 Years of Recuperation of the Situationist International*. New York: Princeton Architectural Press, 2008.

Wolf, Bryan Jay. *Vermeer and the Invention of Seeing*. Chicago: University of Chicago Press, 2001.

THREE

THE CHALLENGE OF ONTOLOGICAL POLITICS

Isabelle Stengers

Preliminaries

Ontology has many meanings, as does politics. The challenge of ontological politics connected to the Zapatista call for "a world where many worlds fit" must mean not clarifying, but taking a stand for some of the meanings of both politics and ontology, and not for others. The stand I will take is not a judgmental one. It is the one I need to think my way as challenged by the ontological politics proposition.

The path I follow will connect politics, as implied by ontological politics, with the old art of diplomacy, rather than with rules ensuring that a choice or decision will prevail over the conflicting opinions of the concerned parties. I am thus disconnecting "politics" from the Greek idea of equality, or isonomia, the affirmation of the homogeneity of the space where citizens gather as members of the same political community. Let us be clear—this disconnection does not mean that "inequality" would come into play. It is from the notion of "opinion" that I am distancing myself, from the idea that since there is no privileged position all opinions should a priori have the same weight, each citizen being free to defend "his" (allochthones, women, slaves, and children being excluded) opinion. In contrast, as we know, diplomats are not meant to defend "their" opinions. They intervene as representatives of a "cause" that transcends them, and they are not free to enter into an agreement without first reporting its terms to those who are empowered to ratify it or to disavow their representatives.

Correlatively, citizens were conceived as what Aristotle called "political animals." When political animals gather and discuss what is good or bad for the city, neither gods nor mountains nor forests have a voice in the process. When the city is extended into one cosmopolitan world, it is a world of which humans are citizens, everywhere at home, not a world where many worlds fit.

A second point to be clarified concerns ontology. It is important to stress that I am a European philosopher, belonging to a tradition for which ontology points toward a highly conflictual adventure of philosophical thinking—what French philosopher Étienne Souriau describes as the most lively, but perhaps the most tendentious, in philosophy: "The most divergent conceptions of existence . . . clash over a single proposition, that 'there is more than one kind of existence,' or conversely that 'the word "existence" is univocal.' Depending on our answer, the entire universe and all of human destiny will change appearance. . . . Doors of bronze swing and pulse—now open, now shut—within the philosophy of great hopes, in the universe of vast domains."[1]

In contrast, the US philosophical tradition, often following the lead of W. V. O. Quine, has turned ontology into a kind of suburb to its capital question, the epistemological question of what we mean when we utter a proposition. For Quine, all ontologies would be equal, as each is relative to a particular language or culture as a whole and its value is only pragmatic, relative to this culture. Physics and mythology are rationally equivalent as epistemic or representational devices to relate to a mute reality, but in order to relate to our technoscientific world, physics is pragmatically better—too bad for those who would have gods' intervention explain the turns of human destiny as the Greeks did. In other words, the Zapatista call is a pragmatic non-sense in our globalized world. Tolerance is what peoples who remained attached to a peculiar ontology may hope for, at best.

To refuse the Quinian trivialization of ontologies is to claim that fitting many worlds into one world will not be done by taming their wild divergence, by reducing that divergence to the incommensurable ways we may frame the understanding of our worlds. Obviously the point is not to extend the passion of the philosophical ontological question to the question of ontological politics. Also, I do not forget that it is possible to associate, as feminist thinker Sandra Harding did, Quine's definition of ontology with an anti-imperialist stand for plurality. This association, however, risks engulfing the question in ethics or politics and the demand that we respect others. If we cannot take seriously—but only respectfully, with what Helen Verran calls "bad faith"—these others' eventual fright at the betrayal of obligations derived from their ontology, we are back to tolerance. We are those who know better, that is, those who can be frightened by nothing—a discreet, well-behaved cosmopolitism.

My point is not to extend the passions of philosophical ontology to political epistemology, but to claim that in order to accommodate "ontology" with ontological politics we need to disentangle it from epistemological presuppositions implying a mute reality available for many worlding and wording ontologies. The problem with ontology is not knowledge or representation, but engagement with and for a world. And this engagement is not an implicit or unconscious one, as epistemological presuppositions are often characterized, but a matter of commitment to obligations that can, if necessary, become a "cause," what you live by and may die for.

Which engagements can we imagine dying for, or at least waging a war for? Twenty years ago, scientists waged such a war against deconstructivist critiques. But the "science wars" were waged not to defend a commitment to obligations or the particular way these scientists engage the world. They were waged in the name of universals such as "reason" or "the advancement of knowledge," and, as such, they excluded the possibility of diplomacy. This question has been central in my writing of *Cosmopolitics*. But before I address it, I will propose a last preliminary point: the importance I will be giving to diplomacy must be understood as "speculative."

In a way, diplomats are by themselves creatures of speculation. They intervene where war seems the logical outcome of a disagreement, and work for a peace that might be possible, for a (partial) articulation between antagonistic commitments. The possibility of a world where many worlds would fit implies that protagonist worlds agree about peace as a possibility, that they agree about "giving peace a chance": this is the condition of diplomatic intervention. Speculation here is defined against the power given to the definition of a state of affairs that logically leads to war. It implies the trust that this definition might not be the last word. Ontological politics, however, implies another kind of speculation, more akin to what physicists call a "thought experiment." There is, indeed, one powerful protagonist that cannot be trusted because it is not equipped for agreeing about peace as a possibility. It is what I would call, among other denominations, the global West.

The global West is not a "world" and recognizes no world. Referring to Deleuze and Guattari, I would rather characterize it as a "machine," destroying both politics and ontologies. No peace is possible with this hegemonic machine, because it knows only, as Bruno Latour emphasized (using another of its names: the advancing front of modernization), "pacification," or police operations. Those who oppose modernization are just "backward" or "misled." The agents of modernization do not wage war against such "bad pupils" and cannot imagine a peace settlement with them. At best they will tolerate them up to the point when they make real nuisances of themselves. As Latour concludes, "Yes, their wars, their conquests, were educational! Even their massacres were purely pedagogical!"[2]

A world-destroying machine cannot fit with other worlds. Whatever its meaning, ontological politics is thus connected with the possibility of resisting our worlds' ongoing destruction. But my speculative stand, what makes my proposition akin to a thought experiment, implies a distinct, complementary hypothesis: the possibility of distinguishing between "agents of modernization," the servants of the machine, and what I will call "modern practitioners," with whom diplomacy might be possible. Even if most modern practitioners would present themselves, even think of themselves, as belonging to the one world with which all the others should agree, I will speculatively address them as captured by, but liable to betray, the destroying machine.[3]

Such a stance may easily be understood as an attempt to exonerate "moderns" from "modernist" crimes. Let me emphasize that the question of innocence or guilt is not my problem. I have no difficulty admitting that right from their beginning modern sciences, for instance, have been complicit with imperialist claims and enterprises. The speculative notion of practice is meant to affirm that their participation in the world-destroying machine did not follow from a logical, even less ontological, necessity, that what came to be called "modern science," rather, results from an operation of capture. It certainly does not deny that this capture was mostly consented, even called for and indeed quite beneficial for those concerned. But to distinguish between modern scientific practices and the institution of Science that results from the capture opens the possibility that practitioners might become able to ally with others who also resist capture and destruction—"also," because, as we will see, characterizing modern practices is also characterizing what is today in the process of being effectively destroyed.

This speculative possibility means resisting the moralistic tale that since they were not innocent, but deeply compromised, indeed they "deserve" the destruction they collaborated in bringing to others. Such a tale has immensely simplified the working of the machine where it could be seen as "progressive," not imperialist ("capitalism opening the way to socialism by destroying what socialism should eliminate anyway"). I will not condone it and thus choose here a resolutely "naturalist," eco-evolutionary stance: it may indeed happen that species are destroyed because what they require is no longer there, but nothing deserves destruction.

Modern Practices

The speculative concept of practices was born at the time of the "Science Wars," with the realization that the belligerent parties, each defending a "cause," were equally indifferent to the possibility of negotiating the terms of their conflict—not to speak of the terms of a peace settlement. In brief, either (physical) reality existed by itself and for itself, or it was only a human construct, reality being mute. It may be remarked that the conflict was not a fully developed one. About other sciences, physicists would rather easily agree with critiques, or endorse a vaguely "reductionist" program—for physicists, "other sciences" are not really sciences, anyway: they just do their best. The tug of war was really the question of reality explaining the success of physics.

It was during this period that I began to envisage the need to "civilize" the way scientists think of themselves, that is, to separate them from hegemonic-order words such as rationality, objectivity, and universality. The correlate was to separate critics of scientific hegemony from their own hegemonic claim that any knowledge is a matter of (human, cultural, linguistic—pick your choice) representation.

The concept of practice I introduced is not meant to be a peaceful one. It rather aims at dividing scientists with regard to their loyalty toward the hegemonic conquest machine called Science, blindly, unilaterally imposing so-called objectivity and rationality over whatever exists. Critical thinkers had very good reasons to be convinced that if they wanted to debunk scientific claims in general, they had to go for the head, to directly attack the authority of theoretico-experimental sciences, among which physics stands as the leader, because these are the only sciences that claim access to "reality" as such. For physicists, other sciences are rather like satrapies, allowed to exist if they pay tribute and help defend the imperium. They even tolerated the skepticism of Quine, since he recognized that science was the only game in town. However, what critical thinkers took for the head of a unique body called Science worked, under attack, rather like a spearhead, the very specific force of which was precisely to be able to counter attacks about objectivity being only a human construct. The critique, instead of weakening Science, contributed to its unification, all satrapies laying claim by proxy to a force of which they are utterly devoid, and which they can only imitate.

Taking seriously this force, but not as a privilege, rather as what specifically engages the passionate commitment of experimental scientists, is the game changer I have proposed in *The Invention of Modern Science*. One can then claim that critics were a bit like bulls charging into a red flag, accepting the propaganda argument that experimental objectivity is heralding a general method for obtaining objective knowledge while it points to a very exceptional achievement specific to the experimental practice.

The possibility of reducing the definition of an experimental object to a "merely human" construction is a critical concern for experimenters themselves. Indeed it may be said that the very condition for the recognition of such objects is their ability to defeat objections implying this possibility, and these objections are produced by experimenters themselves.[4] For them, objecting is a way of participating in an eventual achievement that matters directly for their own work because this work will eventually rely on it. The verification of the ability to defeat objections is thus a crucial part of the collective effort of practitioners for whom reliability is not a simple matter of methodology but a crucial claim on which the future of their research depends.

It is thus no surprise that experimenters felt insulted but were not at all impressed by the attempted critical "deconstruction" of their claims. This deconstruction attacked not a misplaced realism but the very meaning of their achievement: what they address has not only been enrolled in an argument (this is easy) but has proved to be able to "endorse" this role, to play the part of a "reliable witness." Certainly this witness has been mobilized by the practitioner—it is a "fact of the experimental art." But it is not a mere "artifact," a human interpretative construct. It has authorized an interpretation of its own mobilization against other possible interpretations. When they denied that "reality" is able to endorse any interpretation, critiques were denying the whole point of the experimental practice: giving reality the power to make a difference in the way it is to be interpreted.

If one takes seriously the specificity of experimental practices, the unity of Science and its epistemological claims becomes a moot point, to say the least. The very term "objective representation" may appear as a betrayal of what these practices aim at. A representation allows secure argument, a secure chain of "ifs" and "thens" and "thuses." The specificity of experimental practices is such that in their case each link of the chain is itself a question, their verification being a matter of suspense—will it obtain its reliable witness? The first word of this practice appears in Galileo's hand, in 1608, when the first experimental event, the enrollment of balls rolling down an inclined plane as reliable witnesses of the way they gain speed, was about to be achieved: *Doveria*—if I am right, this is the result that should be obtained, and no other characterization of their movement will then be able to undo the created link, to reduce it to a human interpretation imposed on a mute reality.

It may be that if critiques had emphasized the very singularity of experimental practices, some experimenters, instead of feeling insulted by the attack, would have realized that the worst insult to their practice is to use the same word, objectivity, to characterize both the general reduction of any situation to objective terms and their own passionate attempt to create experimental situations empowering a difference between relevant questions and unilaterally imposed ones. This was indeed the very point of my characterization of experimental practices—to thwart the way they are taken as a model to be blindly, that is, methodologically, extended. How indeed to extend a practice which demands that what is mobilized, actively framed in the terms of the question it should answer, be nevertheless able to reliably endorse its mobilization? From the fact that experimental achievements happen, it can only be concluded that some ingredients of "reality" lend themselves to this demand. But, even then, their "objective definition" is strictly relative to the experimental conditions that enabled them to reliably answer the experimenter's question. To take an example, the "objective definition" of genetically modified soybeans or cotton does not cover at all what they will be able to become part of "outside of the lab," in the fields or in living bodies. More generally, as soon as it becomes an ingredient of matters of common concern, an experimental being is no longer liable to an "objective" definition.

In other words, what is created in experimental laboratories are fragile and partial connections, but relevant ones. If, instead of a general ideal of objectivity, the thread uniting scientific practices had been the commitment to create situations that confer on what scientists address the power to make a crucial difference with regard to the value of their questions, relevance and not authority would have been the name of the game. What would have been produced then is a positive, radical plurality of sciences, each particular scientific practice answering the challenge of relevance associated with its specific field, each crafting the always particular achievement that it will eventually call a scientific fact, each presenting itself in terms of its specific achievement.

If "Science" in the singular was to be used, it would be in the sense of what Gilles Deleuze and Félix Guattari called a rhizome, growing through local, always particular and partial connections. A kind of ecological anarchy, certainly, but not a free-for-all connectivity, because while connections may be produced with any part of what will be called "reality," they must be effectively produced. Such productions are events that are and will remain plural, not the witnesses of a potential unity.

This corresponds to the speculative idea of "civilized scientific practitioners," practitioners who would know that it is an insult to their practice to characterize it in terms of general attributes such as objectivity and rationality—this way of presenting themselves implying that their achievements are "normal," that their only difference with regard to "others" is that those others are lacking objectivity or rationality; practitioners who would know that what follows from their achievements should never claim to replace the answers others give to their own questions because the answers they themselves get are affirmatively situated, relative to the situations which allowed them to claim relevance, that is, the situations which enabled the addressee to "take a position" about the way they are addressed. As such, "civilized" sciences would participate in a "world in the making" through the creation of connections with a specificity related to what commits them: the question of what, how, and under which conditions we can "learn from" what we address.

This is a very specific commitment indeed, as "learning from" is not a common human concern. People more usually learn with or learn together. As such, the scientific commitment, to abstract and extract what will be brought back to the "colleagues" as having been "learned from," and what will sustain, one way or another, the collective learning enterprise proper to their common field, is not an innocent one. I would dare to propose that sciences are, from this point of view, entrepreneurial practices, in the sense that entrepreneurs are the children of the possible, which is a potentially predatory passion. What has then to be attentively taken care of is the easy transformation of "it might be possible" to "it must be possible," or to "whatever the price, we have to make it possible."

More generally, I would call civilized practice a practice able to exhibit its own, never innocent, "divergence": in the pragmatic space it creates, the specific way in which its practitioners world and word their world, as Haraway would say. The way a practice diverges characterizes not its difference from others but the way it has its own world mattering, the values that commit its practitioners, what they take into account and how. It communicates with the idea of an "ecology of practices"—not a stable harmony or a peaceful coexistence but a web of interdependent partial connections. Ecology is about the interrelations between heterogeneous beings as such, without a transcendent common interest, or without an arbiter distributing the roles, or without a mutual understanding. Conflicts of interests are the general rule, but the remarkable events (without which only the triviality of predator-prey relations would exist) are the creation of symbiosis or the weaving of coevolutions—that is, the making of connections between "beings" whose interests, whose ways of having their world matter, diverge but who may come to refer to each other, or need each other, each for their own "reasons." Agreements without a common definition or without an understanding reaching beyond divergence is an ecological trope, disappointing the idea of "true," nonpartial connection. It is also a trope for a "diplomatic peace."

However, such a peace, as a speculative possibility, requires practitioners, not scientists functioning as parts of the hegemonic machine. If there is something of a tragicomedy in the Science Wars, it is that at the very time they happened, while furious practitioners were insulting each other and I was beginning to speculate about an ecology of practices and diplomacy, the tug of these wars was being disposed of through completely different means. This is what Donna Haraway understood when she asked us to think in the presence of OncoMouse, the patented mouse created to suffer for women. Second-millennium science is no longer the practice of experimenters such as Robert Boyle. We already knew that conquering, destroying, blindly objectifying never needed reliable relevant knowledge. But we have now to understand that competitiveness and innovation are also generally indifferent to reliable knowledge, and rather require flexibility. Scientists have now to accept that the knowledge they generate is good enough if it leads to patents and the satisfaction of stakeholders. The hegemonic machine is now destroying the practices that claimed to be indispensable for the "modernization" of the world. It does not need those who presented themselves as the very soul of "progress," as it does not need a general trust in progress either.

If the so-called "knowledge economy" has its full way, what had been an insult for scientists, the idea that their knowledge is a matter of representation only, will be verified. It is not, however, the kind of verification critical thinkers should be happy with. It means indeed that the social fabric required by the concern for relevant knowledge has been destroyed. Scientists will no longer need that their colleagues object and test their claimed achievements, as there will be other, easier and more rewarding, means to succeed, which depend on other interests, on promises liable to attract industrial partners. If objections to the weakness of a particular claim may lead to a general weakening of the promises of a field, nobody will object too much. Dissenting voices will then be disqualified as minority views that need not be taken into account, as they spell unnecessary trouble. What may well prevail then is the general wisdom that you do not saw off the branch on which you are sitting together with everybody else. And what is bound to happen has already got a name, "promise economy," when what holds protagonists are glimmering possibilities of innovation nobody is interested in assessing any longer. A knowledge economy is indeed a speculative economy, a bubble-and-crash economy taking control of the production of scientific knowledge.

The same is true for all modern practices, which, we discover, were just surviving, on borrowed time, as flexibility has become the general rule, and ways of diverging synonymous with rigidity. It does not mean that the speculative ideas of "civilized practitioners" and of an "ecology of practice" have lost relevance. They can still make a difference when addressing practitioners oscillating between despair, revolt, angry cynicism, and easy submission. But more than anything, they may protect those who fight the hegemonic machine from the temptation of taking seriously the idea they have to fight against "objective facts," "rationality," "universality," or a Western ontology when they often deal with lying puppets. And finally they bring me to cosmopolitics, my access to the question of ontological politics.

From Cosmopolitics to Ontological Politics

I conceived the "cosmopolitics" proposition as a European philosopher, not a decolonizing anthropologist. Like Bruno Latour's "Parliament of Things" in *We Have Never Been Modern*, but much more explicitly so, it is a speculative idea since it presupposes civilized modern practitioners.

The Parliament of Things modified the Greek idea of politics in two main ways. First, those who gather are not "naked humans" with conflicting opinions, but "spokespersons" for "things," situated by what they have learned "from" them. Second, they gather around an "issue" that should be given the power to problematize each diverging contribution and discover if and how it is relevant in this case, for this issue.

To me, giving an issue the power of having people thinking together resonates with the wide resistance against the use of genetically modified organisms (GMOs) that has developed on European soil. We have seen the beginning of an effective redistribution of expertise and a collective enlargement of imagination and sensibilities. The strength of the movement, its capacity to make "official" experts stammer and to make the imperative of competitive modernization lose some of its grasp, comes from the collective realization that there is not one, but many, good reasons to resist GMOs. Learning from others why they resisted and realizing the interdependence of their respective reasons was transformative. Young urbanites have learned to care about what they eat, not for health reasons only but as a way to continue the fight against the enclosures associated with the industry's property rights over seeds, while farmers have learned that some biologists could be their allies against industrialized monocultures, and environmentalists that their concern could enter into a geopolitical alliance with African and Indian peasants. As for scientists in general, they were divided, with some discovering that the so-called rationalization of agriculture was not that rational at all.

The Science Wars taught me to speculate about the relevance of diplomacy, but what I have come to call the "GMO event" taught me the crucial and actual relevance of activist politics. Giving an issue the power to make concerned people think and act together, enabling each to connect with the ways others come to be concerned, is what activists aim at. And it would also be the political achievement of an issue-centered, not opinion-centered, Parliament of Things gathering "civilized" concerned protagonists, able to disentangle their argument from claims about rationality or objectivity, agreeing that each of them has a legitimate voice and is entitled to contribute to the issue that concerns them all.

However, would those "civilized" people be able to listen to those who would claim that the issue as such does not concern them, that they do not wish to contribute, but refuse eventual consequences of what may be decided? Would they listen to those who would cry: we cannot be part of your political deliberation process because it will consider eventually disposing of what nobody is free to dispose of? To those who cry: if you decide this, you will destroy us! Or: if you decide this, it will mean war!

Here is where I felt the need to slow down, to recognize a limitation of the "Parliament of Things" proposition, as conceived by Bruno Latour. The Parliament of Things keeps from Greek politics the definition of a gathering of people who feel free to negotiate an issue, of people whose knowledge and experience may diverge as much as one can wish, but who accept that it belongs to the political process of collective deliberation to assess the way the knowledge and experiences of each will contribute to the issue that gathers them all. However, those who disrupt deliberation by objecting without contributing, by presenting some aspects involved in the issue as nonnegotiable, may well be rejected as mere nuisances.

I forged the word "cosmopolitics," adding the prefix "cosmo-" to "politics" in order to think with the need to overcome this limitation. The prefix "cosmo-" aims at making the disruption matter. It proposes to characterize the disruptive event as the entering on the scene of human deliberation of "causes" that do not accept dependence on a regime of deliberation and transaction. The cosmos is not an argument and nobody can purport to be its spokesperson, but it signals that together with issues, worlds are in the balance. It "makes present, helps resonate the unknown affecting *our* questions, an unknown that our political tradition is at significant risk of disqualifying."[5]

Those who protest but refuse to contribute are those who need diplomats, since for them what is at stake in the political process is a question of life and death, of peace and war. It is important to emphasize that they are not specifically "nonmoderns." It is the issue that determines who will feel free to contribute to the transaction and who are potentially its victims. It is also important to emphasize that cosmopolitics was not proposing a full recognition on the political scene of "more-than-human" causes. It was only demanding a slowing down of the political process. It called for the political scene to accept being inhabited, even haunted, by those who present themselves as not interested in the creation of partial connections, not forced to think together with the others by the issue. It might well be that the disruptive cry would be in vain, but the slowing down means that it should not be ignored, that it should be heard in its frightening intensity, without the protection of any argument justifying that, even if tolerated, it is not to be taken into account. Cosmopolitics means that politics should proceed in the presence of those who will bear the consequences, who will be the victims of political decisions, in the presence not only of "humans" but also of the multiple divergent worlds they belong to, which this decision threatens.

From the ontological politics point of view, cosmopolitics is badly limited. The cry "you will destroy us," even if it may cause fright in the political assembly, even if, as amplified by diplomats, it may effectively disrupt the collective deliberation and maybe reorient it toward new horizons, is still defined as a disruption, political deliberation being now defined as what must accept disruption. Accept or tolerate? What is lurking is nothing other than the curse of tolerance, a tolerance that would have "us" accept the crucial importance of "causes" for "others" while, except for very special cases, "we" would be "free."

This is why I would take ontological politics as corresponding to the reverse situation, when "causes" would not mean only the disruption of political deliberation. If politics is ontological, ontological clashes would have to be anticipated everywhere as no issue can any longer be considered as a matter of free deliberation, putting into brackets the worlds it implies and the way it matters in these worlds. It would be diplomacy all the way down. There are certainly other definitions of ontological politics, but this definition, avoiding the harmless notion of "representation," accepts that ontology is a matter of commitment. As such, it challenges the idea that the problem with ontological politics is only a question of the long, entrenched life of colonial thought habits.

I will take as a first approach to this challenge a story by Tania Katzschner about the Cape Flats Nature project in the Cape Town area, a project that aimed at preserving an ecologically significant dune system. The cause of preservation in South Africa often clashes with the cause of the struggle for emancipation of (poor, black) communities—communities only too aware that preservation has usually meant fencing them away from what is to be protected. "The project chose a process of open-ended dialogue, and knew very well that in doing so there was a chance that they might lose the dunes."[6] This risk, losing the dunes, was a necessary condition if their preservation and the empowerment of the community were not to stand as rival causes. The project thus implied that the dunes' preservation would not be obtained by protecting them "against" the community but by betting that the community could become an actor in this preservation if it learned to trust those who entered into dialogue with them. The central challenge was thus a creation and nurturing of trust. Trust is transformative, and the process had an impact beyond the dunes: "new young, vocal black conservators" were born from the process, community champions whose voice "has shifted the possibilities for the excluded and powerless to be part of the process of biodiversity conservation, and in turn has changed the fora themselves."[7] About another case, Katzschner writes, "The project itself engaged many sensibilities: head and heart, perception, intuition, feeling and imagination. In this way it also shifted and changed all that it touched."[8]

We may feel that Katzschner tells us a "good ontological politics story," in contrast with those numerous ones in which "nature" is "protected," whatever the consequences for local peoples. But this appreciation should not authorize us to take it as a model. It may, for instance, be objected that conservationists are certainly strongly committed to the defense of biodiversity but that it is a matter of strong concern, rather than of a "cause." For them the dune system was "a" dune system, however ecologically precious. But substituting the "a" with a name, the name of a dune-being, respected and feared as such, would change the whole story. Such substitution obviously entails many other substitutions—it is a fictional hypothesis, abstracted from the geopolitical state of affairs. It is only proposed in order to dramatize the challenge of ontological politics.

When what is at stake are causes that cannot be a matter of human negotiation, there is never a model or a warrant, only the uncertainty of diplomacy together with the practices whereby concerned peoples convoke and consult the nonhuman others to whom belongs the power to accept or refuse eventual diplomatic propositions. Despite their wish to become civilized, it is hard for modern practitioners to accept this suspense.

It is all the more hard that today those practitioners are under stress and may well feel that whatever the niceties of ontological politics, all inhabitants of the Earth are facing a common challenge, which calls for urgent recognition and action. The climate disorder that the functioning of the hegemonic extractive machine has triggered, and which now affects all peoples on this earth, thus threatens to induce a new "pedagogical" position. Peoples all over the Earth are already affected in always specific ways, but "we" know that what affects them is one and the same global change brought by the rise in the emission of greenhouse gases. In other terms, modern practitioners are those who belong, whether they like it or not, not only to the fossil-burning world that bears responsibility for the trouble but also to a world able to formulate the problem, define what is globally at stake, and conclude that unanimous mobilization is necessary, whatever our divergences. In this situation they might well be tempted to discuss and assess the capacity of ontological politics to rise to the occasion and demonstrate that it can be entrusted to generate its own way of answering the climate challenge: other-than-humans are acceptable if they collaborate.

In order to resist this temptation, it may be useful to recall the obvious, which is forgotten by this entrepreneurial urge for unanimous mobilization. Assessing ontological politics would mean that, if it is found lacking, we should have to accept the necessity of a global political answer short-cutting those who resist it. But political deliberation has already been found lacking in this case. In fact, the only protagonist that is well equipped to rise to the occasion—and to turn this occasion into fully developed barbarism[9]—is the hegemonic machine, and it is already at work, demanding that indigenous peoples act as dutiful, strictly controlled stewards of their lands to "save the planet." Those peoples have many reasons to distrust the idea that the trouble with the climate is, or should be, a matter of "shared, mobilizing concern."

However, I think that we academics cannot ride piggyback on their reasons and deny that we "know" something is coming with a rather awful speed that will put into question the ways of life of most inhabitants of this earth—while we also know that this knowledge situates us in our own temporality, which should not engulf other peoples.[10] We cannot dream—let alone think—this tension away with sophisticated arguments about cosmopolitics or ontological politics. We have to accept and think with this perplexing situation.

In the first part of this text I have proposed considering scientists as "entrepreneurs who might be civilized." But I have now to include in this characterization myself as well as those who argue about "ontological politics," together with all other critiques of scientific imperialism. I will claim that we academics cannot deal with this perplexity without interrogating our own situation in our own worlds from an ontological politics perspective, and first remember a world marked by the destruction of the arts of sustaining and entertaining a consistent relation with our own causes—we may be perplexed, but we do not know whom we should consult in this matter. The desperate cries of all those who are separated by neo-management and its imperative of flexibility from what caused them to feel their work as worth doing imply that "causes" are still among us. We just do not know any longer how to name, honor, and defend them. We may feel indignant but not frightened at the prospect of betraying them. Should we not, as perplexed academics, learn to share fright, rather than exchange arguments?

I am taking "fright" in the sense I have learned from the ethnopsychiatry of Tobie Nathan, which actively involves "other-than-humans." Fright would not be a psychological experience, rather the experience "that some 'other' has intruded, has influenced or modified us, possibly even caused our metamorphosis. . . . The essential fright is that the truth of what I perceive, of what I feel, of what I think resides in an Other."[11] What metamorphosed us into the "frightless ones"?

Can We Feel Fright?

Staging "us" academics as the frightless ones is not a denunciation but an "active proposition," meant to make us feel and think. Moreover, this proposition is not addressed to all. It might not concern contemporary field anthropologists who have accepted experiences through which they have learned that fright is something more than a psychological affect—and who have learned also how difficult it is to report that in the academic milieu. But I am certainly not excluding from this address an anthropologist such as Philippe Descola, who proposes to put on the same quadri-partitioned plane Euro-modern so-called naturalists, together with animists, totemists, and analogists. Only—and Descola agrees on this—what he calls a naturalist would imagine without fright such a plane on which other peoples' ways of perceiving and thinking are distributed on the basis of materials extracted and brought from faraway worlds to be organized in a Parisian office. And only a scientist, speaking in the name of science, would confront without fright other scientists, proposing to recognize that what they (rather sloppily) address as "nature" identifies them as belonging to one of his own four compartments.

As for those who are bystanders when scientists' contradictory arguments thunder, they may certainly wonder whether giving to neurons the power to explain our ways of organizing and understanding our world is a case of "naturalism," or whether the organizing quadri-partitioned schemes should be explained in terms of some neuronal attractors. What they know well is that they cannot intervene in those fights any more than a mortal could intervene in the Olympian gods' quarrels. Even philosophers, although they are self-proclaimed inheritors of Greek reason, and theologians, inheritors of the monotheistic creed, have no voice in the matter. Let us not speak of the old lady with a cat, claiming that her cat understands her. She probably knows that her account of her relations with her cat is only "tolerated," as a matter of private belief, that her claim has no purchase in the fighters' world, and that it will probably fare no better with critical academics. Maybe she even knows the pejorative characterization she would deserve in the academic worlds—she entertains "animist beliefs."

As we all know, whatever their scholarship, the diverse definitions given to animism bear the stamps of their origins and can hardly be disentangled from pejorative colonialist associations. But I would claim that those associations also work upon us as commitments. They committed the colonizers of the past to "civilize" others, to have them accepting the hard truth that makes us human: that we are alone in a mute, blind world. But if we are the frightless ones, it may well be that we are still today compelled by this commitment, bound to resist what would mean betraying it. "Do not regress" is a commandment devoid of biological or even ethological connotation. For the fighters, the old lady's stubbornness is rather a witness to the power of ever-resurging illusions, that is, also to the permanent and heroic character of the commandment it is their duty not to betray.

I thus propose to take seriously the power of the "thou shall not regress" commandment, which is alive and well among us, even if the science of biological evolution has left far behind any idea of regression. When the objection resounds—"But this would be animism!"—no particular reference is made to past or present scholars' definitions. I propose taking seriously that this objection may well activate a peculiar fright, as provoked by a transgression. Animism equals regression; it is what we are committed to resist.

As may now be emphasized, my initial propositions—about civilized modern practitioners, the ecology of practices, or cosmopolitics—did not directly contradict this commandment. Cosmopolitics simply complicated its meaning, demanding that an issue be considered in the presence of those who could be the victims of its negotiated formulation. The term "issue" itself is significant. The power conferred on issues, to have people thinking together, is certainly a transformative one, but the transformation is not an answer to something that would have in itself the power to question us. We do not practice arts of consultation. Rather, the power conferred by the question "What does this issue demand?" is considered as a collective human achievement. I myself did not face the question of "other-than-human beings" but rather evaded it, or tamed it, like many "posthumanist" authors. We all feel the commandment even if we are trying to negotiate its consequences. It would seem that we are afraid, indeed frightened, that, if we squarely transgress it, all our resources for thinking will be destroyed—a kind of Dostoyevskian fright may be felt that "everything would be permitted!" A very interesting case of reverse cosmopolitics indeed: when ontological politics demands that we take seriously the existence and power of other-than-human beings, it is we who cry: do not demand that we do that when we ourselves are concerned, or you will destroy us. A strange equality is at last achieved—we are frightened to betray what we are.

This fright may well point to a figure (a strange one) that Bruno Latour has crafted.[12] According to Latour, what we have called "progress" or "emancipation" would not make us look forward; rather, it makes us look backward, as if, running toward the future, we were escaping something horrible, a monster that would take advantage of any weakness, any "opening of the door," and engulf us. What is called "emancipation" would then mean quasi-exclusively the destruction of the so-called "shackles of the past."

With Tobie Nathan, I have learned that peoples who know how to relate with other-than-human entities know well that such entities have to be recognized and honored if they are not to become devouring, furious powers. Civilized, cautious relations with them have to be established and sustained—the gods, spirits, or ancestors must be fed. Bruno Latour's backward-looking flight toward the future correlates with this diagnosis. It seems that the commandment not to regress has such a furious power over us—for instance, possessing us with a compulsive reliance on the power of critical deconstruction. As if making the difference between what is entitled to "really" exist and what is not were our only safeguard against the monstrous grip of illusion.

Such a possession cannot be directly related to scientific practices, as I have characterized them, because their questions are positively situated ones—for instance, the surprise that such a seemingly ghostly existent as the Newtonian force is not just a human construction but a scientific event with no negative correlate. But Science is certainly possessed, as well as critical thought. The power over us of "really" may well be related to the propaganda that wipes away the situated character of any "scientifically authenticated existent," but this does not account for the passionate importance given to the exclusion of what cannot demonstrate its "real" existence. It could be said that we have turned into a compulsive duty the craft and concern of testators who, in the past, tested, in the service of a prince, the gold alchemists paid by this prince presented to him. They knew that all that glimmers is not (really) gold. The monster that we fly away from is indeed glimmering, seductive, inviting us to wallow in illusion.

That "Science" has taken upon itself the testator commitment may be associated with the event the historian Robert Darnton associated with the end of Enlightenment, when the "monster" made its appearance under the guise of the crowd of agitated enthusiasts seduced by the promise of Anton Mesmer's magnetism.[13] Putting their craft in the service of public order, a set of distinguished experimenters accepted the job of demonstrating that Mesmer's magnetic fluid, whatever its impressive effects, "did not really exist." Science served as a rampart against the dangerous gullibility of people ready to follow quacks and miracle workers, just as the testators defended the princes against the alchemists' tricks.

The use of "really" thus denotes the passionate commitment of both Science, at the service of public order, and critical thought, denouncing the normative character of public order, to defeat what tricks us into believing. If ontology is to be related to a sense of commitment, ours is a testator ontology. "Naturalism," in Descola's sense of the term, would be a rather incoherent assembly of what survived, always on borrowed time, the testators' dissolving agents. And I would add that those who would claim to be animists, if they affirm that rocks "really" have souls or intentions as well as we do, could be devoured by the same passion. I would guess that peoples categorized as animists by anthropologists have no word for "really," for insisting that they are right and others are victims of illusions.

Let us emphasize that the modern testators' commitment is all the more passionate as it cannot rest on its efficacy, only on a duty that should never be betrayed. The old testators successfully devised effective dissolving agents, and they are often considered the precursors of modern chemistry. In contrast, whatever the verdict against Mesmer's magnetic fluid, magnetism kept generating a strong interest during the nineteenth century, blurring the well-guarded frontiers between what was opposed as natural and supernatural. Nature was made mysterious, and supernature was populated by messengers bringing news from elsewhere to mediums in magnetic trance—a very disordered situation, which understandably provoked the hostility of both scientific and church institutions. It has even been proposed that psychoanalysis was not the subversive "plague" that Freud boasted about, rather a restoration of order, because it provided the means to explain away, or dissolve, mysterious cures, magnetic "lucidity," and other demonic manifestations, now pigeonholed as purely human and bearing witness to a new universal cause, the Unconscious, deciphered by Science.[14]

Today as yesterday, healers and people looking for a healing path joyfully betray the commandment. However, this betrayal is tolerated. We take it for granted that people who are looking for healing and, by extension, those who take charge of healing by unorthodox, not data-based, means, are somehow lost, unable to bear their duty not to regress. This is why New Age healing, as welcoming as it may be to animist creeds, is not an answer to the challenge of ontological politics as we discuss it on academic grounds, that is, grounds populated by testators. This challenge does not demand either that we repudiate right away the "do not regress" commandment—a rather bad idea if it has over us the power of an "other-than-human" injunction. It is the way this injunction works that perhaps should interest us—the position it proposes us to occupy. We academics have learned to consider that without our commitment to critique, "everything would be permitted." Diffracting the way in which we have learned to occupy this position, breaking it up into the many occasions when it was the only safe position against such insidious words as "Do you 'really' believe that . . . ?" may bring us to address our milieu as what separates us from the possibility of honoring and feeding what makes us feel and think.

Reclaiming Animism?

It is important to first emphasize that this diffracting operation is not a matter of reflexive critique, a typical testator exercise. I received as a shock, an active transforming proposition, the cry of neopagan witch Starhawk: "The smoke of the burned witches still hangs in our nostrils."[15] Certainly the witch hunters of the past are no longer among us and we no longer take seriously the accusation of devil worshipping that witches were the victims of. Rather, our milieu is defined by the modern pride that we are now able to interpret both witchery and witch hunting as a matter of social, linguistic, cultural, or political (glimmering) construction or beliefs. We are those who know that neither the devil nor "true" witches, whatever this means, really existed. And we forget that we are the heirs of an operation of social and cultural eradication—the forerunner of what was committed elsewhere in the name of civilization and reason.

The point is obviously not to feel guilty. It is rather to open up what William James, in his *Will to Believe*, called a genuine, effective option, complicating the power of the injunction "not to regress," demanding that we situate ourselves with respect to this eradication: will we side with those who "normalize" this eradication, or will we reclaim this past? And here comes the efficacy of Starhawk's cry. Reclaiming the past is not a matter of dreaming to resurrect some "true," "authentic" tradition, of healing what cannot be healed, of making whole what has been destroyed. It is rather a matter of reactivating it, and first of all, of feeling the smoke in our nostrils—the smoke that I felt, for instance, when I hurriedly emphasized that, no, I did not "believe" that the past could be resurrected. Learning to feel the smoke is to activate memory and imagination regarding the way we have learned the codes of our respective milieus: derisive remarks, knowing smiles, offhand judgments, often about somebody else, but gifted with the power to pervade and infect—to shape us as the ones who will be among those who sneer and not among those who are sneered at.

However, to reclaim is not only to feel the way the devouring infection works. It is also to recover, that is, to approach in another, not accusatory, way what has been turned into a devouring power.

Here I will call to my help another ally, David Abram, whose *Spell of the Sensuous* proposes an "animist" account of rationality.[16] Animism, here, is no longer an anthropological category. David Abram's learning from and with shamans was grounded on the mutually recognized relation between their craft and his own being, among other things, a sleight-of-hand magician. The point was not, however, to reduce this craft to a matter of illusion. For Abram, what "illusionists" artfully exploit is the very creativity of our senses, "the way the senses themselves have of throwing themselves beyond what is immediately given, in order to make tentative contact with the other sides of things that we do not sense directly, with the hidden or invisible aspects of the sensible." Our senses throwing themselves beyond the given do not explain magic away. As Abram characterizes them, they rather respond to "suggestions offered by the sensible itself."[17] Magic has nothing to do with credulity; it is a witness for our senses not being at the service of detached cognition but existing for participation, for sharing the metamorphic capacity of things that lure us or that recede into inert availability as our manner of participation shifts—shifts but, he insists, never vanishes: we never step outside what he calls the "flux of participation."[18]

What is so interesting here is that this approach allows Abram to conclude that we ourselves could legitimately be called "animists." When we look at small black signs and experience that they are speaking to us, we are both animated by the signs and animating them. Instead of talking about the disenchantment of the modern world, Abram thus emphasizes the strong enchantment of the written text, more precisely of the alphabetic text, the only text that presents itself as self-sufficient, as able by itself to have us "hear spoken words, witness strange scenes or visions, even experience other lives." And he proposes that this efficacy might be recognized as an animating magic—a strong magic, as he experienced himself when he came back to New York from countries where the written letters do not rule, and felt fading away the lure of the stones or the birds or the rivers he had learned to listen to and talk with. "Only as our senses transfer their animating magic to the written word do the trees become mute, the other animals dumb."[19]

If, as Abram claims, our senses make us animists, we nevertheless are not animists in the sense of anthropologists, because we do not honor or recognize what animates us. Alfred North Whitehead wrote that after *The Symposium*, where Plato discusses the erotic power of ideas animating the human soul, he should have written another dialogue, called *The Furies*, which would deal with the horror lurking "within imperfect realization."[20] The possibility of an imperfect realization, that is, of not recognizing and honoring as such animating powers, at the risk of turning them into devouring ones, is certainly present whenever transformative, metamorphic forces make themselves felt. It may well be, however, that it is dramatically so when ideas are concerned, as testified by our violent history, during which wars, including academic wars, have been waged in the name of written-down ideas.[21]

Once "written down," indeed, ideas entice us with the temptation to assimilate them to the expression of the author's intention and to enter into discussion with this author, thus turning what had been the animating experience of reading into the expression of the writer's intentions. A human author has been writing about something and we, the readers, are replaying, in order to understand or criticize, alternative versions of this purely intentional human activity. How then can we grant this kind of intentionality to other beings? Not only the text imposes itself as of human provenance only, but we are put in a position to test its author's ideas, to assess how they are addressing the issue they deal with. This, at least, is the case since the written text has become a printed text, since "authors" are no longer, as in medieval times, "authorities" to be carefully quoted and commented on, but entrepreneurs, rivaling in the conquest of readership.

David Abram nevertheless writes, and passionately so. I would propose to take the experience of writing—not writing down preconceived ideas—as a first antidote against the compulsive insistence of the "either . . . or" unpalatable alternatives: either reducing the reading experience to a cognitive performance or accepting that an "other-than-human" entity is "really" addressing us as an intentional subject would. Writing is an experience of metamorphic transformation. It corresponds to one of those situations that make one feel that something "other-than-human" is addressing us, but not as an intentional subject, rather as demanding its own realization, requiring from the author some kind of cerebral, that is, bodily, contortion (making us larvae, wrote Deleuze) whereby any preformed intention is defeated.[22]

For me, as a philosopher, this first antidote brings with it the temptation to relate animism, as characterized by Abram, to such philosophical ideas as Gilles Deleuze and Félix Guattari's idea of an assemblage, as developed in *A Thousand Plateaus*. Indeed, an assemblage, for Deleuze and Guattari, is the coming together of heterogeneous components, and such a coming together is, for them, the first and last word of existence. I do not exist and then enter into assemblages. The manner of my existence is my very participation in assemblages. I am not gifted with agency, the possessor of intentions or initiative. Animation, agency, intentionality, or what Deleuze and Guattari called "desire," belong to the assemblage as such, including those very particular assemblages, called reflexive ones, that produce an experience of detachment, the enjoyment of critically testing the ins and outs of what we feel or think in order to determine what is "really" responsible for what.

I may also be tempted to relate assemblages to William James's radical empiricism, with its affirmative, not demystifying, promotion of experience—of the full fact of experience, not of experience as critically purified, dismembered into an experiencing subject and an experienced object. Experience as an ongoing flux of participation.

However, relating animism to the efficacy of "assemblages" is a dangerous move because it may well reassure us a bit too easily. When pondering such sophisticated philosophical ideas, we do not fear the suspicious gaze of the inquisitors; we do not feel the smoke in our nostrils. We are protected by the academic assemblages we participate in. But most of all we are protected by the fact that we are pondering what Deleuze and Guattari have published—it is what they meant to mean that matters.

This is why it may be better to revive more compromising words, words that have been academically restricted to metaphoric use only, without ins and outs. "Magic" is such a word, and we freely speak of the magic of an event, of a landscape, of a musical moment. . . . Protected by the metaphor, we may then express the experience of an agency that does not belong to us even if it includes us, that does not address us as intentional agents, but us as lured into feeling by something else, by something which may or may not be intentional—we do not know and, what is more important, we do not "really" care.

Reviving magic, depriving ourselves of the protection of the metaphor, will attract the gaze of the inquisitors and also, inseparably, activate the sad, monotonous critical or reflexive voice that whispers that we should not accept being mystified. This voice may also tell us about the frightening possibilities that would follow if we gave up critique, the only defense we have against fanaticism and the rule of illusions. And this is precisely one of the reasons why neopagan witches call their own craft "magic": naming it so, they say, is, in itself, an act of magic because by experiencing the discomfort it creates, we may feel the smoke in our nostrils. Worse, they have learned to cast circles and invoke the Goddess, She who, the witches say, "returns," She to whom thanks will be given for the event that makes them, each of them and all together, capable of doing what they thus call "the work of the Goddess." So doing, they put us to the test: how can we accept such a return of, or regression to, supernatural beliefs?

The witches' ritual chant—"She changes everything she touches, and everything she touches changes"—could surely be commented on in terms of assemblages because it resists the dismembering attribution of agency.

Does change belong to the Goddess as "agent" or to the one who changes when touched? But the first efficacy of the refrain is in "she touches." The recalcitrance against dismembering is no longer conceptual. It is part of an experience which affirms that the power of changing is not to be attributed to our own selves, nor to be reduced to something "natural" or "cultural." It is part of an experience that honors change as a creation. Moreover, the point is not to comment. The refrain must be chanted; it is part and parcel of the practice of worship.

Chanting, one no longer wonders whether we have to "believe" that the Goddess that contemporary witches invoke and convoke in their rituals "really exists." The commandment "not to regress" is floundering, losing its grasp, because those who chant know the little skeptical voice inside us perfectly well.[23] Indeed, if one told them, "But your Goddess is only a fiction," they would probably smile and ask us whether we are among those who ignore that fiction has the power to shape us. And if one wondered about the danger of fictions that may capture and enslave, it may well be that they would answer that the debunking of illusions is a rather poor defense against such dangers. What they themselves cultivate, as part of their craft (as it is probably a part of any craft involving other-than-humans), is a practice of immanent attention, an empirical practice of "realization," to use Whitehead's word, experiencing what may be toxic—an art of diagnosis which our addiction to "the truth that defeats illusion" has too often despised as too weak and uncertain. Contemporary witches resist this addiction. They are pragmatic, radically pragmatic, experimenting with effects and consequences of a craft that, they know, is never innocent and, as such, involves care, protections, and attention.

This might well be what we are separated from—what the testators suggest the prince is devoid of—the pragmatic art of immanent attention, of discrimination between the toxic and the helpful. The devouring power of the commandment "not to regress" would then be related to the fact that we have not honored what makes us capable of this art, that we have not learned how to foster and sustain it—leaving to the testators' truth the charge of protecting us. This, at least, is what David Abram and neopagan witch Starhawk both inform me of. If magic is to be reclaimed as an art of participation, or of luring assemblages, if we have to reclaim the risky business of honoring change, the assemblages we participate in, inversely, are to become a matter of empirical and pragmatic concern about effects and consequences, not a matter of general consideration or textual dissertation.

I would thus claim that we, who are not witches, do not have to mimic them in order to discover how honoring change exposes one to academic sniggering. We also, like the witches, have to learn how to cast circles that protect us from our insalubrious, infectious milieu, without isolating us from the work to be done, from the concrete situations to be confronted. Turning into an academic argument the Zapatista call for a world where many worlds would fit may be rewarding, as it may give the feeling that we relay this call, that we bring it into the very heart of the enemy fortress, under the very gaze of the testators. But challenging their gaze may not be an end in itself any longer. I have insisted on "us" academics, because for us recognizing and honoring the power of ideas may still matter. But how long will they matter when the princes whom testators serve do not give a darn any longer about the difference between true gold and what just glimmers? How to avoid the temptation to join with the testators lamenting the end of our (academic) world?

Donna Haraway has borrowed from Anna Tsing the thought-provoking formula of "living in the ruins."[24] Eduardo Viveiros de Castro recalls us that for other peoples the "end of the world" is a foregone topic, and living in the ruins is what they have learned. I certainly do not deny that some ruins are much more comfortable than others, but the question of how to live in the ruins is now raised everywhere, and the challenge of ontological politics should not be abstracted from the question of activating this question in the academic ruins.

Ruins are not safe places. Distressed colleagues lurk, made furious by the destruction of what they took for granted, of their "ways of assessing as usual," and caution is needed when you meet them—they may have turned into cannibals, whose only satisfaction is to attack those who threaten the certainty of their despair. But ruins may also be alive with partial connections, connections that do not sustain great entrepreneurial perspective but demand a capacity to learn from and learn with, and to care for what has been learned from.

It may well be that to me, as a European city dweller, alphabetized to the core, a daughter moreover to philosophy, which is an adventure of (written) ideas, a mountain is just a mountain and a fish just a fish. But an idea is not just an idea, it is a metamorphic power, and I have to reclaim the capacity to honor this power just as Ecuadorian peasants honor their land and mountain. In the ruins of our world, reclaiming ideas is remembering that ideas cannot be trusted as such, that they need to be fed, connected with something other than entrepreneurial "thuses" and "therefores," which are always liable to turn their power into an authority or into a weapon. I may align as many thuses and therefores as anybody else to justify the need to struggle against the machine that is turning our many worlds into a devastated "cosmopolitan" desert, but the reclaiming witches taught me the need to cultivate, where we are, what we struggle for, to relay what we have learned and have rendered each other capable of. The idea of ontological politics needs the transformative magic of tales, rituals, modes of palaver, ways of thinking-feeling with, which reworld our ruins and open them to partial connections with other worlds. This is also the only legacy we can leave to the next generation, what can perhaps help them make a difference between living in the ruins and just surviving.

NOTES

1. Étienne Souriau, *The Different Modes of Existence*, trans. Erik Beranek and Tim Howles (Minneapolis: Univocal, 2015), 100–101.

2. Bruno Latour, *War of the Worlds: What about Peace?*, trans. Charlotte Bigg (Chicago: Prickly Paradigm, 2002), 26, also available at http://www.bruno-latour.fr/sites /default/files/85-WAR-OF-WORLDS-GB.pdf.

3. Bruno Latour has since attempted a similar operation, but with other means, in his *Inquiry into Modes of Existence*. At the time I wrote *Cosmopolitics* (1996–97), I borrowed from him a tool he has now dropped, that of the factish (which English readers saw appearing in *Pandora's Hope*, the translation of the *Petité Réflexion sur le culte moderne des dieux fétiches*, published in 1996, having waited fourteen years). Bruno Latour, *An Inquiry into Modes of Existence: An Anthropology of the Moderns*, trans. Catherine Porter (Cambridge, MA: Harvard University Press, 2013); Bruno Latour, *Pandora's Hope: Essays on the Reality of Science Studies* (Cambridge, MA: Harvard University Press, 1999).

4. See Isabelle Stengers, *The Invention of Modern Science*, trans. Daniel W. Smith (Minneapolis: University of Minnesota Press, 2000).

5. Isabelle Stengers, *Cosmopolitics II*, trans. Robert Bononno (Minneapolis: University of Minnesota Press, 2011), 355.

6. Tania Katzschner, "Cape Flats Nature: Rethinking Urban Ecologies," in *Contested Ecologies: Dialogues in the South on Nature and Knowledge*, ed. Lesley Green, 202–26 (Cape Town: HSRC Press, 2013), 221.

7. Katzschner, "Cape Flats Nature," 222.

8. Katzschner, "Cape Flats Nature," 221.

9. See Isabelle Stengers, *In Catastrophic Times: Resisting the Coming Barbarism*, trans. Andrew Goffey (London: Open Humanities, 2015), free access online.

10. Déborah Danowski and Eduardo Viveiros de Castro give us what I read as a very salubrious and perplexing warning here in "Is There Any World to Come?," *e-flux journal*

65 (May–August 2015), http://supercommunity-pdf.e-flux.com/pdf/supercommunity /article_1231.pdf.

11. Tobie Nathan, quoted in Stengers, *Cosmopolitics II*, 325.

12. Bruno Latour, "An Attempt at a 'Compositionist Manifesto,'" *New Literary History* 41, no. 3 (2010): 471–90. See also Bruno Latour, *Facing Gaia: Eight Lectures on the New Climatic Regime*, trans. Catherine Porter (Cambridge, MA: Polity, 2017).

13. Robert Darnton, *Mesmerism and the End of the Enlightenment in France* (Cambridge, MA: Harvard University Press, 1986). I analyzed this episode in Leon Chertok and Isabelle Stengers, *A Critique of Psychoanalytic Reason: Hypnosis as a Scientific Problem from Lavoisier to Lacan*, trans. Martha Evans (Stanford, CA: Stanford University Press, 1992). Let us emphasize that "mesmerized crowds" do not initiate "the fear of the monster," rather reactivate it, as fanatic Nazis or so many others will also do. As Stephen Toulmin proposed in *Cosmopolis*, we may have to turn to the Renaissance in order to meet the prototypical monster that moderns have been flying away from ever since. Stephen Toulmin, *Cosmopolis: The Hidden Agenda of Modernity* (Chicago: University of Chicago Press, 1990).

14. It is worth recalling that, with André Breton, surrealism was originally associated with automatism, as practiced by mediums and clairvoyants. Breton's conviction that the milieu of art should foster what science rejected was, however, an appropriative one, marked by a typically modernist triumphalism. To him, art was supreme, not a craft among other crafts, but the final advent of the surreal, finally purified of superstitious beliefs. He fully obeyed the commandment that we not regress.

15. Starhawk, *Dreaming the Dark: Magic, Sex and Politics* (Boston: Beacon, 1982), 219.

16. David Abram, *The Spell of the Sensuous: Perception and Language in a More-Than-Human World* (New York: Vintage, 1996).

17. Abram, *The Spell of the Sensuous*, 58.

18. Abram, *The Spell of the Sensuous*, 59.

19. Abram, *The Spell of the Sensuous*, 131.

20. Alfred N. Whitehead, *Adventures of Ideas* (New York: Free Press, 1967), 148.

21. David Abram proposes that what we have called "idea" since Plato cannot, whatever Plato's distrust for writing, be disentangled from the new Athenian literate intellect and the detached reflection that the writing technology induces.

22. The French philosopher Étienne Souriau speaks about a "questioning situation," the progressive exploration of the answer to be given to an enigmatic insistence. See Étienne Souriau, "On the Work to Be Done," in *The Different Modes of Existence*.

23. A similar point is beautifully made by Tanya Luhrmann in *When God Talks Back: Understanding the American Evangelical Relationship with God* (New York: Vintage, 2012). Contemporary Evangelicals are aware not only that for many the voice of God they experience inside themselves is a delusive product of self-suggestion, but that the problem of discriminating what comes from God and what comes from them is part and parcel of their experience.

24. Donna Haraway, *Staying with the Trouble: Making Kin in the Chthulucene* (Durham, NC: Duke University Press, 2016).

Abram, David. *The Spell of the Sensuous: Perception and Language in a More-Than-Human World*. New York: Vintage, 1996.

Chertok, Leon, and Isabelle Stengers. *A Critique of Psychoanalytic Reason: Hypnosis as a Scientific Problem from Lavoisier to Lacan*. Translated by Martha Evans. Stanford, CA: Stanford University Press, 1992.

Danowski, Déborah, and Eduardo Viveiros de Castro. "Is There Any World to Come?" *e-flux journal* 65 (May–August 2015). http://supercommunity-pdf.e-flux.com/pdf /supercommunity/article_1231.pdf.

Darnton, Robert. *Mesmerism and the End of the Enlightenment in France*. Cambridge, MA: Harvard University Press, 1986.

Haraway, Donna. *Staying with the Trouble: Making Kin in the Chthulucene*. Durham, NC: Duke University Press, 2016.

Katzschner, Tania. "Cape Flats Nature: Rethinking Urban Ecologies." In *Contested Ecologies: Dialogues in the South on Nature and Knowledge*, edited by Lesley Green, 202–26. Cape Town: HSRC Press, 2013.

Latour, Bruno. "An Attempt at a 'Compositionist Manifesto.'" *New Literary History* 41, no. 3 (2010): 471–90.

Latour, Bruno. *Facing Gaia: Eight Lectures on the New Climatic Regime*. Translated by Catherine Porter. Cambridge, MA: Polity, 2017.

Latour, Bruno. *An Inquiry into Modes of Existence: An Anthropology of the Moderns*. Translated by Catherine Porter. Cambridge, MA: Harvard University Press, 2013.

Latour, Bruno. *Pandora's Hope: Essays on the Reality of Science Studies*. Cambridge, MA: Harvard University Press, 1999.

Latour, Bruno. *War of the Worlds: What about Peace?* Translated by Charlotte Bigg. Chicago: Prickly Paradigm, 2002.

Luhrmann, Tanya. *When God Talks Back: Understanding the American Evangelical Relationship with God*. New York: Vintage, 2012.

Souriau, Étienne. *The Different Modes of Existence*. Translated by Erik Beranek and Tim Howles. Minneapolis: Univocal, 2015.

Starhawk. *Dreaming the Dark: Magic, Sex and Politics*. Boston: Beacon, 1982.

Stengers, Isabelle. *Cosmopolitics II*. Translated by Robert Bononno. Minneapolis: University of Minnesota Press, 2011.

Stengers, Isabelle. *In Catastrophic Times: Resisting the Coming Barbarism*. Translated by Andrew Goffey. London: Open Humanities, 2015.

Stengers, Isabelle. *The Invention of Modern Science*. Translated by Daniel W. Smith. Minneapolis: University of Minnesota Press, 2000.

Toulmin, Stephen. *Cosmopolis: The Hidden Agenda of Modernity*. Chicago: University of Chicago Press, 1990.

Whitehead, Alfred N. *Adventures of Ideas*. New York: Free Press, 1967.

FOUR

THE POLITICS OF WORKING COSMOLOGIES TOGETHER
WHILE KEEPING THEM SEPARATE

Helen Verran

Indigenous cosmopolitics? In a rather straightforward way, in this chapter the phrase refers to the politics of working indigenous and other cosmologies together and separately in a particular time and place. Cosmology as I use it here is the anthropologists' cosmology, effected as relativizing. It is not the philosophers' nor the theoretical physicists' cosmology, which, as I tell things, are accomplished as absolutes. Here I am concerned with the working together/keeping distinct of a Yolngu Aboriginal Australian cosmology and the Western cosmology that is expressed in a modern mathematics curriculum. Cosmologies know partially, and they know parts of the multiverse. Note that I am using "multiverse" differently than James, who invented the term (as a synonym for pluriverse). James was pointing to the many moral worlds that could be constructed by humans necessarily living in nature—nature is a multiverse for James.[1] In contrast, the multiverse, whose variable boundaries I negotiate, refers to multiple possible forms of human and nonhuman collective being: multiple forms of life. My multiverse renders James's as parochial. For me, concepts (and I have already introduced quite a few in my first paragraph) are the achieved working units of cosmologies, clotted as routine sets of practices, necessarily in the workings of a particular cosmology. Concepts can be made to cohere well enough in such working and, importantly, they can also be made to cohere well enough between cosmologies. Concepts are a means to negotiate the flimsy boundaries of the multiverse.

In 2006, the famous anthropologist Mary Douglas suggested that it was now too late for anthropologists to study cosmologies. Modernity had become too pervasive. She felt that other cosmologies no longer wait out there for anthropologists to happen upon.[2] The several claims implicit in her assessment would have been vehemently opposed by the Yolngu elders and teachers I worked with in the 1980s and 1990s, and they would still be disputed today. First, the idea that cosmologies have ever been somehow hermetically sealed from each other and so could be something anthropologists found as whole and pure worlds would have been hotly disputed. And second, the idea that an indigenous cosmology is somehow inevitably weakened by a modern Western cosmology would likely have been met by invitation to participate in a ceremony—a funeral, or a boys' initiation, or even a workshop held as part of mathematics education. Yolngu cosmology is alive and well and actively inventing new forms of cosmopolitics as it does the multiverse through its concepts.[3]

This chapter is about mathematics education in a small group of Yolngu schools in Australia's Northern Territory. Across the period 1987–96, a curriculum came to life that, as a cosmopolitics, strategically worked cosmologies together while simultaneously assiduously keeping them separate. As I experienced and puzzled about the working together and separately of these two cosmologies, a third minimalist translating cosmology began to emerge, and this chapter tells of an episode in that process of emergence.

Ethical and Political Practices Entailed
in Indigenous Cosmopolitics

The translating cosmology I have begun to outline here is better named as a methodology. Here I mobilize and to some extent develop this as an analytic in telling of the working together/keeping distinct of a Yolngu Aboriginal Australian cosmology and the cosmology embedded in a modern mathematics curriculum. As a cosmology, my translating framing is minimalist, concerned solely with epistemic practices and epistemology; what it values is limited to knowledge making. While I recognize that I do need to fully specify what it offers in this regard, that must wait for a different occasion. Since I write here under the topic of indigenous cosmopolitics, what I specify prior to telling my stories is the ethos that is entailed for a collective that mobilizes such a methodology (cosmology) in doing cosmopolitics as analysis, that is, in explicitly negotiating the boundaries of the multiverse. I offer consideration of this ethos as a means to partially specify ethical and political practices entailed when analysts participate in indigenous cosmopolitics.

Cosmopolitics is necessarily a collective matter and requires nurturing a collective ethos committed to respectfully enacting dissensus that goes along with active accord making. In rhetorics, ethos defines a relation between a giver and a receiver of news, of information, of knowledge, of advice, of exhortation, and the rest. This relation is necessarily nurtured in a working cosmology through situated, cultural, and epistemic encounters and engagements. The forms of such relations are often implicit in shared histories, but, albeit less comfortably, they can and must be explicitly articulated when contesting histories encounter and engage. In cosmopolitics, all participants are both givers and receivers.

Ethos concerns the credibility, in a particular situation, of givers' characteristic modes of giving information or knowledge, which includes explanations given, for example, by teachers. Ethical practice, expression of the ethos in cosmopolitics, requires good faith and bad will of givers when it comes to epistemics. Dissensus arising in expressions of epistemic bad will and good faith is the ethical order of the day. Epistemic bad will is required since participants must refuse to go along with the various common senses that are, inevitably, at play; refusing to go along with what everyone knows is mandatory, since in cosmopolitics there are no everyones who know, and there is nothing given to be known. Yet at the same time, epistemic good faith is required. Principled refusal to go along with what everyone knows requires givers to know what they know (as knowers of a parochial cosmology), to know how they know it, and to have a developed capacity to articulate it. Knowing what I know and how, and trusting others to know what they know and how, leads to possibilities of active accord making while respecting dissensus. It makes it possible to go along doing our differences together in the light of freely given assent to particular agreed matters in the here and now.

Dissensus and active accord making and keeping (or not keeping—withdrawing assent) is the default ethos of a collective engaging in cosmopolitics. Enacting this default ethics explicitly is one element of political practice in working cosmologies together while keeping them separate—of cosmopolitics. Let us imagine political practices as managing the going on together along three axes, three power-laced continua of collective

action. One axis stretches between persuasion and coercion, another between cooperation and competition, and a third between dissensus and consensus. An ethos that cultivates dissensus—imposed in the epistemics of
the methodology (my minimalist translating cosmology)—necessarily also
cultivates persuasion and cooperation. Political practices of cosmopolitics
are by derivation, those which cultivate dissensus and yet require continuous active assent to particulars. This in turn requires cooperation and persuasion. Cosmopolitics is a particular enactment of political possibilities.

Mutual Encounter and Engagement in Developing
a Novel Mathematics Curriculum

Here I re-present an account of mutual encounter and engagement between
members of the Yolngu Aboriginal Australian community at Yirrkala, and
the Northern Territory state Department of Education. I use both "encounter" and "engagement" here, for I want both the "contra" (against) that lurks
within "encounter," and also the links back to "gage"—pledging oneself, of
engaging. Both are required in order to go on together doing difference. I
write as a partial participant in the action, one who was a member on the
modern education side—a teacher and researcher of mathematics education.

First, I relate the encounter and engagement of the curriculum in a general way, attending in particular to the concepts that the curriculum entailed. Then I tell of an episode where I became aware in a new way of the
cosmopolitical significance of some epistemic aspects of an ethos committed to dissensus and active assent to particular epistemic accords. The story
tells of my coming to recognize that as a teacher educator of the emerging
curriculum, I was (mis)using my authority as a mathematics educator in
proposing something that was not assented to. In performing myself as a
giver of knowledge in the collective, my practice of the required ethos was
wanting. My practice was both ethically wrong and bad cosmopolitics. As
a knower of the cosmology embedded in the modern mathematics curriculum, at the time I experienced this episode as the falling to bits of the ontic
and epistemic commitments that had enabled me as a teacher of science and
mathematics for many years. This experience precipitated the puzzling that
would eventually enable me to articulate what here I name as a minimalist
translating cosmology—a methodology for indigenous cosmopolitics.

In the late 1980s, the Australian polity quite uncharacteristically engaged explicitly with political change. Environmental policy, workplace

relations, political rights of Australia's indigenous peoples, gender equality, and multiculturalism—all became important political issues, and administrative change followed. Difference was not only recognized, but policies were formulated to support and even foster different development trajectories for indigenous institutions, among others.

For nearly a decade, indigenous educational institutions expanded, and innovation thrived. Bilingual education had been growing in Northern Territory schools since the 1970s and by the mid-1980s was well funded and confidently extending to more and more schools. The particular project I describe here grew out of this bilingual curriculum and pedagogy and culminated in what became known as the Garma Maths Curriculum. This curriculum, with its associated syllabi, was officially recognized as a state-endorsed curriculum by the Northern Territory Department of Education Board of Studies in 1992. The children learning through this curriculum showed improved achievement in standard mathematics tests. But by 1996, almost all trace of this curriculum had vanished from the small group of schools in which it had been established, along with the bilingual program, which was abolished. New public management policies struck, and radical cost cutting became the order of the day. Indigenous languages and bilingual education are still largely absent from Northern Territory state schools.

In the particular group of schools where I found myself working in the late 1980s and early 1990s, an Action Group of Aboriginal teachers was formed to administer the school on a week-to-week basis, working in close collaboration with a school principal appointed by the Department of Education. Both of these administrative arms were subject to governance by a devolved school council of elders, a group whose work was funded by the state and supported by government officers under a policy of local control of schools. The project to develop a radically new mathematics curriculum and pedagogy was initiated in recognition of the failure of conventional mathematics education to promote effective learning in the school. So inadequate and indeed counterproductive was conventional mathematics education judged to be that in beginning the work of imagining a new mathematics curriculum the School Council banned mathematics teaching for a year.

In 1992 our curriculum was described this way:

In the 1980s, after Yirrkala school introduced a program of Aborigi-
nalization, Yolngu community elders were asked to come to the
school to help develop a "both-ways" curriculum for the schools at
Yirrkala and the Laynha Homelands.

The community elders came to meetings at the school to tell the
Yolngu teachers in the Action Group what their school curriculum
should be like.

The first thing these elders did was to give us several Yolngu words
to guide the development of the maths curriculum. These words, or
metaphors, reflect the knowledge of the Yolngu elders, about how
maths in the Yolngu world and maths in the Balanda world can be
taught side by side, so that one does not crowd out the other. Three
of the metaphors through which curriculum planners have learnt
to understand "both ways" mathematics are Garma, Ganma, and
Galtha. . . .[4]

Garma is a place, a ceremonial area, but not for secret ceremonies.
It is for open ceremonies that everyone can participate in. . . . If a
ceremony has been properly negotiated and produced in full view of
everyone, it will be performed in the Garma ceremonial area. Yolngu
can sit and watch a Garma ceremony and read from it the network
of connections between people, places, songs and totems that make
up this particular ceremony. Garma is an open forum where people
can talk . . . ideas, differences, agreement. The old people who su-
pervised the making of the curriculum told the Action Group that the
School should be like this Garma area.

. . . Where might a Garma Maths curriculum start? . . . The recursive systematic kinship system [which all Yolngu children know
and use before they come to school] by which the Yolngu world is
routinely given order and value can be placed alongside the recursive
system of English numbers [which equally Yolngu children can recite
and sometimes use before they come to school]. In Garma Maths
students spend as much time extending their knowledge in exploring
ways of representing and interpreting their own Yolngu systems on
paper, as they do exploring the ways in which Western maths is used
to give order and value in white Australian life.[5]

The new curriculum had four elements, and over the years a full syllabus for all the school years of the primary school and the lower years of secondary schooling were laid out. In articulating the theory of the curriculum, we used the term "mathetics" (rather than mathematics).[6] Using the everyday term "maths" in the curriculum title might look like a colloquialism, but for us it expressed a serious challenge to the epistemic hegemony of mathematics. The four areas of the curriculum were named Djalkiri, the footsteps of the ancestors; Gurrutu, the Yolngu kinship system; Space Grid, Cartesian grid and navigation; and Tallying Number, arithmetic, measurement, and calculus. Mathetically, Gurrutu and Tallying Number were understood as analogous, as were Djalkiri and Space Grid; culturally, Gurrutu and Djalkiri belonged together on the Yolngu side and Tallying Number and Space Grid worked together on the modern mathematics side.

It is self-evident that, experientially, Gurrutu and its practices are profoundly different from Tallying Number and its practices: the worlds they order as routine sets of practices feel incommensurable. As elements of disparate cosmologies in commonsense terms, it is not obvious how they might be connected. Similarly, Djalkiri, committed as it is to physical orientation of embodied (and other) humans (and nonhumans) and places through stories of spirit ancestors, differs from physical orientation achieved through the technologies of Cartesian coordinates as theorized and practiced in Space Grid. The differences were and are so obvious that in the emerging Garma Maths Curriculum difference looked after itself. The mathetic concepts we devised as connections in the curriculum—recursion and positionality—name a family likeness respectively between the kin relations of Gurrutu and the numbers of arithmetic, and positional relations systematically coded in Djalkiri on the one hand and modern navigation on the other.

The core concepts in each of these curriculum areas are best understood as relations. In one mathetical domain of the curriculum, relational concepts are effected in practices of doing recursive series of names, as numbers, and on the one side as reciprocal kin names. In the other mathetical domain, practices of positioning as conceptual point-field relations are enacted in the grid-tracking technologies of modernity and in the doings of people-places as routinely enacted in Yolngu life. Mathetically, the curriculum as a whole effects a variable set of relations of relations. The core logic of the curriculum mobilizes a Wittgensteinian relational logic of family likenesses.[7]

The Garma Maths Curriculum inducted children into mathetical think-ing, without always obliging them to think modern, which is not to say that modern thinking was not being taught in Garma Maths. In thinking modern, we are working with a set of figurations that are usually invisibly imposed on modern thinkers. In this the modern order of things system-atically and invisibly enacts our obligations to a particular past then-there. This is actually a then-there quite far away from the here-now of 1980s Yolngu Aboriginal Australia. The conceptual figurations of modern think-ing clotted in the fury of the competing knowledge authorities of Europe's seventeenth century, as feudalism faded as a form of governance and Chris-tendom tore itself apart. Not surprisingly, the cosmology of modern-era institutions—which the mathematics curricula of modern primary schools faithfully express—was instituted through achieved formulations that, among other things, separated off knowledge and politics, and knowledge and gods. Neither of these separations feature in Yolngu cosmology.

I have given a brief account of the working imaginary of our Garma curriculum and in concluding, as an aside, I alert readers to an element in the historical situation of the curriculum that I have missed in my tell-ing so far. Unlikely though it seems, this curriculum initiative in northern Australia had one of its beginnings in some primary school classrooms of Yoruba land in southwestern Nigeria, where I had worked earlier in the 1980s. Yoruba teachers had demonstrated that there is a difference between Yoruba numbers and the numbers of the primary school curriculum and si-multaneously shown that these disparate numbers could be connected.[8] In articulating what I had been shown, it took me some time to recognize that I did not know how to articulate that difference-sameness as generative. As I am about to reveal, I experienced a similar blindness when I began working with Yolngu teachers and their advisors. It was not until I was stopped in my tracks by the dead of a colonial massacre that I saw that cosmopolitics requires a more sophisticated doing of difference-sameness than what I have just proposed in describing the curriculum. What I have just offered is a particular description of what was known in the epistemic practices of the Garma Maths Curriculum—a relatively uncontroversial ac-count of the curriculum's working ontology. As you are about to see, while that might have been adequate for the mathematics curriculum authorities who viewed the curriculum as cross-cultural mathematics education, it is not sufficient when the curriculum is more properly understood as cosmo-politics. To get at the epistemic requirements that recognizing the curriculum as cosmopolitics entails, we need to go further and problematize both the configurations of the entities known in the curriculum and the figure of the knower.

Learning from Disconcertment

I am taking cosmopolitics as the politics of collectively doing cosmologies together and separately. In working my way toward articulating some practices entailed in partially participating in cosmopolitics as an analyst, I began by considering the ethos of such a collective. I proposed that what is required is the nurturing of a collective ethos committed to respectfully enacting dissensus that goes along with active accord making. Ethos is tied up with the epistemic demeanor of participants as knowers, especially those who participate as analysts, and by extension also what they know, and how, and how they know they know, and why they value that particular knowing.

In this section, I turn my attention to beginning consideration of the epistemic demeanor that goes along with engagement in a cosmopolitics. I propose that epistemic demeanor is something that can be cultivated, although it usually is not. In describing the Garma Maths Curriculum in the previous section, I adopted an epistemic demeanor appropriate for conducting an argument in mathematics education. In concluding that section I proposed that, as such, it was inadequate for participating in Garma Maths when more properly understood as cosmopolitics. Here, in working toward articulating what is an appropriate epistemic demeanor in participating in cosmopolitics as an analyst, I tell of meeting the dead of Gängan, a small Yolngu homeland settlement. Meeting these dead came to pose the problem of how these dead, as expressions of Gurruṯu, were to participate in our maths teaching and learning. How to carry the dead of Gängan along in the Garma Maths Curriculum? My story centers on the configuration of what is known and on the figure of the knower in the curriculum. It punctures the comfortable epistemic assumptions of the mathematics teacher-educator working as a curriculum development advisor—the author-in-the-text of the previous section. My story tells of what for me became a continuing, profoundly uncomfortable moment of the curriculum work.

A Story

Southwest from Yirrkala, a small town in Australia's northeastern Arnhem Land, it takes about half an hour in a light plane to get to the Yolngu homeland settlement of Gängan. For me, adopted into the Marika clan, Gängan is in the homeland of my mother's clan. On this visit I was to feel shame that in the past my lot, Australians of Anglo descent, had taken a fatal interest in this adoptive family of mine. Somewhat at odds with this shame, simultaneously I felt a strong professional concern over what Yolngu adults consider proper as the content of a junior primary school reading primer. The disconcerting mutual interruption of those two judging figures, plural versions of the modern knower as removed, judging observer, is my main focus in this telling. My story of learning to work a disconcertment elicited by a story of the dead of Gängan led me to recognize the inadequacy of some ontological assumptions I had not previously concerned myself with. I recognized that my epistemic practice as a participant in the Garma Maths Curriculum cosmopolitical collective was flawed.

I arrived in Gängan along with Yolngu *yapa*, teachers who are sisters for me. We had come, together with other teachers, both Balanda and Yolngu, for a workshop in the recursion strand of the curriculum. The curriculum was developing well. In the recently established statewide tests, the students of this region had performed better than expected; the children were learning. This is not to say the curriculum was uncontroversial—it remained contested by members of the wider Yolngu world, in particular senior clan members there at Gängan, who justifiably feared the betrayal of the sacred meanings of Gurruṯu and Djalkiri by the explicit analogizing with tally number and the cartographic grid. In this workshop, we were to consider the syllabus for the older children, and explicitly how to develop ideas of quantifying valuation in the tallying number strand of the curriculum. Working with the children and teachers of this very small outstation school, we rehearsed the teaching of the practices of the base ten pattern using boxfuls of straws. But the main focus was linguistic. What are the English and Yolngu terms that should be engaged to teach quantifying valuation, and how can we specify with enough precision how these terms should be introduced and expressed in pedagogical practices?

Buildings of corrugated iron sheets held up with bush timber flank the airstrip. A teacher from the school meets the plane, and, accompanying us on the walk to the school, he tells us that these old buildings were retrieved from the first Gängan settlement established in 1970, over there to the west, closer to the river. They were moved when the airstrip was built, east-west across a small rise. Houses with sand verandas face outward from the communal shower and telephone box. The Telecom logo seems oddly out of place—so orange. Set on a small hummock over to our right and behind us as we walk, screened by bushes, are a steel tower with its dish and an array of solar panels. The light green Colorbond school buildings face each other across a wide connecting veranda where we'll sleep. It funnels the breeze into the classrooms through open louvers. Wurran, the black-legged crane, is painted on the outer east-facing wall of the school building here at Gängan. Its wings are outspread, its head atop the long neck turned to one side, dancing. Many of the children who learn in this building are Wurran, or maybe their mother identifies as Wurran. As we muddle about selecting our sleeping positions, in openly acknowledging my adoptive position, a young woman, mother for me, promises that tomorrow she will show me the country.

The next day, our morning work goes smoothly, and after lunch as a group we visit the lagoon, seemingly the center of life in Gängan, a wide deep waterhole where the sweet-fleshed baypinnga, lungfish, and large barramundi live. We strangers all wade in along with the children. Our hosts do not, and we are teased. When our sweat, the sweat of strangers, is carried downstream, a tremendous storm will blow in, we are told—this place is cared for in that way. We impetuous visitors retreat back to the edge, and to no one's surprise a storm does blow in later in the afternoon, whipping the sheets of butcher paper on and through which our negotiations are being conducted off the wall where they've been secured with masking tape.

Later in the afternoon, as she promised, my young plump mother shows me the country. The *yati* (ritual ground) with its huge tree, the river that feeds the lagoon. About halfway along the lagoon we visited at lunchtime, we stop at a sandy spot, naturally clear of bush, dominated by a large, shady fruiting tree. "It was through there," my mother indicates, "along that rise you see there across on the other side of the lagoon, that Bilarni [Bill Harney] and his men rode." She points back toward the yati. "All the men were doing men's [sacred] business, way back there."

This is the story of a 1920s massacre in which the Dhalwangu clan was very nearly wiped out, from which today it still struggles to recover. As she goes on, tears begin to stream down my cheeks, quite unbidden. The place becomes its history. My young mother gestures, making a map of the horror, pointing out the landscape features that had their place in the killing, the dying, the surviving. The hollow water lily stems through which some of those who take to the water breathe; the huge rotting log behind which the rifle shooters kneel; the trees behind which the Dhalwangu men stand as they prepare to throw their spears. The shots crack noiselessly around me. Invisible children fling themselves into the water as it remains undisturbed. The young woman, member of my adoptive mother clan, becomes a distressed crane, dragging her broken legs, furrowing the sand we stand on.

Later, back at the schoolrooms, my guide goes into the teachers' storeroom and brings me a small green booklet. The story she has told me has been written down in both Gumatj and English. Gruesome amateurish line drawings illustrate it.[9]

> All the men were at a private ceremony site in the bush nearly. The children and women were at the camp. The other women and children had gone gathering yams, berries, goannas, and freshwater turtles.
>
> None of them knew that a party of men with guns were riding towards the camp on horses. They were led by Bill Harney, a yellafella from the Roper River area. The armed band of men rode into the camp and shot the older women. The men heard the shot[s] from their gathering spot and ran to see what was happening at the camp. There they saw their wives being shot dead so they attacked the killers with their spears. The rifles were too much for the spears and they were driven back to a large lagoon nearby. Some of the men who went in the water were shot and killed.
>
> Meanwhile other women were shot and killed at the camp. While some escaped with their children, where they were joined by the men who escaped. The other young women, children and men were captured by [the] men. Bodies were lying everywhere. Those in the bushes watched as Bill Harney and his men started their journey back, taking with them the captives, back the way they had come from.
>
> That was not the end of the story though, Bill Harney returned the next year and collected the skulls of the people he had murdered. And later sold them to a museum in southern cities and made a lot of money.

When I finish reading this small book, my young mother, a teacher at Gängan school, comments that even though they, as a homelands school, do not have an official bilingual program, among the children it is one of their most popular reading primers. "They read it again and again," she says proudly. "It's taught so many children to read English!" The odd bodily feeling of profound wrongness which that remark evokes in me is certainly the most vivid memory I retain of that Garma Maths Curriculum workshop.

Making Something of the Story

The story with its dual performances, as narrated enactment in place and as enthused-over reading primer, continued to haunt me. For me it brought to the fore two sets of tensions in the collective epistemic work of the Garma Maths Curriculum. One concerned the entity known and taught in the various elements of the curriculum; the other concerned the figure of the knower. These tensions were embedded in a politics that was the world known in a cosmopolitical Garma Maths Curriculum—its dual cosmologies.

The story of the dead of Gängan doing work in helping their young lively kin to learn to read reminds me that these dead I have just shed tears over are Gurrutu. Every one of the dead is related in a particular nameable way to all those who are embodied as a Gurrutu position, and a learner in the Garma curriculum, even I, partial though my Gurrutu embodiment might be. The dead as a whole are a part of the vague Yolngu whole, one of many such parts, although of manifestly different provenance than most of the Yolngu world's identifiable parts. This is how the logic of Yolngu life works—every individual and every place are uniquely nameable as a Gurrutu position by every Yolngu person and are set in a complex reciprocal relation with every place. (Of course, that semiotic logic also attaches to the much less institutionally formalized working of kin positions in mainstream Australia—I am my mother's daughter, but, in modernity, application of that logic is severely constrained, very patchy and partial in its coverage.)

Garma Maths is a curriculum in which names of reciprocating Gurrutu positions and names of numbers conjure up concepts that are rendered equal through a focus on the material practices of recursion; both numbers and Gurrutu positions become as mathematical objects. In the practical here and now of classroom life, this holds well enough as a connection for the curriculum to work. Yet perhaps we should not be surprised that inevitably, despite attempts to keep things separate, numbers begin to work with the material semiotic logic of Gurruṯu positions, and vice versa. We find that the dead of Gängan can and clearly do become in the present as a number in Yolngu life (albeit never a precise number). The dead of Gängan are present in the curriculum as a number of people; in fact, if the story told in the reading primer is to be believed, as several numbers: shooters, dead, survivors, and money are all numbers that continue to have life in Gängan (albeit rarely named as numerals). In a form of restorative justice in Gängan, the Garma curriculum must recognize number as the dead of Gängan, and their killers, and the supposed rewards they got. Each of these is necessarily a singular number, unlike every other number, but one that, willy-nilly, is always present. The curriculum must carry along these onto-logically singular numbers with it—as numbers. Number as enacted in other aspects of Australian life (including the conventional mathematics curriculum) has enumeration as representing the dead and the shooters, rendering them as safely in the past, and as not inhabiting the present.[10] Yet in our ontologically dangerous curriculum, numbers that are taken for granted as indexes and taught as such must sometimes become something else—icons.

And of course it works in the other direction too. When it comes to the curriculum, what the elders of Gängan worry about is that Gurruṯu positions might be taken to be mere indexes. Gurruṯu position as an entity known in the Garma Maths Curriculum might be taken solely as a sign, leaving bodies, places, and here and nows out of contention. For the elders, what is important about Gurruṯu is that the names are the thing named—Gurruṯu positions are icons. For most of those people who are Gurruṯu as well as numbered (indexed) modern Australian citizens, to render Gurruṯu positions as indexes is profoundly wrong. And I could make analogous arguments for the Djalkiri and Space Grid domains of the curriculum. Carrying along the dead of Gängan in our curriculum is important in all four of its mathetical domains. These ontological challenges around the con-figurations of entities known in the Garma Maths Curriculum are where dangers need to be continually actively managed as a politics between cosmologies in the present.

In continuing to make something of this story, I turn now to an ontolog-ical issue that is prior to the politics over what is known—the topic that has concerned me in the previous paragraphs. Shifting to what many might see as subjective aspects, here I am concerned with questions of how knowers are configured. I begin by noting that, predictably, I had cried when faced with the place of a massacre. I was strongly affected by words uttered and gestures enacted in a place where years ago entire families had been mercilessly slain. It was around the time my mother was born as the very first Australian in my family, setting her apart from her Scottish brother, so clearly my family was not involved. So why should I feel shame? And should one be skeptical about the veracity of reports of skulls being sold to museums after a massacre in the twentieth century? Such questions of individual and institutional responsibility are not what concerns me here.

After the workshop, I would moil around in conflicting emotions for days. The precisely imagined horror of the story set against the idyll of Yolngu family life in a homeland that I had briefly experienced held me in its thrall in one moment, and then suddenly I was plunged into paroxysms of worry about whether children should be exposed to such horror stories as part of the effort of learning to read. I found myself inhabiting simultaneously two intensely felt, but somewhat contradictory, modern knowing figures—an extreme form of disconcertment. I felt judgment was needed in both cases but was unable to formulate such a judgment because I did not know which figure to prioritize or how such a decision could be made. It took some time for me to see that it was the generic figure of the modern knower that was the problem here. In seeing that, I recognized that the form of conceptual knowing required in the Garma Maths Curriculum requires that the figure of the knower be dissolved into practices in the here and now, no less than the entity known.

The story of the dead of Gängan, in both its enacted form by the lagoon and its enthused-over reading primer, was not presented in the time and place of the Gängan workshop all those years ago with the intention of producing disconcertment. It was not that the young narrator felt I needed reminding of the horrors perpetrated by my mob who had arrived unbidden and taken over as the colonizing frontier progressed with considerable violence and bloodshed across lands known and owned by others. The story of Gängan's dead is a story of that place, one of many, and the story can be told in infinitely many ways, with many morals, we might say. The moral I foreground is not the usual demand for restorative justice; rather, it is tensions associated with epistemic assumptions. A set of easy assumptions about universally configured knowers and what they know began to dissolve, to fall into their constituent bits, as I stood there on the veranda of a school building, transfixed by a small reading primer whose lime-green cover featured an amateurish drawing of crossed spear and rifle. The story as I tell it here, as packing a double punch, took some time and much puzzling over before its lines became clear. While it had been clear to me for some time that in the Garma Maths Curriculum we were working prior to the tense mathematical objects of the curriculum clotting as concepts, as tense mathetical relational entities, I had up to that point failed to see that knowing subjects were likewise dissolved in the curriculum to become as bundles of practices and ephemerally clotted as cosmopolitical knowers in particular moments of learning and teaching. The form of disconcertment I experienced in Gängan, a discomfort born as a knower configured as a modern removed judging observer was forced to simultaneously inhabit an interrupting personae, was revelatory.

Conclusion: Cosmopolitical Epistemic Practices

Engaging in cosmopolitics entails cultivating an ethos that in turn is expressed in the epistemic demeanor of participants as knowers. Recognizing this is especially important for those who participate in cosmopolitics as analysts. What is epistemic demeanor, and what is an appropriate demeanor for engaging in cosmopolitics as an analyst? An epistemic demeanor may be assertive, dogmatic, or tentative. It might be confidently tentative or timidly tentative. It can be cultivated, as it sometimes is when someone giving or receiving in communicative interaction aims to misinform or prevaricate. Much of the time, however, epistemic demeanor is not knowingly cultivated. Demeanor arises in the word "mien"—the form in which something is expressed. In writing of epistemic demeanor, I propose that form of expression and epistemic practice are intimately connected. If we wish to ask about collective epistemic practices, we must ask about the figure of the knower, about what they know and how, and how they know they know, and why they value that particular knowing.

If we could imagine the unlikely event that the questions articulated in such a typology were to be answerable in empirical description, we would have met an empirical account of a cosmology.[11] But the actuality is that such empirical questions one might ask of a working cosmology—"What is known?" (ontology); "How is it known?" (methodology); "Who knows?" (how the knower is configured); "How is it known to be known?" (epistemology); "Why is this knowing valued?" (axiology)—are only ever answered partially in collective enactment. Cosmopolitics is no different: there as everywhere enacted answers are the collective, partial emergent and contingent epistemic practices that eventuate.

Nevertheless, claiming the modest privilege that arises in her skills as analyst, which carry with them special response-abilities and responsibilities, a participant analyst in cosmopolitics, in wearing her minimalist translating cosmology on her sleeve, might, in assuming a confidently tentative epistemic demeanor, propose an answer to the final question: Why, in cosmopolitics, is it appropriate to adopt the demeanor that goes along with claiming that the epistemic practices appropriate in cosmopolitics are collective, partial, emergent, and contingent? Why is that knowing valued in cosmopolitics? The answer is circular and takes you back to the beginning of my chapter. Yet in that claim lies hope, hope that an ethos that is generative of dissensus might be nurtured again, and again.

NOTES

1. "Visible nature is all plasticity and indifference, a multiverse as one might call it, not a universe." William James, "Is Life Worth Living?," *International Journal of Ethics* 6, no. 1 (1895): 10.

2. See Allen Abramson and Martin Holbraad, "Introduction: The Cosmological Frame in Anthropology," in *Framing Cosmologies: The Anthropology of Worlds*, ed. Allen Abramson and Martin Holbraad, 1–28 (Manchester: Manchester University Press, 2014), 5.

3. Endre Dányi and Michaela Spencer, "Common Ground: Centres, Scales and the Politics of Difference," paper presented at the 4S/EASST Conference BCN-16: Science + Technology by Other Means, Barcelona, August 31–September 3, 2016.

4. See Michael Christie and Helen Verran, "Digital Lives in Postcolonial Aboriginal Australia," *Journal of Material Culture* 18, no. 3 (2013): 299–317, for a treatment of all three metaphors.

5. Michael Christie and Yirrkala School Action Group, *Garma Maths* (Yirrkala, Australia: Yirrkala Literature Production Centre, 1992). In addition to a series of curriculum documents and explanatory pamphlets published by the Yirrkala Literature Production Centre, a set of videos edited from the amateur video footage generated by Yolngu teachers recording various workshops and events was produced by feminist documentary film maker Merle Thornton in the 1990s. Papers on this curriculum include Helen Watson (Verran), "The Politics of Knowing and Being Known," *Arena: A Marxist Journal of Criticism and Discussion*, no. 92 (1990): 125–38; Helen Verran-Watson, "We've Heard You Teach Mathematics through Kinship? Mathematics Curriculum Development in the Laynhapuy Schools," in *Kauna Public Lecture Series 1991*, 53–76 (Adelaide: Aboriginal Research Institute, 1991); Helen Verran, "Logics and Mathematics: Challenges Arising in Working across Cultures," in *Mathematics across Cultures: The History of Non-Western Mathematics*, ed. Helaine Selin and

Ubiritan D'Ambrosio, 55–78 (Dordrecht: Kluwer Academic, 2000). The work was funded by research grants from the Australian Institute of Aboriginal and Torres Strait Islands Studies, University of Melbourne Research Office, and the Australian Research Council, with ongoing funding from the Northern Territory Department of Education

6. The term "mathesis" currently features in theorizing of mathematics education that draws on Deleuze for inspiration. For example, Holdsworth offers an account of mathematics education informed by "Deleuze's general views about . . . the *mathesis universalis.*" He proposes that the experience of mathematics education can be "an encounter with complexity that takes us . . . to a political space in which we encounter the forces of creative intensity." He sees Deleuze as "reinforcing the view that despite the *univocity of being,* mathematical and scientific practices are actualised *plurivocally.*" David Holdsworth, "Philosophical Problematisation and Mathematical Solution," in *Deleuze and Education,* ed. Ina Semetsky and Diana Masny, 137–54 (Edinburgh: Edinburgh University Press, 2013), 138.

7. This logic is argued in Helen Watson (Verran), "A Wittgensteinian View of Mathematics: Implications for Teachers of Mathematics," in *School Mathematics: The Challenge to Change,* ed. Nerida Ellerton and Ken Clements, 17–30 (Geelong, Australia: Deakin University Press, 1989).

8. As I was beginning the work with Yolngu teachers, their elders, and Department of Education advisors in the late 1980s, the book I had been assembling for some time about my experience with different numbers in Yoruba classrooms, provisionally titled *Numbers and Things,* was disintegrating. See Helen Verran, *Science and an African Logic* (Chicago: University of Chicago Press, 2001); Helen Verran, "Comparative Philosophy and 'I,'" *Confluence: Online Journal of World Philosophies* 3 (2015): 171–88.

9. Bronwyn Wuyuwa Yunupingu, *A True, Bad Story,* ed. Brian Devlin (Yirrkala: Yirrkala Literature Production Center, 1981). See the *Living Archive of Aboriginal Languages,* http://laal.cdu.edu.au/record/cdu:34418/info/.

10. Numbers constituted in such a semiotic logic are of course quite common in mainstream Australian life—they constitute the life of the Australian Stock Exchange, for example.

11. This is a teaching typology. I developed it as a pedagogical trick to alert listeners to the actuality that although rarely articulated as questions, these questions are answered all the time in our collective going on. Note the author in the text of Latour's *An Inquiry into Modes of Existence* sets off on a quest to do just this for the cosmology collectively enacted by the moderns. Bruno Latour, *An Inquiry into Modes of Existence* (Cambridge, MA: Harvard University Press, 2013).

BIBLIOGRAPHY

Abramson, Allen, and Martin Holbraad. "Introduction: The Cosmological Frame in Anthropology." In *Framing Cosmologies: The Anthropology of Worlds,* edited by Allen Abramson and Martin Holbraad, 1–28. Manchester: Manchester University Press, 2014.

Christie, Michael, and Helen Verran. "Digital Lives in Postcolonial Aboriginal Australia." *Journal of Material Culture* 18, no. 3 (2013): 299–317.

Christie, Michael, and Yirrkala School Action Group. *Garma Maths*. Yirrkala, Australia: Yirrkala Literature Production Centre, 1992.

Dányi, Endre, and Michaela Spencer. "Common Ground: Centres, Scales and the Politics of Difference." Paper presented at the 4S/EASST Conference BCN-16: Science + Technology by Other Means, Barcelona, August 31–September 3, 2016.

Holdsworth, David. "Philosophical Problematisation and Mathematical Solution." In *Deleuze and Education*, edited by Ina Semetsky and Diana Masny, 137–54. Edinburgh: Edinburgh University Press, 2013.

James, William. "Is Life Worth Living?" *International Journal of Ethics* 6, no. 1 (1895): 1–24.

Latour, Bruno. *An Inquiry into Modes of Existence*. Cambridge, MA: Harvard University Press, 2013.

Verran, Helen. "Comparative Philosophy and 'I.'" *Confluence: Online Journal of World Philosophies* 3 (2015): 171–88.

Verran, Helen. "Logics and Mathematics: Challenges Arising in Working across Cultures." In *Mathematics across Cultures: The History of Non-Western Mathematics*, edited by Helaine Selin and Ubiritan D'Ambrosio, 55–78. Dordrecht: Kluwer Academic, 2000.

Verran, Helen. *Science and an African Logic*. Chicago: University of Chicago Press, 2001.

Verran-Watson, Helen. "We've Heard You Teach Mathematics through Kinship? Mathematics Curriculum Development in the Laynhapuy Schools." In *Kauna Public Lecture Series 1991*, 53–76. Adelaide: Aboriginal Research Institute, 1991.

Watson (Verran), Helen. "The Politics of Knowing and Being Known." *Arena: A Marxist Journal of Criticism and Discussion*, no. 92 (1990): 125–38.

Watson (Verran), Helen. "A Wittgensteinian View of Mathematics: Implications for Teachers of Mathematics." In *School Mathematics: The Challenge to Change*, edited by Nerida Ellerton and Ken Clements, 17–30. Geelong, Australia: Deakin University Press, 1989.

Yunupingu, Bronwyn Wuyuwa. *A True, Bad Story*. Edited by Brian Devlin. Yirrkala: Yirrkala Literature Production Center, 1981.

FIVE

DENATURALIZING NATURE

John Law and Marianne Lien

If we talk only of singular Man and singular Nature we can compose a general history, but at the cost of concealing the real and altering social relations.
—RAYMOND WILLIAMS, *Problems in Materialism and Culture*

What if there are Nature-wholes made real, and what if these "Natures-made-real-as wholes" matter? What if there are Nature-wholes made real in relation to, as well as a consequence of, other practices, wholes and entities?
—KRISTIN ASDAL, "Enacting Things through Numbers:
Taking Nature into Account/ing"

It is important to understand how what we sometimes call the modern makes itself smooth, singular, and overwhelming, but it is also a mistake to take this at face value. Instead, its crevices and cracks deserve exploration, both because they are crucial to its techniques of power and because they suggest strategies of resistance.[1] In short, so-called modernity is both coherent and not coherent at all.[2]

In this chapter, we develop this argument in one particular context by exploring how a set of contemporary northern practices naturalize nature. Our answer, inflected by science and technology studies (STS), is that this happens in an intricate play within and between practices. On the one hand, these work on the assumption that nature is a single reality separate from culture and that nature is given. On the other hand, they simultaneously operate to generate natures in multiple and divergent forms. In this chapter, we trace some of these practices as they unfold in relation to salmon aquaculture in west Norway. The argument is that these both/and practices naturalize nature. Nature, in other words, is neither given nor made, but rather the stubborn outcome of myriad practices that together conjure and confirm its existence. In the closing part of the chapter, we extend the argument to suggest that these practices also naturalize reality, enacting this as both multiple and singular. Feminists taught decades ago that biology is not destiny, and our argument is similar in form. Naturalization works to reaffirm political limits: if the world is a certain way, then this means that it cannot be otherwise. There is no point in trying to change it. But what follows if this is not the case? Any response will be contingent, but it is likely that instead of reenacting nature or reality as single and coherent, it would sometimes be better to press on modernity's noncoherences, to denaturalize its single and multiple realities and consider how those might be rendered less repressive.[3]

In part because it teaches that a complex world is best understood as sets of specificities, sts works with particular events, materials, and processes. Anthropology similarly insists on paying attention to the particular. We follow these traditions by working ethnographically with a specific case.[4] But unlike many committed to postcolonial concerns, we work at a site strongly associated with the industrial or the modern or the North. Even more, we work with salmon aquaculture, the belly of the beast in relation to global capitalist food production.

Ontological interventions in relation to nature have drawn heavily on Amerindian perspectivism but sometimes leave the so-called modern unexplored, because they apply a kind of strategic essentialism to underscore ontological difference (in relation to the nonmodern).[5] This essay is an attempt to trace the making of nature in the so-called modern. Our object is to apply the same open-ended curiosity in relation to the "tribe of 'the Moderns'" as proponents of the postcolonial apply elsewhere.[6] Our journey through the ethnography and history of salmon farming in Norway could be mobilized to demonstrate that, just as there is no singular universe, there is no universal modern. The most common anthropological intervention would be to say that modernity is multicultural too. While this is not entirely wrong, it is also too simple, because it brackets the ways in which, despite their particularities, a broad range of heterogeneous practices work together to conjure up this stubborn (modern) singularized beast often referred to as nature. Let us open our argument by briefly considering how Norwegian nature appears in tourist literatures.

Nature Untouched

Between 2011 and 2013, Norway's official tourist travel guide told the world that Norway is "powered by nature."[7] As we write, this slogan is still an important part of its campaign. Indeed, wherever Norway is sold to tourists, this is the message. In practice, however, the story is a little more complex. So the campaign showed stunning photographs and movie shots of mountains, clouds, fjords, lakes, snow, rain storms, forests, and waterfalls, together with pictures of wildlife, including whales, ospreys, polar bears, and moose, as well as the midnight sun and the aurora borealis. But it showed human activities too, including rafting, canoeing, fishing, skiing, walking, and skating. Perhaps potential visitors were meant to understand that these are ways of bringing people into contact with nature. This would explain why the ships, trains, ski lifts, and motorbikes came with scenic backdrops. Then there were photos of art galleries, theater performances, people in national costume, and pictures of chef-prepared dishes. Obviously these were pointing in the direction of culture.

We will return to the question of culture briefly at the end of this piece, but for the moment we want to attend to Norwegian nature. So, for instance, next to a photo of Nærøyfjord the website says, "There are mountains plunging into the sea from hundreds of meters, fjords, tall mountain peaks, northern lights and midnight sun."[8] It also describes the "magic" northern lights as a "mystical experience" and tells us, "Nearly 85 per cent of Norway's national parks are mountains. The mountain landscape varies from endless gently rolling high plateaus to sharp peaks, ravines and glaciers."[9] The story is that if we want to see nature, we should visit Norway. Nature may be silent, untouched, or magic, and visiting it can be a mystical experience. We are in the presence of a large binary: in these particular representations, nature becomes something other. In particular, it belongs where culture does not.

Many have noted that this is an imaginary that is indeed more or less imaginary. In his pioneering 1972 essay "Ideas of Nature," Raymond Williams wrote that "the idea of nature contains . . . an extraordinary amount of human history."[10] Linking nature to monotheism, he added, "What was being looked for in nature was an essential principle. The multiplicity of things, and of living processes, might then be mentally organized around a single essence or principle: a nature."[11] But as Williams reminds us (see the opening quotation), there are social relations in nature too. William Cronon pressed the point in his brilliant polemical essay on US versions of wilderness.[12] Though nature and wilderness are not identical, his argument is similar. Tracing the history of wilderness from biblical wasteland via sublime terror through nineteenth-century near-Edenic domestication in different versions of Romanticism, Cronon adds that the idea of natural authenticity reappears in many contemporary quasi-religious versions of environmentalism. And, again like Williams, he shows how the wild Other is done differently in different locations. Nature, then, is both singular and multiple, and in the Western imaginary it is very powerful, but how does this work in practice? To think about this question, we move to the world of salmon farming.[13]

Nature: A World without Domesticated Salmon

In Norway, salmon farming is a large industry, with around 380 million farmed salmon in 2014.[14] Between 1998 and 2015, it is estimated that over six million salmon escaped from Norwegian fish farms.[15] Averaging about half a million per year between 1998 and 2006, the figure has fallen to around 340,000 per year since 2007, but either way the proportion that escaped is small. Thus, in 2011 (a bad year, when 365,000 made it into the wild) the figure was only around one in a thousand. But how are the farmed salmon kept in? How are they kept separate from their wild cousins? How is nature actually done in farming practice?[16] Our argument is that this involves many practices. The first of these takes us to a world of nets, ropes, tanks, walls, pipes and filters, fishy habits, and human labor. The salmon are enclosed in pens or tanks, kept in place, and there are physical barriers between nature and culture (figure 5.1). But how to think about these barriers?

STS tells us that they are generated in practices. The latter are not just about people. Instead, they are materially heterogeneous and more or less repetitive relational patterns of association and dissociation. STS thus asks us to attend to pipes, tanks, and nets as well as people, and to attend to the patterning of the heterogeneous associations and arrangements on

FIGURE 5.1. Keeping (aquaculture) separate from nature. A circular pen on the salmon farm. Photo by John Law.

the farm. The object is to trace the web or network of relations that keep the salmon in place. It is this web of associations that gives things shape, and STS treats whatever emerges—in this case a boundary between nature and culture—as a more or less secure or insecure effect of those practices.[17]

This is a line of reasoning that moves us to the realm of ontology because it explores what is being made real or realized.[18] The interest is in what there is in the world that is being enacted in this practice or that. Thus, in this case a division between the farm and the world is being enacted that distinguishes between objects that belong to (aqua)culture and those that belong to nature. So if nature is that which is pristine or untouched, then the conclusion is that this nature is being done here in a very particular way, as a world that is in principle physically untouched by domesticated salmon. In this dualist world, there are two physical or geographical domains: nature is outside; culture is within. If we were to visualize this, it might look like figure 5.2.

But what does such a nature contain?

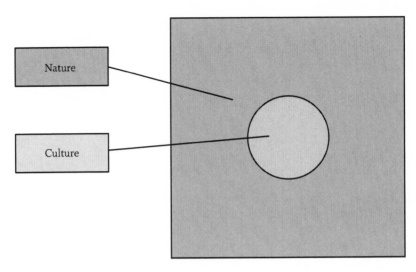

FIGURE 5.2. Culture contained within nature.

Nature: A Salmon That Didn't Come from a Farm

One way of populating nature is to tell stories about wild salmon. To do this, we take our cue from fly-fishing people.[19] Fly-fishing is also a large industry. Around 80,000 Norwegians and 35,000 overseas visitors enjoy recreational salmon fishing in Norway each year, and the sport is worth at least NoK 1.3 billion (well over $200 million) annually.[20] But for those who fish, what is it all about?

There are many answers, but one is that recreational salmon fishing carries its own romance. Here is a tourist blurb: "Norwegian salmon fishing is a fantastic experience. Being so far north, fishing days can be long with almost 24 hours of daylight in midsummer. It has a well deserved reputation as a BIG fish country and every year lucky anglers beat their personal record by catching fish of 30lb's [sic] plus with some real monsters hooked and lost."[21]

But if fly-fishing is a form of Romantic subjectivity, it is also a set of embodied skills. Indeed, it is a set of practices that array—and enact— particular kinds of people, rivers, salmon, and circumstances: "The total experience is what matters; from observing river conditions and choosing a fishing strategy and equipment, to actually fooling the salmon into taking your fly. The more difficult the conditions, the bigger the challenge, and the bigger the joy when the take finally happens!"[22] Contest, tug-of-war, fight, game of deception, feint, and counterfeint—these are some of the images that characterize the joy of fly-fishing. The wild salmon is being enacted, and so too is his or her adversary—the skilled angler.[23] And the sport is materially heterogeneous too. The person and the fish and the condition of the river and the time of day and the technical equipment are all important.

But what are these recreational fisher-people catching? The Norwegian Salmon River Association publishes a pocket guide to the "silver-covered nomad."[24] Wild salmon or domesticated? That is the question. The guide tells us, "Rounded and often split fins, shortened gill covers and deformed fins and jaws are common characteristics of escaped farmed salmon. More stippling below their median line makes them easy to confuse with sea trout. Vaccination marks and abdominal adhesions may also be detected when the fish is cleaned."[25] "Split," "deformed," and "shortened"—the language tells us that the benchmark is the wild salmon in its assumed primordial or original state: pristine and untouched. It is only when human beings have intervened that this noble fish emerges deformed with "adhesions" or "marks." So what is farmed salmon to the fisher-person? Our friends who fish tell us that it is not cultivation as such that makes a difference.[26] Rather, it is the rampant profit-driven interventions associated with large-scale industrial fish farming. The escapee, once it is identified as such, is already stigmatized, forever marked as matter out of place. It does not matter if the fish in question is healthy and in good shape.

"Lykke til!" says a poster (see figure 5.3). "Good luck!" Why? Because it is the wild fish at the top that you want to catch, not the inferior domesticated specimen at the bottom: "Steffen [caught] . . . a 7 kilo . . . [salmon] on the Mosand beat, [but] this turned out to be a farmed fish, [so] the celebration did not take off because of this."[27] In the world of fly-fishing, an escaped farmed salmon is a disappointment. Indeed, it behaves differently too. It is not strong enough and fails to put up a proper fight.[28] Unsurprisingly, it also turns out that people will not pay—or will not pay as much—when they catch farmed salmon, though even here the practices that distinguish wild salmon from domesticated *oppdrettslaks* are multiple.[29] The locals guiding visiting anglers may find that they have to tell the latter that they have just caught an oppdrettslaks, or perhaps they keep quiet about it, because the distinction is not always clear, and domesticated salmon lose many of their stigmata after a couple of years at sea and become very difficult to identify by inspection. So what to do? In some rivers you can send scale samples to the Norsk Institutt for Naturforskning (Norwegian

FIGURE 5.3. "Good luck!" How to distinguish between wild and farmed salmon. Reproduced with the kind permission of the National Veterinary Institute, the Veterinærinstituttet, http://www.ngofa.no/files/Hvordan-skille-villfisk-og -oppdrettsfisk-revidert.pdf.

Institute for Nature Research) for genetic analysis and wait for the answer, a procedure that generates yet another version of the nature/culture divide.

Here, then, we are seeing a second version of the boundary between nature and culture. This fly-fishing nature maps onto the world of nets and pipes and tanks and walls of the fish farm: both are versions of a nature without domesticated salmon. It maps, too, onto the world of genetics. At the same time it is different, for by the time you are standing on the riverbank, the battle to contain culture has been lost: alongside the wild salmon, the *villaks*, there are many salmon in the river that are not "natural."[30] This means that the distinction has to be done fish by fish. First you catch a fish, and then you look for the signs of (aqua)culture. Only then can you draw the vital boundary between nature and that which does not belong. So pristine nature is everywhere, still. Unfortunately, however, escapees are swimming around inside nature and have to be picked out of it, instance by instance. We might visualize this as in figure 5.4.

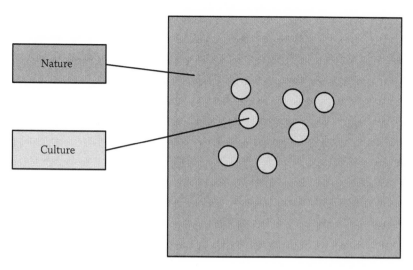

FIGURE 5.4. Culture within nature.

Nature: A World without (Many) Sea Lice

A third practice for dividing nature from culture takes us to the sea louse, *Lepeophtheirus salmonis*. This marine parasite attacks all salmonids and is a problem for both fish and farmers because it breeds and spreads fast in the crowded pens of the fish farms.[31] Fish with sea lice suffer irritation, and if the lice get out of control, they cause injury and distress to the salmon, and the farmers lose money because the salmon stop growing. Worrying that salmon migrating from the rivers to the open sea will pick up lice as they pass down the fjord, the Norwegian food safety authority implements mitigation strategies that include obligatory lice counts and sets permissible upper limits of sea lice per salmon. The farmers control lice by insecticides, breeding, and biological control using wrasse.[32] The wrasse or *rensefisk* (cleaning fish)—in west Norway they are called *leppefisk* (literally, lipfish)—eat the lice off the salmon, and this works quite well.[33] But sometimes the state-stipulated fortnightly farm inspections reveal that the levels of lice are too high, and more immediate measures are called for, often involving insecticides. The farmworkers then pull the net at the bottom of the pen up so the salmon are close to the surface and hang a tarpaulin skirt around the whole pen to stop the insecticide being washed away too quickly. Then they pull the net even further in so that the fish are right at

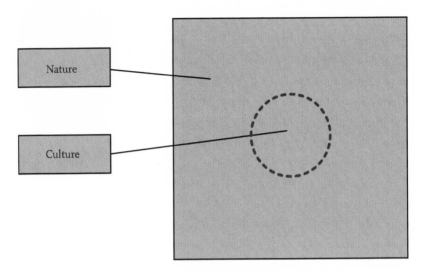

FIGURE 5.5. Nature and culture with permeable boundaries.

the surface, pour insecticide into the water, and wait for half an hour. All of this involves heavy manual handling.

Here the boundary between nature and culture is different yet again. Nature is a world that does not contain sea lice in such high concentrations as it often does in the pens, where there are plenty of salmon to feed on. It is a world that contains healthy populations of (equally healthy) salmon. Nature becomes a world in balance, where salmon are not seriously threatened by large populations of sea lice. The boundary between nature and culture has to do with parasite populations and is permeable and statistical. Indeed, if everything is going well, it is not there at all. Perhaps we could visualize it as in figure 5.5.

Nature: A World of Thriving Populations of Wild Salmon

There are around 800,000 salmon on the farm where we did our fieldwork, and a few die each day. Beginners on the farm such as ethnographers are given the unskilled job of collecting these dead fish, the *daufisk*.[34] They are sucked out of the pen and their number is noted on water-resistant paper, taken to the control room, tapped into a spreadsheet, and sent to the head office. But there are many other figures on the farm.

As well as the number of dead fish, the spreadsheet shows monthly statistics for incoming deliveries of fish by number and biomass; fish sent for slaughter; current biomass and numbers of fish; how much the fish have grown since they arrived; how much they have been fed; and a figure called the economic feed conversion ratio (FCR). All of these numbers are important. The FCR is crucial to profitability because it tells the firm how efficiently feed is being converted into fish flesh.[35] Biomass goes into this, but the figure is also relevant to regulation because the state specifies the maximum biomass of farmed salmon for any given license and location. So the firm creates and aggregates figures, but so too does the state. All of these figures and a lot more go to the authorities. These are precisely the kinds of practices that make it possible to produce statistics that tell us that in 2014 in Norway there were around 1,260,000 tons of biomass, with a grand total of nearly 422 million fish.[36]

Nature is taking shape here differently again. As with the sea lice, it is being done statistically, but the statistics not only draw from the farms but also rest on figures for wild salmon. For the latter there is no possibility of a census. Instead there are models and guestimates. The Vitenskapelig Råd for Lakseforvaltning, the Norwegian Scientific Advisory Committee for Wild Salmon, dips its toe into these murky waters to generate a figure for salmon at sea, the PFA or Pre-Fishery Abundance. This is derived from river catches of salmon minus the oppdrettslaks and a series of assumptions including the proportion of spawning salmon caught in the rivers, how much the fishermen are underreporting their catches, and the proportion of salmon taken in the sea (though the council is particularly wary about the last of these statistics).[37] And the estimate for 2014—475,000 wild salmon in Norway.[38] This figure set alongside the figure of 422 million domesticated salmon enacts the world as one of populations, some belonging to culture and others to nature. Nature exists within a conceptual statistical space, and in this space nature is dwarfed by aquaculture. It is almost as if the fisher-person's world is being stood on its head: what is being conjured up is a world that is almost entirely cultural. Nature, as pristine or untouched, has been rendered small (see figure 5.6).

If a narrative is added—for instance, about sea lice, global anthropogenic climate change, acidification, or river engineering—then we enter a world in which nature is being progressively squeezed by culture, though it is also possible to nuance this conclusion by generating geographical

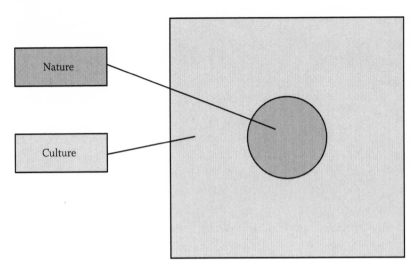

FIGURE 5.6. Nature rendered small by culture.

difference, in which case the finding is (for instance) that nature is being squeezed more in west Norway than in the far north.[39]

Nature: A Prelapsarian World Filled with Salmon

The distinction is statistical, and it is also synchronous. However, time can be added to the statistics (see figure 5.7). The graph comes from the Vitenskapelig Råd for Lakseforvaltning. The top line suggests that in 1983 around a million salmon were returning from the North Atlantic to Norwegian coastal waters. In 2008, the estimated figure was around half that: over the last few decades the population has suffered what scientific literature describes as a "slow and steady decline."[40] Partly this is an artifact of the fact that there is less sea fishing—priority is being given to salmon fishing in the rivers—and partly it is a consequence of falling sea temperatures in the North Atlantic. But it is also because human activity is bad for wild salmon: "a combination of factors associated with human activities including overexploitation, habitat destruction, salmon aquaculture and as well as . . . changes in the natural environment."[41]

Other long-term studies tell much the same story.[42]

In these stories and statistics, nature is under pressure from culture and tends to belong to a receding past. In short, the narrative takes

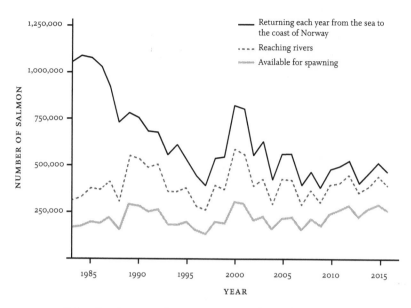

FIGURE 5.7. Scientific advice on salmon management. Copyright Norwegian Scientific Advisory Committee for Atlantic Salmon. Reproduced with permission from the committee. Wild salmon returning each year from the sea to the coast of Norway (top line), plus salmon reaching rivers (middle line) and available for spawning (bottom line). Redrawn from an original with the kind permission of NINA, the Norwegian Institute for Nature Research.

that common Western form: it is lapsarian. There are no fish in Lucas Cranach's version of the Garden of Eden, but the message is similar (see figure 5.8).

Before knowledge and industry and the weight of human numbers—before culture—the seas and the rivers were filled with salmon. Nature was untouched, but then it started to give way to culture. A boundary is being drawn in time. Perhaps the fall was in the late eighteenth century and coincided with the moment of conquest and colonial invasion, or at the beginning of the twentieth century with an emergent global fishing industry, or indeed in the 1970s in west Norway, when salmon were enrolled in expansive industrial domestication.[43] The particular answers differ, but the narrative form does not: the beginning of the end lies somewhere in the past. This is where nature untouched is to be found and the present—however lively—is only a pale reflection of what once was. The story is familiar. Donna Haraway's deconstruction of Carl Akeley's gorilla diorama

FIGURE 5.8. Lucas Cranach the Elder, *The Garden of Eden*, 1530, Gemäldegalerie Alte Meister, Dresden, Germany.

at the American Museum of Natural History counts as an exemplary case.[44] And a boundary diagram of this dystopian divide between nature and culture might look like figure 5.9.

But what of the future? Again, it depends. Dystopian narratives are matched by redemption stories. For some, including those who created or re-created wilderness in the form of the US national parks, paradise will be regained with appropriate conservation measures.[45] For others it depends on the work of gods or magic.[46] Either way, we might draw the redemption narrative as in figure 5.10.

Nature: A Genetically and Behaviorally
Unmodified World of Salmon

There are no genetically modified salmon in Norway, but the industry uses selective breeding. The breeders select for around a dozen attributes that fall into three large groups. First, they look for growth: the fish farmers want fish that will grow quickly and convert feed to flesh efficiently. Sec-

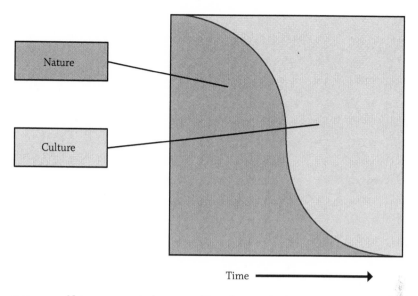

FIGURE 5.9. Nature progressively squeezed by culture as time passes.

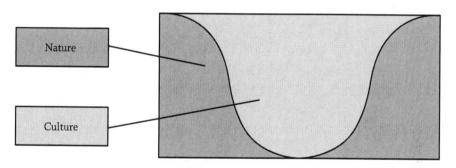

FIGURE 5.10. Nature squeezed by culture, and then redeemed.

ond, they breed for disease resistance. And third, they also select for flesh quality because they want to avoid fatty salmon.

As a result, farmed salmon are genetically and behaviorally different from their wild cousins, and since they escape from the farms, this is also a major problem. Escaped domesticated salmon breed less successfully than their wild cousins, and they reduce the breeding success of the latter.[47] However, when they do breed, their offspring are more aggressive and likely to take risks, and since they grow faster, they also tend to dominate wild salmon. The problem, then, is that domesticated genetic profiles (that is, those selected for their advantage in relation to aquaculture settings) are displacing those that are wild, contributing to less genetic variation in the population at large. Indeed, on some projections wild salmon—or wild genes—will be in a minority in the rivers of three of Norway's regions by 2050.[48] This is a dystopian future because:

> If escaped farmed salmon spawn in rivers containing wild salmon and cross-breed with them, the wild salmon strains may lose their unique adaptation to the particular river system from which they come. Offspring from such hybrids between farmed and wild salmon compete for food with the local salmon parr. . . . Many scientists believe that, in the long term, continual infusion of farmed salmon into the wild salmon strains will lead to the differences between the original salmon strains, which have become adapted to the environment through natural selection over a long time, being erased.[49]

In this story, nature is multiple, no longer one but many. But the way it multiplies is singular: the story is Darwinian. In nature, genes and behaviors adapt to fit particular ecological niches, but now we are witnessing a genetic version of Gresham's law. Ill-adapted domesticated genes and behaviors are in the process of driving out natural but better-adapted genes and behaviors, and natural genetic diversity is being replaced by a cultural genetic uniformity. Perhaps we might visualize the genetic nature/culture boundary as in figure 5.11.

This division has been written, albeit controversially, into the formally adopted Norsk Svarteliste (Norwegian Blacklist), which in 2007 defined the domesticated Atlantic salmon, *Salmo salar*, as an alien species in Norway even though it is only forty years since the fish farmers created their original brood stock by catching wild salmon from the rivers that are now being protected.[50] In this world, nature is natural only if it remains unimproved—though this itself is also a source of controversy, because Norwegian river owners have been restocking their rivers for at least a century with little regard for differences between those rivers.[51]

Mutual Inclusion and Ontological Politics

We have argued that these practices (together) generate a single nature, out there untouched, pristine, clean, remote, and nonhuman, but at the same time they are generating multiple natures.[52] So what follows?

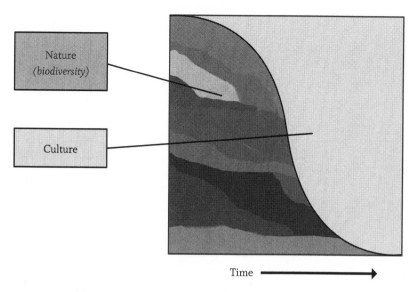

FIGURE 5.11. Culture progressively squeezing nature and its diversity as time passes.

One answer is that to understand what nature is in any particular location, it becomes important to explore how different practices and objects interact at that location. Such interaction may be coherent or it may not. Think, for instance, of fly-fishing. As we saw above, its practices draw on and reproduce Romanticism as it searches for unmediated access to the pristine.[53] But within fly-fishing, both nature and culture also take non-Romantic forms, for instance in the shape of technologies, texts, and genetics. The paradoxical lesson is that unmediated access to nature is possible but only via mediating technical and social practices: as an expression of Romanticism, fly-fishing rejects many forms of aquaculture, while selectively including others.[54]

This is not a complaint or criticism. If practices are multiple, then we will expect to discover paradoxes and tensions when they intersect. So, for instance, the matter-of-fact work of keeping the salmon contained within the farm reflects—or includes—imperatives that are simultaneously economic, political, genetic, environmental, and Romantic. Unsurprisingly, there are other contexts in which there are tensions between the natures enacted in population genetics, the genetics of breeding, fly-fishing, and the business of rearing salmon in captivity. To take just one example, offspring from salmon brood stock sourced prior to the expansion of aquaculture are currently being produced in local hatcheries and released into

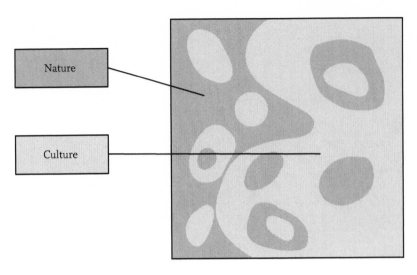

FIGURE 5.12. The mutual inclusion of nature and culture.

the Vosso River in west Norway as eggs, fry, and smolt. The hope is that endangered stocks in those rivers—and their genes—may be preserved.[55] Though there are dissenters, the assumption at work here is that this kind of hatchery production and breeding fit with environmental and Romantic versions of nature—and this despite the fact that in other contexts fish farming counts as a major threat to both. These overlaps, tensions, and paradoxes all suggest that the picture we need to draw if we want to visualize the boundaries between nature and culture will often take the form of mutual inclusion (see figure 5.12). Indeed, there is no reason to suppose that this process of mutual inclusion would not continue if we were to turn up the magnification. Perhaps we also need to draw fractal-like patterns.[56]

So the boundary contingencies are just that—contingent. Boundaries become complex. Press on one matter of concern, and the implications elsewhere are likely to multiply in ways that generate noncoherent distinctions between nature and culture. But this has political implications. Earlier we cautiously suggested that, faced by a messy both-and modernity, it might sometimes make sense to insist on the noncoherence and differences that make up the latter. This becomes important for the conduct of postcolonial politics because it suggests that it will often be a mistake to treat modernity (or any of its world-system analogues) as monoliths. As we have mentioned in relation to postcolonialism, there will be moments for (what feminists call) strategic essentialism: moments to argue that modernity is a dangerous and repressive force. Nevertheless, to enact the modern as if it were a single and coherent system has the major disadvantage that it tends to add to its apparent invincibility. World systems become world systems in part because they are treated as world systems.

Second, and as a part of this, to treat naturalization as a monolith is also to miss the possibility of using multiple natures as potential places of leverage and to forgo the opportunities opened up by an ontological politics or a politics of what it is to do without the idea that other (natural) worlds are possible.[57] Although the case can be made both ways, there are circumstances where recognizing ontological difference will be a progressive political move—for instance, in postcolonial contexts where other realities may suggest either tactics for resisting incorporation into hegemonic schemes or procedures for recognizing the former in ways that make it possible for different realities (in Helen Verran's phrase) to go on well together in difference.[58]

The Science of a Singular World

So the boundary between nature and culture may be multiple, complex, and not particularly coherent, but is also persistently reproduced. Nature singular and untouched remains a powerful Western imaginary. But why is it so powerful? One answer is that natural science treats it that way.

The graph in figure 5.13 comes from a short management-oriented scientific review that describes the effect on salmon of the acidification of the rivers and lakes of southern Norway.[59] The abstract in part runs thus:

> Due to acidification, 18 Norwegian stocks of Atlantic salmon are extinct and an additional eight are threatened. In the two southernmost counties, salmon is eradicated. Due to the high acid sensitivity, production of salmon was greatly reduced as early as 1920, several decades before acid rain was recognized as an environmental problem. International agreements on reduced atmospheric emissions will reduce acidification effects in Norway. . . . However the extreme acid sensitivity of salmon makes the destiny of this species in Southern Norway uncertain. Liming is an effective measure to protect and restore fish populations in acidified waters.[60]

As this paragraph suggests, the article describes a series of objects or actors and the processes that link them together. The term "nature" does not appear, but the article talks of "an environmental problem," and therefore, by

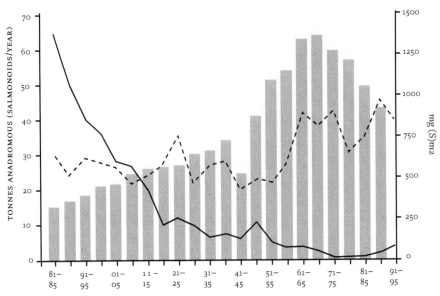

Historical oxidised sulphur depositions and fish catches in five-year periods, 1881–1995

FIGURE 5.13. Deposition of sulfur and catches of salmon. Bars: Estimated historical deposition of oxidized sulfur in southern Norway. Continuous line: catches of salmon in seven rivers along the southern coast. Dotted line: Catches of salmon in twenty-nine rivers on the western coast. This figure is redrawn from an original, with kind permission, from Steinar Sandøy and R. M. Langåker, "Atlantic Salmon and Acidification in Southern Norway: A Disaster in the 20th Century, but a Hope for the Future?," *Water, Air and Soil Pollution* 130, nos. 1–4 (2001): 1344.

implication, it is modeling a single environmental world. But what is the context for this? How is it possible to do this?

The answer is a historical contingency. In an important essay, Kristin Asdal traces part of the genealogy of nature in Norway and shows how pollution became an issue in the 1950s when agricultural damage was linked to emissions from the country's aluminum smelters. The result was a set of procedures that generated an abstract space in which factories came to exist within a natural environment.[61] She then shows how this reality was transmuted by the European Monitoring and Evaluation Programme (EMEP) in the 1970s and 1980s in the context of what became known as the acid rain problem, a development that was in large measure driven by Norwegian concerns about forest dieback and falling salmon stocks.[62] Her argument is one that we have picked up in this chapter. It is that though different versions of nature were enacted in the EMEP apparatus, the result was also a unified nature generated by weaving meteorology, environmental chemistry, and financial accountability and budgeting together within a particular institutional context.[63] We would add that what was created can also be understood as a single space or a volume within which objects, causes, and effects are located. It is this version of reality that makes the article by Sandøy and Langåker possible. It is simply being taken for granted that there is a single volume covering Norway (and Europe) over a period of a century. A volumetric world is being enacted, and its contents are being modeled. The world is being done as a single space-time box.

But the scientists and policy makers in the EMEP program did not invent this singular reality *de novo*. This, too, has its genealogy. To trace this in detail would take us beyond the scope of this chapter. However, both Raymond Williams and Cronon stress the importance of the Judeo-Christian tradition for the creation of a single real nature: "Nature in Western culture is the product of a monotheistic religious tradition; it is often unrecognizable for people whose cultures have not taught them to worship a lone deity."[64] In this cosmogony, God imposed an order on formless matter to create a single cosmos with a particular nature. Though God was mysterious, this did not prevent medieval European scholars from speculating about the character of that order. With the birth of modern science, this interest in the character of cosmic order was connected to empirical inquiry. Indeed, in natural science it ultimately survived the disappearance of the divine creator, and the universe became orderly in the absence of a God. After the scientific revolution, the idea of order was embedded in the heterogeneous movement of the Enlightenment, and the idea of a single nature that might be known and managed was carried over into the specialist natural sciences, including the nineteenth-century discipline of ecology.[65] The mechanisms in nature might be unclear in particular cases, but the assumption throughout was that nature and the cosmos are out there, singular, and are endowed with specific mechanisms behind the complexities of appearance that might in principle be revealed.[66] It was the task of the natural sciences to characterize those mechanisms, and indeed it is this historical context that renders natural science inquiry possible. This is the metaphysics that underpins and is reproduced in the great majority of contemporary scientific publications, and it is this that makes it possible for Sandøy and Langåker to write, "The purpose of this paper is to give an overview of the status of Atlantic salmon in Norway."[67]

This is metaphysics in practice. A small scientific article carries and reproduces the weight and the resources of European intellectual practice. It would not be possible to have an overview of nature at all if reality were vague, fluid, or indeterminate, or if the mechanisms that underpin reality did not hold steady between different locations.[68] Neither would it be possible if the fundamental mechanisms at work in the world changed over time, or if the claims made by the authors were only valid at the location in which they were written.[69] All of these operating assumptions are a historical contingency, and they could be different. To write an essay in the traditions of Western science is thus to assume, enact, and reaffirm the existence of a single world or a universe. And this is why we want to say that modern Western natural science does not simply naturalize nature. It also naturalizes reality and enacts the real. It performs, and institutionalizes, a kind of essentialism that works hegemonically, facilitating other papers, and tightening the web of associations upon which it simultaneously relies. This is another both/and but contingent feature of modern practices. In the dominant practices of natural science in publishing, multiverses are simply not possible.[70]

Romanticism

The both/and generation of many realities that are also naturalized and singular extends beyond natural science. Similar processes are at work in many contemporary Western everyday practices where routinization and rationalization have profoundly shaped daily conduct.[71] But what of the pristine realities of Romanticism that we saw at work in Norwegian tourism and fly-fishing? Do these also imply multiple versions of a singular reality?

As a historical movement, Romanticism was heterogeneous and diverse, but it was often a more or less privileged European reaction to secular changes that included industrialization, bourgeois commitments to commoditization and economic calculability, Enlightenment rationalism, and the Napoleonic attempt to impose that rationalism on large parts of Europe by force.[72] In addition, it was often deeply affiliated with nationalist political agendas and inspired the efforts of urban elites to both chart and shape the character of new nation-states. Like the Enlightenment, Romanticism sought truth, but it tended to value ways of knowing that were concrete, intuitive, embodied, qualitative, holistic, organic, culturally specific, and attuned to qualitative historical and cultural difference. It often celebrated the need for each individual to find his or her own personal version of the truth. As a part of this, it powerfully operated to create a new aesthetic of nature. Cronon and Williams both show that wilderness, previously experienced as ugly, barren, and dangerous, became a source of the sublime for the Romantics. A terrifying but transcendental place of emotional or spiritual encounter between the individual and a landscape, wilderness made possible direct apprehension of, and awe for, the overwhelming character of natural reality.

But the distinction between nature and culture was not always sharp. The iconic painting *Brudeferden i Hardanger* (Bridal party in Hardanger), by Norwegian artists Adolph Tidemand and Hans Gude, was commissioned in 1848 as a backdrop for a theater in Oslo (see figure 5.14). In the nineteenth-century struggles to articulate a Norwegian national, cultural, and linguistic identity, the painting became iconic for a particular Romantic, privileged, and urban nationalist vision. Its version of the sublime visualized an imagined authentic rural culture that would act as a source for a nation that had been tainted by centuries of Danish urban-based rule. Perhaps we might say that the peasants themselves were being naturalized.

But what of singularity? What was happening when Romantics came face to face with the sublime? One answer is that there was no overall Romantic response.[73] The inspiration might be Christian, in which case a monotheistic God lay behind the terror, and the sublime became a privileged way of coming face to face with Him in all His impossible and unitary majesty. At the same time, for other writers and poets reality was polytheistic. In Norway, Norse mythology was enrolled as player in the Romantic version of the attempt to create an authentic national history appropriate to an aspirant nation-state. Indeed, the Jotunheim massif, "the home of the Jotun giants," was thus named in 1862 by Romantic poet and lawyer A. O. Vinje.[74]

Perhaps, then, and especially given the preferentially solitary character of the sublime encounter with nature, we need to say that Romanticism made space for the multiplicity of realities without always insisting on this. But how did this work in practice? The answer lies in part in the encounters between Romanticism and (a more pragmatic) rationalization.

FIGURE 5.14. Adolph Tidemand and Hans Gude, *Bridal Procession on the Hardangerfjord* (*Brudeferden i Hardanger*), 1848, National Museum of Art, Architecture and Design, Oslo.

The complexities of the Norwegian political, cultural, and social struggle to create a national identity are beyond the scope of this chapter, and we do not have the resources that would allow us to link them directly to salmon fishing.[75] However, in a parallel case Gro Ween and Simone Abram describe how hiking or "mountain wandering" grew to enact an influential and partially Romantic version of Norway.[76] They show how Den Norske Turistforening (DNT, the Norwegian Trekking Association), established in 1868, reflected urban Romantic-nationalist agendas by locating authentic national identity in narratives about the rural, and in particular in the higher and wilder parts of nature.[77] As with *Brudeferden i Hardanger*, these narratives, organized in part around Romantic historical and mythological stories, also folded in the imagined virtues of peasants. So how did they do this?

The answer is that DNT progressively, laboriously, and meticulously created and then maintained a network of mostly high-altitude long-distance paths and skiing trails that spanned the length and breadth of the country. To do this, the organization used a meticulous set of practical but completely routinized techniques that included signage, cartography, field guides, and huts. Local specificities, forms of knowledge, and ownership rights were more or less swept away by these standardized techniques for knowing, appreciating, and moving in the landscape. Here is the paradox. Though historically there was a range of reasons for trekking in Norway, the DNT's efforts can also be seen a thoroughly rationalized project for achieving goals that were in part Romantic in inspiration.[78] The DNT worked to create a consistent set of material practices and subjectivities that facilitated particular forms of appreciation already endorsed by an adventurous urban elite committed to mountaineering.[79] Through their practices, and inspired by an egalitarian ethos, the DNT made these experiences accessible to all, but only as part of a standardized package. By the time the DNT had finished its national network of paths and ski trails, the apprehension of mountains and nature was both individual and routinized or collective, and thus readily available for further appropriation as iconic symbols of the nation. A single Romantic nature and a uniform Romantic world had been generated for all, which is surely how it is, with minor variations, in the practices of recreational fishing, with its logistical arrangements, its infrastructures, its technologies, its recourse to field guides and handbooks, and the way in which it draws on resources of genetics. Indeed, and more generally, the parallels between the business of recreation and the story of the scientific EMEP mapping project are striking. There are specificities in each (different pHs for different rivers, and different particular narratives about different landscapes), but the ways in which these are framed overall are uniform. If there is multiplicity, then this is a multiplicity that has been domesticated within a larger and partially pragmatic, hegemonic framework that is also, in part, nationalist.

None of this should surprise us. Romanticism and rationalism were woven together in Europe and took specific forms in the different projects of nineteenth-century nation building.[80] But our argument is that when Romanticism intersected with egalitarian individualism and nation building, it started to enact a single nature and a single reality. There is space in Romanticism to generate a pluriverse, but when it was standardized and routinized, it enacted nature as a singularity, resilient but also in need of protection—at which point we are back where we began. Culture

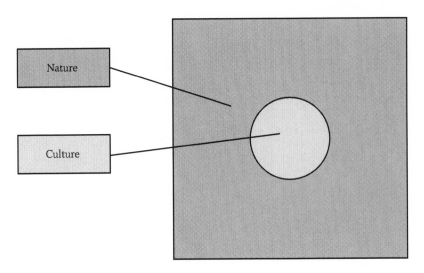

FIGURE 5.15. Culture contained within nature.

is being contained and encapsulated within a nature that is untouched (see figure 5.15).

Afterword

Since Nietzsche announced the death of God, parts of Western philosophy have been seeking to repattern our understanding of reality and move us from singularity.[81] This is a golden thread that also runs through parts of contemporary STS, anthropology, feminism, and postcolonialism.[82] So how does it help us to think about the sticky webs of the modern world and their both/and commitment to ontological singularity? How might we visualize this predicament? Figure 5.16 presents one possibility.

Starting from the middle of figure 5.16, we know that culture is multiple. This we expect. Indeed, this is the stock in trade of anthropology. But as we shift to the second term, nature, things start to change. For while we may practice a nature multiple (often unknowingly, and in our tacit material engagements with the world), we find it difficult to recognize or talk about it. As Viveiros de Castro and others have painstakingly taught us, multinaturalism is a very odd beast for most forms of modern common sense.[83] Because it is so odd, nature becomes resilient. But then with the third term we move again, and this time to reality. This is the general fram-

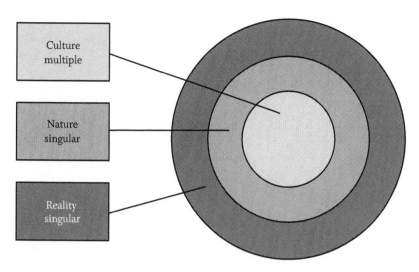

FIGURE 5.16. Multiple culture contained within a single nature and a single reality.

ing, the general ground of everything. As we have been rehearsing, in the modern Western imaginary this is usually endowed with a particular order, even if its character is obscure. Reality becomes a single volume containing not-yet-known—and possibly unknowable but determinate—realities. That container defines the conditions of possibility for knowing those realities: categories that include time, space, causality, and singularity. Such is the job lot that comes with the propensity to pattern and singularize reality.

But this is starting to change. For now, as we attend to practices and the ontological work that they do, we are slowly beginning to learn that it does not have to be that way. Isabelle Stengers draws on neopaganism to challenge the Western academy to rediscover its "cemetery of destroyed practices."[84] She is thinking of the repressive brutalities of the European witchcraft trials, but her point is political and ontological. Through her work, and that of many others, we are beginning to see that there are multiple both/and natures, that nature is not singular, and that frameworks of a single real are starting to lose their grip. For once we put the practices that do realities alongside one another and start to take those practices seriously, once we start to insist that differences are not just matters of perspective, once we start to insist that what the practices do is real in the context of those practices, once we do all of these things, then we start to discover multiple times, multiple spaces, multiple relations, multiple origins, and multiple modes of causality or noncausality. We find, in short, that reals start to multiply and the framing assumption that there is a single reality, a universe, starts to dissolve.

But the fact that reality is not destiny is not simply an interesting analytical discovery. It is also a political opportunity. For, as we have hinted with our ethnographic examples above, the internal colonization of what we call modernity by modernity was never complete. The lesson that we can take from this is that it is time to rearticulate the subordinate sensibilities, sensibilities embedded in and enacted by those caught up in the practices of modernity. It is time to rearticulate and reassert those sensibilities both ethnographically and politically. For other worlds exist, even within modernity.

ACKNOWLEDGMENTS

We are grateful to the anonymized Sjølaks AS for their kind agreement to let us locate our study within the firm, and for their additional generous practical support. We would like to thank all those who work for Sjølaks (they too are anonymized) for their warm welcome, their help, and their willingness to let us watch them at work. In very many cases their kindness vastly exceeded any reasonable expectation or need. We are grateful to Kristin Asdal, Mario Blaser, Marisol de la Cadena, Arturo Escobar, Judith Farquhar, Casper Bruun Jensen, Wen-yuan Lin, Andrew Mathews, Annemarie Mol, Knut Nustad, Hugh Raffles, Vicky Singleton, Heather Swanson, and Gro Ween for discussion and advice. The project, Newcomers to the Farm, was funded by Forskningsrådet, the Norwegian Research Council (project number 183352/S30), with additional research leave and financial support from Lancaster University, the Open University, Oslo University, and the Centre for Advanced Studies, Oslo. We are grateful to all these institutions. Finally we are grateful to Mario Blaser and Marisol de la Cadena for the invitation to participate in the Sawyer Seminar series, where an earlier version of this chapter was presented.

NOTES

1. In order not to overburden the text, in what follows we do not normally place the terms "modernity" or "the modern" in quotation marks. However, given the both-and character of the processes glossed as modern, we have considerable reservations about the wisdom of using these terms. Most large-scale categories—for instance the "postcolonial," which we also use—are in need of similar qualification.

2. For a clear expression, see Bruno Latour, *We Have Never Been Modern* (Brighton: Harvester Wheatsheaf, 1993).

3. The argument is developed for biomedicine in Annemarie Mol, *The Body Multiple: Ontology in Medical Practice* (Durham, NC: Duke University Press, 2002).

4. The authors usually did joint fieldwork, sharing field notes, discussing, and sometimes combining those activities. We cultivated the principle of naive observation, assuming that we did not know beforehand what a salmon is, and paid particular attention to the heterogeneous networks and relational practices that make up the realities that are often otherwise taken for granted by coworkers and fieldworkers alike.

5. Eduardo Viveiros de Castro, "Cosmological Deixis and Amerindian Perspectivism," *Journal of the Royal Anthropological Institute* 4, no. 3 (1998): 469–88; Mario Blaser, "The Threat of the Yrmo: The Political Ontology of a Sustainable Hunting Program," *American Anthropologist* 111, no. 1 (2009): 10–20.

6. See "Explore the Oslo Region," Norway: Powered by Nature, 2017, https://www .visitnorway.com/about/; David Berliner, Laurent Legrain, and Mattijs van de Port, "Bruno Latour and the Anthropology of the Moderns," *Social Anthropology* 21, no. 4 (2013): 435.

7. See, for instance, the video at Visit Norway's Facebook page, October 3, 2012, available at https://www.facebook.com/VisitnorwayUSA/videos/10152130732285063/.

8. "Must-See Nature Attractions," Norway: Powered by Nature, 2017, https://www .visitnorway.com/things-to-do/nature-attractions/.

9. "Northern Norway: The Kingdom of Light," Norway: Powered by Nature, 2017, https://www.visitnorway.com/places-to-go/northern-Norway/. The text of this page (without photographs), accessed August 31, 2017, is archived at https://web.archive.org /web/20130802153136/http://www.visitnorway.com/us/what-to-do/attractions-culture /nature-attractions/national-parks-in-norway/.

10. Raymond Williams, "Ideas of Nature," in *Problems of Materialism and Culture*, 67–85 (London: Verso, 1980), 70.

11. Williams, "Ideas of Nature," 68.

12. William Cronon, "The Trouble with Wilderness: or, Getting Back to the Wrong Nature," in *Uncommon Ground: Rethinking the Human Place in Nature*, ed. William Cronon, 69–90 (New York: Norton, 1995).

13. The Newcomers to the Farm project, from which we draw much of the material in this chapter, rests on the idea that while sheep and goats have been domesticated for at least six thousand years, for salmon this has been true for only forty (for an extended discussion, see Marianne Lien, *Becoming Salmon: Aquaculture and the Domestication of a Fish* [Oakland: University of California Press, 2015]). The assumption is that many of the processes lost in prehistory for land animals are at work in a temporally telescoped version in aquaculture; that domestication and its other—the wild or the natural—are evolving at high speed and that new ways of doing the natural are therefore being invented in and around the practices of salmon farming. In the project, Gro Ween went to the Deatnu/Tana River in northern Norway to look at practices—indigenous and otherwise— involving *villaks*, or wild salmon, while Marianne Lien and John Law worked together on the fish farms of the fjord country of west Norway and Kristin Asdal explored the historical paper trails associated with the emergence of Norwegian farmed cod.

14. This figure comes from "Atlantic Salmon, Rainbow Trout and Trout—Grow Out Production," Norsk Fiskedirektoratet [Norwegian Directorate of Fisheries], March 2,

2018, https://www.fiskeridir.no/Akvakultur/Statistikk-akvakultur. It refers to salmon in saltwater grow-out sites only, and does not include the cohorts raised in tanks that have not yet reached the transformation that adapts them to saltwater, called smoltification.

15. Do salmon actually escape? The answer is probably not, as most escape incidents are human-induced accidents or mishaps that break the nets. Unlike cod, which are known as the Houdinis of aquaculture, salmon, as far as we are aware, do not actively make attempts to break out. To classify these fish as escapees is of course a further way in which nature is being done, but one we do not elaborate here. For discussion, see Lien, *Becoming Salmon*, 161–62. Statistics sourced from "Atlantic Salmon, Rainbow Trout and Trout—Grow Out Production," Norsk Fiskedirektoratet [Norwegian Directorate of Fisheries], March 2, 2018, https://www.fiskeridir.no/Akvakultur /Statistikk-akvakultur.

16. Nature and culture are being done in representational practice too—as, for instance, in the present chapter, in the tourist texts, and in relation to biodiversity; see Marianne Elisabeth Lien and John Law, "'Emergent Aliens': On Salmon, Nature and Their Enactment," *Ethnos* 76, no. 1 (2011): 65–87. For the moment, however, we choose to bracket this complication and focus on farming and farming-relevant practice. On the performativity of representation in a quite different domain, see John Law, "Seeing Like a Survey," *Cultural Sociology* 3, no. 2 (2009): 239–56; and on the politics of the actor-network or material semiotic version of STS in the context of salmon farming, see John Law and Vicky Singleton, "ANT and Politics: Working in and on the World," *Qualitative Sociology* 36, no. 4 (2013): 485–502.

17. Though particular metaphors are troubling in particular contexts (see, for instance, Susan Leigh Star, "Power, Technologies and the Phenomenology of Conventions: On Being Allergic to Onions," *Sociological Review* 38, no. S1 [1991]: 26–56), we take it that there is no overall reason for preferring one metaphor for the patterns of weblike association over any of the others. Actor-network theory tends to talk of networks, though Bruno Latour links ANT to Deleuzian rhizomes (see Bruno Latour, "On Recalling ANT," in *Actor Network and After*, ed. John Law and John Hassard, 15–25 [Oxford: Blackwell and the Sociological Review, 1999]). Donna Haraway has written about cat's cradles (Donna Haraway, "A Game of Cat's Cradle: Science Studies, Feminist Theory, Cultural Studies," *Configurations* 1 [1994]: 59–71), and (though rather differently) Tim Ingold tweaks ANT's tail by talking of spiders' webs (Tim Ingold, "When ANT Meets SPIDER: Social Theory for Arthropods," in *Being Alive: Essays on Movement, Knowledge and Description*, ed. Tim Ingold, 89–94 [Abingdon: Routledge, 2011]). No doubt all of these terms have their advantages and inconveniences. See also Marilyn Strathern's comment on the bias to continuity of the ANT version of association (Marilyn Strathern, "Cutting the Network," *Journal of the Royal Anthropological Institute* 2, no. 3 [1996]: 517–35).

18. The argument is standard in material semiotic versions of STS. Sources include Michel Callon, "Some Elements of a Sociology of Translation: Domestication of the Scallops and the Fishermen of Saint Brieuc Bay," *Sociological Review* 32, no. S1 (1984): 196–233; Bruno Latour, *The Pasteurization of France* (Cambridge, MA: Harvard University Press, 1988); Donna Haraway, *When Species Meet* (Minneapolis: University of

Minnesota Press, 2008); Mol, *The Body Multiple*; John Law, *Aircraft Stories: Decentering the Object in Technoscience* (Durham, NC: Duke University Press, 2002); and Karen Barad, *Meeting the Universe Halfway: Quantum Physics and the Entanglement of Matter and Meaning* (Durham, NC: Duke University Press, 2007).

19. Some avid fly-fishers appeared on our aquaculture field site as farmhands. Others were mobilized by our master's students, who positioned themselves in relation to major salmon rivers. See Anita Nordeide, "Møte mellom menneske og laks: Om lakse-fiskepraksiser i Namsenvassdraget [Meeting between human and salmon: On salmon fishing practices in the Namsen watershed]," master's thesis, University of Oslo, 2012; Line Dalheim, "Into the Wild and Back Again: Hatching 'Wild Salmon' in Western Norway," master's thesis, University of Oslo, 2012; and Merethe Ødegard, "I samme båt: Stakere, fluefiskere og maskulinitet i laksefisket i Alta," master's thesis, University of Oslo, 2013. In addition, we draw on the many websites on the topic.

20. Yajie Liu, Jon Olaf Olaussen, and Anders Skonhoft, "Wild and Farmed Salmon in Norway—a Review," *Marine Policy* 35, no. 3 (2011): 413, 415.

21. Max Sardi, "Norway—a Guide to Salmon Fishing," Sportfish, 2017, https://www.sportfish.co.uk/norway-a-guide-to-salmon-fishing.

22. Jan-Erik Granbo, "Salmon Behaviour in Relation to Water Temperature and River Level," 2015, http://www.granbo-flyfishing.no/_english-edition/laksens-adferd.html.

23. Knut Gunnar Nustad, Cato Berg, and Rune Flikke, "Human-Fish Temporalities in Aurland, Norway," paper delivered at the annual meeting of the American Anthropological Association, San Francisco, November 14–18, 2012.

24. Anonymous. "The Incredible Wild Salmon: Norway's Silvery Inheritance." Accessed March 2, 2018, archived at https://web.archive.org/web/20160429211146/http://www.lachsverein.de/pdf/norwegen/wild_salmon.pdf.

25. Our translation of text sourced at Norske Lakseelver, "Norske Lakseelvers guide til villaks-gjenkjenning," accessed January 29, 2018, http://prohd.no/Bilder/Laks%20Oselva%202010/Villaks%20gjenkjenning/Villaks%20gjenkjenning.pdf.

26. Salmon have been subject to hatchery experiments for more than a century.

27. Jan-Erik Granbo, "Fishing Diary," Granbo Flyfishing, September 11, 2001, http://www.granbo-flyfishing.no/_english-edition/fiskedagbok.php?start_from=5&ucat=&archive=&subaction=&id=&.

28. Nordeide writes, "Fishermen say that farmed salmon are fish with little strength, and they come straight up with no fight, like a cod. Escaped farmed salmon are thus in sharp contrast with a wild salmon, which is vigorous and untamed." Nordeide, "Møte mellom menneske og laks," 83, our translation.

29. Liu, Olaussen, and Skonhoft, "Wild and Farmed Salmon in Norway"; Nordeide, "Møte mellom menneske og laks."

30. Figures for the percentages of farmed salmon in the spawning populations of salmon in Norwegian rivers range from 14 to 80 percent, depending on the river. See Liu, Olaussen, and Skonhoft, "Wild and Farmed Salmon in Norway," 315.

31. For a further account of delousing and the problems of sea lice, see John Law, "Notes on Fish, Ponds and Theory," *Norsk Antropologisk Tidsskrift* 23, no. 3–4 (2012): 225–36.

32. There were around 24 million of the latter in the pens of the fish farms in Norway in 2014. Statistics from "Cleaner Fish," Norsk Fiskedirektoratet [Norwegian Directorate of Fisheries], March 2, 2018, https://www.fiskeridir.no/Akvakultur/Statistikk-akvakultur.

33. For details see Lien, *Becoming Salmon*.

34. For a fuller account of daufisk, see John Law and Marianne Elisabeth Lien, "Slippery: Field Notes on Empirical Ontology," *Social Studies of Science* 43, no. 3 (2013): 363–78.

35. The mass of the food eaten divided by the body mass gain, over a specified period, is the FCR. See Marianne E. Lien, "Feeding Fish Efficiently: Mobilising Knowledge in Tasmanian Salmon Farming," *Social Anthropology* 15, no. 2 (2007): 169–85.

36. "Atlantic Salmon, Rainbow Trout and Trout—Grow Out Production," Norsk Fiskedirektoratet [Norwegian Directorate of Fisheries], March 2, 2018, https://www.fiskeridir.no/Akvakultur/Statistikk-akvakultur; and https://www.fiskeridir.no/content/download/7620/95513/version/30/file/sta-laks-mat-07-utgbeh.xlsx.

37. Vitenskapelig råd for lakseforvaltning, *Status for norske laksebestander i 2012* [Scientific advice for salmon management in 2012] (Trondheim: Vitenskapelig råd for lakseforvaltning, 2012), 123.

38. Vitenskapelig råd for lakseforvaltning, *Status for norske laksebestander i 2015*, rapport fra Vitenskapelig råd for lakseforvaltning no. 8 (Trondheim: Vitenskapelig råd for lakseforvaltning, 2015), 29.

39. See, for instance, Ola H. Diserud, Peder Fiske, and Kjetil Hindar, *Regionvis påvirkning av rømt oppdrettslaks på ville laksebestander i Norge* [Regional impact of escaped farm salmon on wild salmon populations in Norway] (Trondheim: Norsk Institutt for Naturforskning, 2010), 33; and Vitenskapelig råd for lakseforvaltning, *Status for norske laksebestander i 2012*.

40. Liu, Olaussen, and Skonhoft, "Wild and Farmed Salmon in Norway," 414. A nonacademic fly-fishing source says that the fall is steeper: from 1.8 million forty years ago to 0.2 million now. Orri Vigfússon, "Norway's Wild Salmon Facing Extinction?," www.karuvaaraflyfishing.com, accessed November 20, 2015, http://www.karuvaaraflyfishing.com/?id=1&s=1243186195251.

41. Liu, Olaussen, and Skonhoft, "Wild and Farmed Salmon in Norway," 414.

42. "Salmon farming is the main threat to the viability of wild salmon due to spread of diseases, escapees, environmental pollution, etc." Steinar Sandøy and R. M. Langåker, "Atlantic Salmon and Acidification in Southern Norway: A Disaster in the 20th Century, but a Hope for the Future?," *Water, Air and Soil Pollution* 130, nos. 1–4 (2001): 1344.

43. Such are the stories often told in so-called settler nations, when the fall becomes a historically significant moment of arrival, such as in the case of Australia, of Captain Cook's arrival in 1776. See Marianne E. Lien, "Weeding Tasmanian Bush: Biomigration and Landscape Imagery," in *Holding Worlds Together: Ethnographies of Knowing and Belonging*, ed. Marianne Elisabeth Lien and Marit Melhuus, 103–21 (Oxford: Berghahn, 2007).

44. Donna Haraway, *Primate Visions: Gender, Race and Nature in the World of Modern Science* (London: Routledge and Chapman Hall, 1989).

45. Cronon, "The Trouble with Wilderness."

46. For a discussion of Australian utopianism, see Lien, "Weeding Tasmanian Bush"; and Marianne E. Lien and Aiden Davison, "Roots, Rupture and Remembrance: The Tasmanian Lives of the Monterey Pine," *Journal of Material Culture* 15, no. 2 (2010): 233–53.

47. Miljøverndepartmentet [Norway's Ministry of the Environment], "St.prp. nr. 32 (2006–2007): Om vern av villaksen og ferdigstilling av nasjonale laksevassdrag og laksefjorder," December 15, 2006, https://www.regjeringen.no/nb/dep/md/dok/regpubl /stprp/2006-2007/stprp-nr-32-2006-2007-/id=442076.

48. Lisbeth Gederaas, Ingrid Salvesen, and Åslaug Viken, eds., *2007 Norwegian Black List: Ecological Risk Analysis of Alien Species* (Trondheim: Norwegian Biodiversity Information Centre, 2007), 33.

49. Gederaas, Salvesen, and Viken, *2007 Norwegian Black List*, 38.

50. Gederaas, Salvesen, and Viken, *2007 Norwegian Black List*, 17.

51. Lien and Law, "'Emergent Aliens,'" 74.

52. Mol, *The Body Multiple*.

53. Many have noted that Romanticism can be understood as a nineteenth-century European reaction to the equally European movement of the Enlightenment—though also one that is also deeply related to the rationalism of the Enlightenment. Karl Mannheim, "Conservative Thought," in *Essays on Sociology and Social Psychology*, ed. Karl Mannheim, 74–164 (London: Routledge and Kegan Paul, 1953); Alvin Gouldner, "Romanticism and Classicism: Deep Structures in Social Science," *Diogenes* 21, no. 82 (1973): 88–107.

54. For instance, selectively bred strains of farmed salmon are rejected, while hatchery practices as such are widely practiced, and indeed often required for fish to be sufficiently abundant to be harvested.

55. Dalheim, "Into the Wild and Back Again"; Bjørn Barlaup, ed., *Redningsaksjonen for Vossolaksen*, vol. DN Utredning 1-2013 (Trondheim: Direktoratet for Naturforvaltning, 2013); Lien, *Becoming Salmon*, 153–58.

56. The logic was explored by Marilyn Strathern, *Partial Connections* (Lanham, MD: Rowman and Littlefield, 199).

57. Mol, *The Body Multiple*; Annemarie Mol, "Ontological Politics: A Word and Some Questions," in *Actor Network Theory and After*, ed. John Law and John Hassard, 74–89 (Oxford: Blackwell/Sociological Review, 1999). On cosmopolitics, see also Isabelle Stengers, "The Cosmopolitical Proposal," in *Making Things Public: Atmospheres of Democracy*, ed. Bruno Latour and Peter Weibel, 994–1003 (Karslruhe: ZKM, 2005). On wildlife, see Steve Hinchliffe, Matthew B. Kearnes, Monica Degen, and Sarah Whatmore, "Urban Wild Things: A Cosmopolitical Experiment," *Society and Space* 23, no. 5 (2005): 643–58.

58. In "making the case both ways," the business of denaturalizing what is taken to be natural is one of the major tactics of climate change denial, where the small minority of scientists who oppose the climate change thesis is cited as sufficient reason for refusing arguments for anthropogenic climate change. Again, there can be no rules, but one way of tackling this is to say that criteria for determining truth in technoscience are being (in many cases deliberately) confused with those that belong to public and political debate. For a version of this argument, see Bruno Latour, *An Inquiry into Modes*

of Existence: An Anthropology of the Moderns (Cambridge, MA: Harvard University Press, 2013). See, for instance, Helen Verran, "Re-imagining Land Ownership in Australia," *Postcolonial Studies* 1, no. 2 (1998): 237–54; Harvey A. Feit, "James Bay Crees' Life Projects and Politics: Histories of Place, Animal Partners and Enduring Relationships," in *In the Way of Development*, ed. Mario Blaser, Harvey A. Feit, and Glenn McRae, 92–110 (London: Zed, 2004); Brian Noble, "Justice, Transaction, Translation: Blackfoot Tipi Transfers and WIPO's Search for the Facts of Traditional Knowledge Exchange," *American Anthropologist* 109, no. 2 (2007): 338–49; Marisol de la Cadena, "Indigenous Cosmopolitics in the Andes: Conceptual Reflections beyond 'Politics,'" *Cultural Anthropology* 25, no. 2 (2010): 334–70; and Cristóbal Bonelli, "Ontological Disorders: Nightmares, Psychotropic Drugs and Evil Spirits in Southern Chile," *Anthropological Theory* 12, no. 4 (2012): 407–26.

59. This boundary between nature and culture is like that of the farming of wild salmon described above. In another case of mutual inclusion, science and technology intervene in nature to re-create the latter.

60. Sandøy and Langåker, "Atlantic Salmon and Acidification in Southern Norway," 1343.

61. Kristin Asdal, "Enacting Things through Numbers: Taking Nature into Account/ ing," *Geoforum* 39, no. 1 (2008): 123–32.

62. This generated the notion of environmental critical load. In the context of acidification, this is the idea that emissions such as SO^2 are buffered by the environment up to but not beyond a critical threshold.

63. This was embedded in state agencies including the Finance Ministry (Finansdepartementet) and the Pollution Control Authority (Statens Forurensningstilsyn).

64. William Cronon, "Introduction: In Search of Nature," in *Uncommmon Ground: Rethinking the Human Place in Nature*, ed. William Cronon, 23–56 (New York: Norton, 1995), 35.

65. Roy Porter, *Enlightenment: Britain and the Creation of the Modern World* (London: Allen Lane, 2000), 138–39; Michael G. Barbour, "Ecological Fragmentation in the Fifties," in *Uncommon Ground: Rethinking the Human Place in Nature*, ed. William Cronon, 233–55 (New York: Norton, 1995); see also Kristin Asdal, "The Problematic Nature of Nature: The Post-constructivist Challenge to Environmental History," *History and Theory* 42 (2003): 60–74.

66. Philosophers and natural philosophers have understood this in different ways, often, for instance, distinguishing between observation (which in many empiricist theories of science is taken to be relatively solid) and inferences or theories built on those observations (which are taken to be conjectural). At the birth of the scientific revolution, Robert Boyle, for instance, distinguished what might be witnessed from the uncertain and possibly variable mechanisms created by God for generating witnessable phenomena; Steven Shapin and Simon Schaffer, *Leviathan and the Air Pump: Hobbes, Boyle and the Experimental Life* (Princeton, NJ: Princeton University Press, 1985), 24. A similar though nondivine division underpins Karl Popper's twentieth-century falsificationism; Karl R. Popper, *The Logic of Scientific Discovery* (London: Hutchinson, 1959). It was only with the work of the nonfoundational historians, best known in the work

of Thomas Kuhn, that the contextual basis of observation was systematically explored. Thomas S. Kuhn, *The Structure of Scientific Revolutions* (Chicago: University of Chicago Press, 1970).

67. Sandøy and Langåker, "Atlantic Salmon and Acidification in Southern Norway," 1344.

68. Particular phenomena (the amount of SO^2 or the health of salmon) will vary, but the assumption is that the basic characteristics of SO^2 or salmon do not.

69. These assumptions are indeed assumptions and could be otherwise, as is the case for the dominant traditions in Chinese classical philosophy. See David L. Hall and Roger T. Ames, *Anticipating China: Thinking through the Narratives of Chinese and Western Culture* (Albany: State University of New York Press, 1995).

70. For a version of this argument using different empirical materials and in the context of social science, see Law, "Seeing Like a Survey"; John Law, "Collateral Realities," in *The Politics of Knowledge*, ed. Fernando Domínguez Rubio and Patrick Baert, 156–78 (London: Routledge, 2011).

71. To catch a train or attend a meeting is to imply—and enact—a space-time box. For a sample of the literatures on the creation of contemporary Western space-time coordination see, for instance, Nigel Thrift, *Spatial Formations* (London: Sage, 1996).

72. For discussion, see Gouldner, "Romanticism and Classicism"; and Mannheim, "Conservative Thought." For a discussion of the relation between Danish and Norwegian Romanticism in relation to the French, see Elisabeth Oxfeldt, *Nordic Orientalism: Paris and the Cosmopolitan Imagination, 1800–1900* (Chicago: Museum Tusculanum Press, 2015).

73. Norwegian nation building, coinciding with national Romanticism in the late nineteenth century, can be described as a heterogeneous assemblage of different projects. Historian Øystein Sørensen has described the period from 1830 to 1860 as consisting of three such projects: the modernization efforts of the Norwegian intelligentsia, the national Romanticist vision of Henrik Wergeland (who wished to emphasize links with the cultural past to European modernization), and finally the national Romanticist nation-building project that located the nation's true identity among contemporary peasants. Øystein Sørensen, "Hegemonikamp om det Norske," in *Jakten på det norske: Perspektiver på utviklingen av en norsk nasjonal identitet på 1800-tallet*, ed. Øystein Sørensen, 26–30 (Oslo: Ad Notam Gyldendal, 1998); Oxfeldt, *Nordic Orientalism*, 105.

74. Gro Ween and Simone Abram, "The Norwegian Trekking Association: Trekking as Constituting the Nation," *Landscape Research* 37, no. 2 (2012): 160.

75. For a brief overview, see Iver B. Neumann, "State and Nation in the Nineteenth Century: Recent Research on the Norwegian Case," *Scandinavian Journal of History* 25, no. 3 (2000): 239–60.

76. Ween and Abram, "The Norwegian Trekking Association."

77. This is a large Norwegian NGO, with a current membership of 240,000. See the Norwegian Trekking Association website, https://english.dnt.no/.

78. For instance, Ween and Abrams discuss the importance of trails and tracks for transhumance agriculture; Ween and Abrams, "The Norwegian Trekking Association," 158–59.

79. For instance, emplacing trails in the landscape is a way of enabling particular views to emerge, or become visible, to the trekker.

80. An example of this is the enlightenment efforts associated with what has become known as the porridge feud. Astri Riddervold and Andreas Ropeid, "Popular Diet in Norway and Natural Science during the 19th Century: The Porridge Feud 1864–1866," *Ethnologia Scandinavica* (1984): 48–65.

81. See, for instance, discussion of William James's notion of the pluriverse in Bruno Latour, "Whose Cosmos, Which Cosmopolitics? Comments on the Peace Terms of Ulrich Beck," *Common Knowledge* 10, no. 3 (2004): 450–62.

82. See, for instance, Donna Haraway, "Situated Knowledges: The Science Question in Feminism and the Privilege of Partial Perspective," *Feminist Studies* 14, no. 3 (1988): 575–99; Haraway, *Primate Visions*; Latour, *We Have Never Been Modern*; Verran, "Re-imagining Land Ownership in Australia"; Dipesh Chakrabarty, *Provincializing Europe: Postcolonial Thought and Historical Difference* (Princeton, NJ: Princeton University Press, 2000); Helen Verran, *Science and an African Logic* (Chicago: University of Chicago Press, 2001); Bruno Latour, *War of the Worlds: What about Peace?* (Chicago: Prickly Paradigm, 2002); Law, *Aircraft Stories*; Mol, *The Body Multiple*; Charis Thompson, "When Elephants Stand for Competing Models of Nature," in *Complexity in Science, Technology, and Medicine*, ed. John Law and Annemarie Mol, 166–90 (Durham, NC: Duke University Press, 2002); Feit, "James Bay Crees' Life Projects and Politics"; Haraway, *When Species Meet*; Noble, "Justice, Transaction, Translation"; Arturo Escobar, *Territories of Difference: Place, Movements, Life, Redes* (Durham, NC: Duke University Press, 2008); Isabelle Stengers, "Experimenting with Refrains: Subjectivity and the Challenge of Escaping Modern Dualism," *Subjectivity* 22 (2008): 38–59; Blaser, "The Threat of the Yrmo"; de la Cadena, "Indigenous Cosmopolitics"; John Law and Wen-yuan Lin, "Cultivating Disconcertment," in *Sociological Routes and Political Roots*, ed. Michaela Benson and Rolland Munro, 135–53 (Oxford: Wiley-Blackwell, 2011); Isabelle Stengers, "'Another Science Is Possible!': A Plea for Slow Science" (Brussels: Université Libre de Brussels, 2011); Vicky Singleton and John Law, "Devices as Rituals: Notes on Enacting Resistance," *Journal of Cultural Economy* 6, no. 3 (2013): 259–77; Law and Lien, "Slippery."

83. Viveiros de Castro, "Cosmological Deixis and Amerindian Perspectivism." Note that we need the Amerindians to grasp these ideas and also to emplace them. When multinaturalism moves closer to home, it sparks far more controversy. See Berliner, Legrain, and van de Port, "Bruno Latour and the Anthropology of the Moderns."

84. Stengers, "Experimenting with Refrains," 55. For a discussion of subordinate practices or resistance within modernity that draws on Stengers, see Singleton and Law, "Devices as Rituals."

BIBLIOGRAPHY

Anonymous. "The Incredible Wild Salmon: Norway's Silvery Inheritance." Accessed March 2, 2018. https://web.archive.org/web/20160429211146/http://www.lachsverein.de/pdf/norwegen/wild_salmon.pdf.

Asdal, Kristin. "Enacting Things through Numbers: Taking Nature into Account/ing." *Geoforum* 39, no. 1 (2008): 123–32.

Asdal, Kristin. "The Problematic Nature of Nature: The Post-constructivist Challenge to Environmental History." *History and Theory* 42 (2003): 60–74.

Barad, Karen. *Meeting the Universe Halfway: Quantum Physics and the Entanglement of Matter and Meaning*. Durham, NC: Duke University Press, 2007.

Barbour, Michael G. "Ecological Fragmentation in the Fifties." In *Uncommon Ground: Rethinking the Human Place in Nature*, edited by William Cronon, 233–55. New York: Norton, 1995.

Barlaup, Bjørn, ed. *Redningsaksjonen for Vossolaksen*, vol. DN Utredning 1-2013. Trondheim: Direktoratet for Naturforvaltning, 2013. http://www.miljodirektoratet.no/old /dirnat/attachment/3072/DN-utredning-1-2013_nett.pdf.

Berliner, David, Laurent Legrain, and Mattijs van de Port. "Bruno Latour and the Anthropology of the Moderns." *Social Anthropology* 21, no. 4 (2013): 435–47.

Blaser, Mario. "The Threat of the Yrmo: The Political Ontology of a Sustainable Hunting Program." *American Anthropologist* 111, no. 1 (2009): 10–20.

Bonelli, Cristóbal. "Ontological Disorders: Nightmares, Psychotropic Drugs and Evil Spirits in Southern Chile." *Anthropological Theory* 12, no. 4 (2012): 407–26.

Callon, Michel. "Some Elements of a Sociology of Translation: Domestication of the Scallops and the Fishermen of Saint Brieuc Bay." *Sociological Review* 32, no. S1 (1984): 196–233.

Chakrabarty, Dipesh. *Provincializing Europe: Postcolonial Thought and Historical Difference*. Princeton, NJ: Princeton University Press, 2000.

Cronon, William. "Introduction: In Search of Nature." In *Uncommmon Ground: Rethinking the Human Place in Nature*, edited by William Cronon, 23–56. New York: Norton, 1995.

Cronon, William. "The Trouble with Wilderness: Or Getting Back to the Wrong Nature." In *Uncommmon Ground: Rethinking the Human Place in Nature*, edited by William Cronon, 69–90. New York: Norton, 1995.

Dalheim, Line. "Into the Wild and Back Again: Hatching 'Wild Salmon' in Western Norway." Master's thesis, University of Oslo, 2012.

de la Cadena, Marisol. "Indigenous Cosmopolitics in the Andes: Conceptual Reflections Beyond 'Politics.'" *Cultural Anthropology* 25, no. 2 (2010): 334–70.

Diserud, Ola H., Peder Fiske, and Kjetil Hindar. *Regionvis påvirkning av rømt oppdrettslaks på ville laksebestander i Norge* [Regional impact of escaped farm salmon on wild salmon populations in Norway]. Trondheim: Norsk Institutt for Naturforskning, 2010.

Escobar, Arturo. *Territories of Difference: Place, Movements, Life, Redes*. Durham, NC: Duke University Press, 2008.

"Explore the Oslo Region." Norway: Powered by Nature, 2017. https://www.visitnorway .com/about/.

Feit, Harvey A. "James Bay Crees' Life Projects and Politics: Histories of Place, Animal Partners and Enduring Relationships." In *In the Way of Development*, edited by Mario Blaser, Harvey A. Feit, and Glenn McRae, 92–110. London: Zed, 2004.

Gederaas, Lisbeth, Ingrid Salvesen, and Åslaug Viken, eds. 2007 *Norwegian Black List: Ecological Risk Analysis of Alien Species*. Trondheim: Norwegian Biodiversity Information Centre, 2007. https://www.artsdatabanken.no/Files/13975/Norsk_Svarteliste _2007_(PDF).

Gouldner, Alvin. "Romanticism and Classicism: Deep Structures in Social Science." *Diogenes* 21, no. 82 (1973): 88–107.

Granbo, Jan-Erik. "Fishing Diary." Granbo Flyfishing, September 11, 2001. http:// www.granbo-flyfishing.no/_english-edition/fiskedagbok.php?start_from=5&ucat =&archive=&subaction=&id=&.

Granbo, Jan-Erik. "Salmon Behaviour in Relation to Water Temperature and River Level." Granbo Flyfishing, 2015. http://www.granbo-flyfishing.no/_english-edition /laksens-adferd.html.

Hall, David L., and Roger T. Ames. *Anticipating China: Thinking through the Narratives of Chinese and Western Culture*. Albany: State University of New York Press, 1995.

Haraway, Donna J. "A Game of Cat's Cradle: Science Studies, Feminist Theory, Cultural Studies." *Configurations* 1 (1994): 59–71.

Haraway, Donna J. *Primate Visions: Gender, Race and Nature in the World of Modern Science*. London: Routledge and Chapman Hall, 1989.

Haraway, Donna J. "Situated Knowledges: The Science Question in Feminism and the Privilege of Partial Perspective." *Feminist Studies* 14, no. 3 (1988): 575–99.

Haraway, Donna J. *When Species Meet*. Minneapolis: University of Minnesota Press, 2008.

Hinchliffe, Steve, Matthew B. Kearnes, Monica Degen, and Sarah Whatmore. "Urban Wild Things: A Cosmopolitical Experiment." *Society and Space* 23, no. 5 (2005): 643–58.

Ingold, Tim "When ANT Meets SPIDER: Social Theory for Arthropods." In *Being Alive: Essays on Movement, Knowledge and Description*, edited by Tim Ingold, 89–94. Abingdon: Routledge, 2011.

Kuhn, Thomas S. *The Structure of Scientific Revolutions*. Chicago: University of Chicago Press, 1970.

Latour, Bruno. *An Inquiry into Modes of Existence: An Anthropology of the Moderns*. Cambridge, MA: Harvard University Press, 2013.

Latour, Bruno. "On Recalling ANT." In *Actor Network and After*, edited by John Law and John Hassard, 15–25. Oxford: Blackwell and the Sociological Review, 1999.

Latour, Bruno. *The Pasteurization of France*. Cambridge, MA: Harvard University Press, 1988.

Latour, Bruno. "Technology Is Society Made Durable." *Sociological Review* 38, no. 1 (1990): 103–31.

Latour, Bruno. *War of the Worlds: What about Peace?* Chicago: Prickly Paradigm, 2002.

Latour, Bruno. *We Have Never Been Modern*. Brighton: Harvester Wheatsheaf, 1993.

Latour, Bruno. "Whose Cosmos, Which Cosmopolitics? Comments on the Peace Terms of Ulrich Beck." *Common Knowledge* 10, no. 3 (2004): 450–62.

Law, John. *Aircraft Stories: Decentering the Object in Technoscience*. Durham, NC: Duke University Press, 2002.

Law, John. "Collateral Realities." In *The Politics of Knowledge*, edited by Fernando Domínguez Rubio and Patrick Baert, 156–78. London: Routledge, 2011.

Law, John. "Notes on Fish, Ponds and Theory." *Norsk Antropologisk Tidsskrift* 23, no. 3–4 (2012): 225–36.

Law, John. "Seeing Like a Survey." *Cultural Sociology* 3, no. 2 (2009): 239–56.

Law, John, and Marianne Elisabeth Lien. "Slippery: Field Notes on Empirical Ontology." *Social Studies of Science* 43, no. 3 (2013): 363–78.

Law, John, and Wen-yuan Lin. "Cultivating Disconcertment." In *Sociological Routes and Political Roots*, edited by Michaela Benson and Rolland Munro, 135–53. Oxford: Wiley-Blackwell, 2011.

Law, John, and Vicky Singleton. "ANT and Politics: Working in and on the World." *Qualitative Sociology* 36, no. 4 (2013): 485–502.

Lien, Marianne E. *Becoming Salmon: Aquaculture and the Domestication of a Fish.* Oakland: University of California Press, 2015.

Lien, Marianne E. "Feeding Fish Efficiently: Mobilising Knowledge in Tasmanian Salmon Farming." *Social Anthropology* 15, no. 2 (2007): 169–85.

Lien, Marianne E. "Unruly Appetites: Salmon Domestication 'All the Way Down.'" In *Arts of Living on a Damaged Planet*, edited by Anna Tsing, Nils Bubandt, Elaine Gan, and Heather Swanson, 107–24. Washington, DC: Island Press, 2017.

Lien, Marianne E. "Weeding Tasmanian Bush: Biomigration and Landscape Imagery." In *Holding Worlds Together: Ethnographies of Knowing and Belonging*, edited by Marianne Elisabeth Lien and Marit Melhuus, 103–21. Oxford: Berghahn, 2007.

Lien, Marianne E., and Aidan Davison. "Roots, Rupture and Remembrance: The Tasmanian Lives of the Monterey Pine." *Journal of Material Culture* 15, no. 2 (2010): 233–253.

Lien, Marianne Elisabeth, and John Law. "'Emergent Aliens': On Salmon, Nature and Their Enactment." *Ethnos* 76, no. 1 (2011): 65–87.

Liu, Yajie, Jon Olaf Olaussen, and Anders Skonhoft. "Wild and Farmed Salmon in Norway—a Review." *Marine Policy* 35, no. 3 (2011): 413–18.

Mannheim, Karl. "Conservative Thought." In *Essays on Sociology and Social Psychology*, edited by Karl Mannheim, 74–164. London: Routledge and Kegan Paul, 1953.

Miljøverndepartmentet [Norway's Ministry of the Environment]. "St.prp. nr. 32 (2006–2007): Om vern av villaksen og ferdigstilling av nasjonale laksevassdrag og laksefjorder." December 15, 2006. https://www.regjeringen.no/nb/dep/md/dok /regpubl/stprp/2006-2007/stprp-nr-32-2006-2007-/id=442076.

Mol, Annemarie. *The Body Multiple: Ontology in Medical Practice.* Durham, NC: Duke University Press, 2002.

Mol, Annemarie. "Ontological Politics: A Word and Some Questions." In *Actor Network Theory and After*, edited by John Law and John Hassard, 74–89. Oxford: Blackwell / Sociological Review, 1999.

"Must-See Nature Attractions." Norway: Powered by Nature, 2017. https://www .visitnorway.com/things-to-do/nature-attractions/.

Neumann, Iver B. "State and Nation in the Nineteenth Century: Recent Research on the Norwegian Case." *Scandinavian Journal of History* 25, no. 3 (2000): 239–60.

"Newcomers to the Farm." UiO: Department of Social Anthropology, December 15, 2018. http://www.sv.uio.no/sai/english/research/projects/newcomers/.

Noble, Brian. "Justice, Transaction, Translation: Blackfoot Tipi Transfers and WIPO's Search for the Facts of Traditional Knowledge Exchange." *American Anthropologist* 109, no. 2 (2007): 338–49.

Nordeide, Anita. "Møte mellom menneske og laks: Om laksefiskepraksiser i Namsen-vassdraget" [Meeting between human and salmon: On salmon fishing practices in the Namsen watershed]. Master's thesis, University of Oslo, 2012.

"Northern Norway: The Kingdom of Light." Norway: Powered by Nature, 2017. https://www.visitnorway.com/places-to-go/northern-norway/.

Nustad, Knut Gunnar, Cato Berg, and Rune Flikke. "Human-Fish Temporalities in Aurland, Norway." Paper delivered at the annual meeting of the American Anthropological Association, San Francisco, November 14–18, 2012.

Ødegard, Merethe. "I samme båt: Stakere, fluefiskere og maskulinitet i laksefisket i Alta" [In the same boat: Oarsmen, fly fishermen and masculinity in salmon fishing in Alta]. Master's thesis, University of Oslo, 2013.

Oxfeldt, Elisabeth. *Nordic Orientalism: Paris and the Cosmopolitan Imagination, 1800–1900.* Chicago: Museum Tusculanum Press, 2015.

Popper, Karl R. *The Logic of Scientific Discovery.* London: Hutchinson, 1959.

Porter, Roy. *Enlightenment: Britain and the Creation of the Modern World.* London: Allen Lane, 2000.

Riddervold, Astri, and Andreas Ropeid. "Popular Diet in Norway and Natural Science during the 19th Century: The Porridge Feud 1864–1866." *Ethnologia Scandinavica* (1984): 48–65.

Sandøy, Steinar, and R. M. Langåker. "Atlantic Salmon and Acidification in Southern Norway: A Disaster in the 20th Century, but a Hope for the Future?" *Water, Air and Soil Pollution* 130, no. 1–4 (2001): 1343–48.

Sardi, Max. "Norway—a Guide to Salmon Fishing." Sportfish, 2017. https://www.sportfish.co.uk/norway-a-guide-to-salmon-fishing.

Shapin, Steven, and Simon Schaffer. *Leviathan and the Air Pump: Hobbes, Boyle and the Experimental Life.* Princeton, NJ: Princeton University Press, 1985.

Singleton, Vicky, and John Law. "Devices as Rituals: Notes on Enacting Resistance." *Journal of Cultural Economy* 6, no. 3 (2013): 259–77.

Sørensen, Øystein. "Hegemonikamp om det Norske." In *Jakten på det norske; Perspektiver på utviklingen av en norsk nasjonal identitet på 1800-tallet* [Seeking out the Norwegian: Perspectives on the development of a Norwegian national identity in the nineteenth century], edited by Øystein Sørensen, 26–30. Oslo: Ad Notam Gyldendal, 1998.

Star, Susan Leigh. "Power, Technologies and the Phenomenology of Conventions: On Being Allergic to Onions." *Sociological Review* 38, no. S1 (1991): 26–56.

Stengers, Isabelle. "'Another Science Is Possible!' A Plea for Slow Science." Brussels: Université Libre de Brussels, 2011.

Stengers, Isabelle. "The Cosmopolitical Proposal." In *Making Things Public: Atmospheres of Democracy*, edited by Bruno Latour and Peter Weibel, 994–1003. Karslruhe: ZKM, 2005.

Stengers, Isabelle. "Experimenting with Refrains: Subjectivity and the Challenge of Escaping Modern Dualism." *Subjectivity* 22 (2008): 38–59.

Strathern, Marilyn. "Cutting the Network." *Journal of the Royal Anthropological Institute* 2, no. 3 (1996): 517–35.

Strathern, Marilyn. *Partial Connections.* Lanham, MD: Rowman and Littlefield, 1991.

Thompson, Charis. "When Elephants Stand for Competing Models of Nature." In *Complexity in Science, Technology, and Medicine,* edited by John Law and Annemarie Mol, 166–90. Durham, NC: Duke University Press, 2002.

Thorstad, Eva B., and Torbjørn Forseth. *Status for norske laksebestander i 2017* [Status of Norwegian salmon stocks in 2017]. Trondheim: Vitenskapelig råd for lakseforvaltning [Norwegian Scientific Advisory Committee for Atlantic Salmon]. https://brage.bibsys.no/xmlui/handle/11250/2446896.

Thrift, Nigel. *Spatial Formations.* London: Sage, 1996.

Verran, Helen. "Re-imagining Land Ownership in Australia." *Postcolonial Studies* 1, no. 2 (1998): 237–54.

Verran, Helen. *Science and an African Logic.* Chicago: University of Chicago Press, 2001.

Vigfússon, Orri. "Norway's Wild Salmon Facing Extinction?" www.karuvaaraflyfishing.com, accessed November 20, 2015. http://www.karuvaaraflyfishing.com/?id=1&s=1243186195251.

Vitenskapelig råd for lakseforvaltning. *Status for norske laksebestander i 2012* [Status of Norwegian salmon stocks in 2012]. Trondheim: Vitenskapelig råd for lakseforvaltning [Norwegian Scientific Advisory Committee for Atlantic Salmon]. http://www.nina.no/archive/nina/PppBasePdf/Rapport%20fra%20vitenskapelig%20r%C3%A5d%20for%20lakseforvaltning/2012/Thorstad%20Status%20Rapport%20fra%20Vitenskapsr%C3%A5det%20for%20lakseforvaltning%204%202012.pdf.

Vitenskapelig råd for lakseforvaltning. *Status for norske laksebestander i 2015* [Status of Norwegian salmon stocks in 2015]. Rapport fra Vitenskapelig råd for lakseforvaltning no. 8. Trondheim: Vitenskapelig råd for lakseforvaltning, [Norwegian Scientific Advisory Committee for Atlantic Salmon]. http://www.nina.no/archive/nina/PppBasePdf/Rapp%20Vitr%C3%A5dlaks/Thorstad%20Status%20RVitr%C3%A5d%20olaks2015-8.pdf.

Viveiros de Castro, Eduardo. "Cosmological Deixis and Amerindian Perspectivism." *Journal of the Royal Anthropological Institute* 4, no. 3 (1998): 469–88.

Ween, Gro, and Simone Abram. "The Norwegian Trekking Association: Trekking as Constituting the Nation." *Landscape Research* 37, no. 2 (2012): 155–71.

Williams, Raymond. *Problems in Materialism and Culture.* London: Verso, 1980.

SIX

HUMANS AND TERRANS IN THE GAIA WAR

Eduardo Viveiros de Castro and Déborah Danowski

What do you do, after you stop pretending?
—DOUGALD HINE, The Dark Mountain Project

There is a growing sentiment in contemporary culture—though by no means a unanimous, let alone consistent, conviction[1]—that the two actants in our mytho-anthropology, "humankind" and "world" (species and planet, societies and their environments, subject and object, thought and being, etc.), have entered a nefarious cosmological or spatiotemporal conjunction associated with the controversial names of Anthropocene and Gaia. The first name designates a new time, or rather a new age of time—a new concept and a new experience of temporality—in which the difference of magnitude between the scale of human history and the biological and geophysical scales has decreased dramatically, if not reversed, with the environment changing faster than society. With that, the near future becomes not only increasingly unforeseeable but perhaps also increasingly impossible. The second name, Gaia, designates a new way of experimenting space, drawing attention to the fact that our world, the Earth, having suddenly become at once exiguous and fragile, susceptible and implacable, has taken on the appearance of a threatening Power that evokes those uncaring, unpredictable, and unfathomable deities of our archaic past. Unpredictability, unfathomability, and a sense of panic in the face of a loss of control, if not of hope altogether: these are no doubt new challenges for modernity's proud intellectual assuredness.

Three authors serve us as guides in our analysis, not only because they recognize the magnitude and gravity of current transformations, but because they insist on the need for a metaphysical reinvention—a reconceptualization and/or refiguration—of the notions of humanity and world elicited by the Anthropocene's and Gaia's bursting on the scene: Dipesh Chakrabarty, Günther Anders, and Bruno Latour.

The Impossible Species

In "The Climate of History," Dipesh Chakrabarty drew attention to the fact that the Anthropocene seems to demand the recovery of the concept, refused outright by critical theories of capitalist globalization, of humanity as denoting the human species. This is because, he claims, the consequences of climate catastrophe are only comprehensible when we think of humans as a form of life, and their more recent trajectory (Holocenic in the strict etymological sense) as part of the long history of life on Earth. That does not mean, of course, that we should subscribe to pre-Darwinian speciesist essentialism, or some kind of sociotechnical teleologism, ignoring the historically contingent character of capitalism and its dependency on the intensive use of fossil fuels. However, we need an understanding of that which, outside the narrow limits of history as an academic discipline, pertains to so-called deep history—the cultural-genetic mutations themselves brought about by oscillations and multicyclical or catastrophic changes in the behavior of the Earth system that created humankind hundreds of thousands of years ago—if we are to come to grips with how dependent we, as a species among others, are on other Earth species, and therefore on the planetary thermodynamic conditions that sustain the present biosphere and which are, as we know, to a large extent reciprocally conditioned by it.[2] Global warming will bring changes that will remain for several tens of centuries, maybe even hundreds of thousands of years. Not even capitalism will last so long—which is at least some consolation, after all.

Whereas responsibility for environmental collapse cannot be uniformly distributed—it is glaringly obvious which geographical regions and social segments benefited historically from the processes that set it in motion—its consequences will be much more so: the Anthropocene, Chakrabarty alerts us, "points to a shared catastrophe."[3] In any case, we all know how the geopolitical landscape is changing in that respect, with the rise of China, India, Brazil, and so on as economic powerhouses with a promising eco-toxic future, and how this veritable arms race as regards the acceleration of growth has played a part in further complicating the diplomatic impasses around the environmental question, already complicated in view of the inertia, intransigence, and greed of core capitalist countries.[4] Everything takes place as if some of the erstwhile victims wished to claim their own share in the now enviable condition (cui bono?) of future culprits of the shared catastrophe.

The polemical note in "The Climate of History" resides in the assertion that the history (historicity) of climate change does not fit within the history (and historiography) of globalization, which entails that the usual critique of capitalism runs the risk of tragically underestimating the real problem: "The problematic of globalization allows us to read climate change only as a crisis of capitalist management. While there is no denying that climate change has profoundly to do with the history of capital, a critique that is only a critique of capital is not sufficient for addressing questions relating to human history once . . . the Anthropocene has begun to loom on the horizon of our present."[5]

It remains the case that the biocosmopolitical consciousness required by the new age would call for a kind of historical subject that Chakrabarty paradoxically regards as impossible: humankind as a species, precisely. According to him, the concept of species, politically mobilized by naturalists such as Edmund Wilson, plays "a quasi-Hegelian role . . . in the same way as the multitude or the masses in Marxist writings," but it is (as opposed to the Marxist masses?) a collective identity that is phenomenologically empty.[6] Human beings, says Chakrabarty, never experience themselves as a species; they can only intellectually apprehend themselves as a case of the concept: "Even if we were to emotionally identify with a word like mankind, we would not know what being a species is, for, in species history, humans are only an instance of the concept species as indeed would be any other life form. But one never experiences being a concept."[7] We admit to our difficulty in following the author's line of reasoning at this crucial juncture. It is possible that what Chakrabarty lacks here, so to speak, is greater attention to those subaltern peoples and discourses that he has analyzed so well elsewhere.[8] What is missing is perhaps a conceptual analogon that could play the role of that originary prespecific and prehistoric, generic nature of the humankind that we encounter in indigenous mythologies, a genericness that, precisely, affords the humankind of reference (the ethnos as concrete universal) the possibility of a phenomenological apprehension, as intense as one may wish, of its own precarious specificity as affectual being, lived corporeality, perspectival subjectivity in perpetual cosmopolitical tension with the other humankinds hidden under the corporeality of other species.[9] The ontological solidarity of the human species (i.e., the ethnos of reference) with the other peoples, collectives, and interests that populate, dispute, and constitute the Earth is not, for many nonmodern people, the inert (conceptual) consequence of a natural history, but an active (experiential) given of the social history of the ensemble of the living as differentiated actualization of a precosmological anthropomorphic potency. Chakrabarty's concept of the Anthropocene, in short, seems to us to need a little more ethnological comparativism and translative curiosity.

This capital text—one of the great merits of which, to our minds, resides in the admission of the insufficiency of the critique of capitalism to account for planetary crisis—thus ends with a surprising confession of perplexity.[10] The human species, Chakrabarty concludes, can perhaps be the provisional name of the subject of a "new universal history of humans."[11] But, he adds, "we can never understand this universal . . . that arises from a shared sense of a catastrophe"—from a shared sense of the imminence, that is, "of a naked apocalypse, an apocalypse without the Kingdom," instead of the glorious transfiguration of the revolutionary apocalypse that prepares the Kingdom, in the Christian and Marxist style.[12] This is a universal that cannot positively subsume particulars, and which for that reason only deserves the name of "a *negative human history*."[13] Which would mean perhaps that humankind's only common finality is its end, its extinction. In fact, for as long as one tacks onto "universal history," taken as self-evident, the ambiguous restrictive qualification "human," it seems to us that it will be difficult to exit the Anthropocene both intellectually and phenomenologically and to pay all the necessary attention to the intrusion of Gaia.

Despite resorting to the notion of species in his reflection on the mutation undergone by humankind with the advent of the nuclear age—namely, our passage from the condition of a "genre of mortals" to a "mortal genre," a species whose end has become metaphysically imminent—Günther Anders insists on the deceiving character of expressions such as "the threat of humankind to itself" or "atomic suicide."[14] These evoke an image of humankind as an entity endowed with a single universal essence, but with a soul that is tragically torn between two possible actions, pushing or not pushing the button of nuclear holocaust, the struggle between which would thus take place inside each one of us, perhaps as a conflict between two opposed inclinations of our soul or generic essence. This conception is attractive to the extent that it allows some room for hope, the hope that our will, this supposedly neutral instance, could exercise the role of judge, making the good choice provided it is informed by reason. Yet Anders thinks, much on the contrary, that we have no right to dissimulate the existence, in the time of the end brought about by the advent of the nuclear age, of two distinct and irreconcilable sides, the culprits and the victims. It is not suicide we are dealing with, but the murder of one part of the species by another part of the same species. At the same time, nuclear technology being what it is, annihilation would eventually extend to all humans indistinctly, so that, according to him, "fission" would dialectically pass over into "fusion": "the effect of nuclear war will no longer bear any trace of duality, as the enemies will constitute a one and only vanquished humankind."[15] Thus, as in Chakrabarty, it seems that there will only be one humankind when there is none— when the last human being has vanished from the face of the Earth.[16]

In the context of climate catastrophe that defines the Anthropocene, the line separating victims and culprits is historically clear from a collective or societal point of view, but much harder to trace from the point of view of individual action. This is because, today, many of us (us humans, and the nonhumans we have enslaved or colonized) are victims and culprits all at once, in each action we engage in, at the push of every button, with every portion of food or animal feed we swallow—even if it is as obvious as it is essential that we do not confuse McDonald's itself and the teenager conditioned into consuming junk food, or Monsanto and the small farmer obliged to spray his genetically modified corn with glyphosate, let alone the pharmaceutical industry and the cattle force-fed with antibiotics and hormones.[17] Even if, as with the nuclear apocalypse, all of us at any rate will, some sooner, some later, become victims of the crossing of planetary boundaries, this does not prevent us from identifying the opposing camps, as Latour points out now and Anders himself suggested: "The time of the end in which we live . . . contains two kinds of men: culprits and victims. We should take this duality into account: the name of our work is 'combat.'"[18]

The author of *Le Temps de la Fin*, in short, calls for a veritable political combat, a war in the sense that Latour will borrow from Carl Schmitt, a

toxic author that was Anders's ideological antipode: war as strictly immanent conflict, where there is no possible intervention from an external arbiter or superior authority, in which it is necessary to confront the enemy
in a scenario where the physical annihilation ("existential negation") of the
other is a real possibility. We have seen that, for Chakrabarty, the two actors
conjured by the Anthropocene are the human species and the Earth, but,
even though humans have become a natural force on a geological scale and
the Earth system has taken on the unpredictable behavior that we attribute
to beasts (the climate beast . . .), the conflict appears to have a clear arbiter,
which is science: climatology, geophysics, natural history. If we wish to
survive the Anthropocene, Chakrabarty seems to say, it is to this transcendent instance that we have to pay heed and obedience. In Anders's nuclear
apocalypse, on the contrary, if we can say that there will be no instance exterior to the interested parties, it is because all are either on the side of the
murderers or on the side of the victims, but also because, at the same time,
all will ultimately be victims, including the world in which the conflict will
unfold. Bruno Latour, in turn, while also speaking of a war that has already
started, stresses that this war must be "officially" declared before peace
talks can begin, not only in order to avoid the "end of the world" through
the generalization of ecocide that follows the expansion of the modernization
front, but also to create or institute a world, a "common world" to be more
precise, a modus vivendi among the inhabitants of a planet heretofore
placed under the sign of Gaia, a "divine character" (theôteros) very dissimilar to nature or divinity in the modern period.[19] A character that above all
has no interest in acting as external arbiter in the conflict between the two
peoples, the two opposing demoi engaged in a struggle to the death around
the nomos (order, distribution, appropriation) of the Earth.[20]

For some time now, Latour has been collecting evidence of the objective historical crumbling of the distinction that founds modernity: that
between nature and politics. More recently, he has indicated planetary environmental collapse as at once the most real result and the most eloquent
proof of the unreality of that distinction—which creates a situation that we
could describe as the multiple organ failure of the cosmopolitical government (nomos) of the moderns. In his 2013 Gifford Lectures, the relation
between the two poles of humankind (anthropos as demos) and world (nature as theos, but also the world as ordered/appropriated by modernity) is
subjected to a detailed analysis. Crucially, they are reconstructed in terms
that seek above all to highlight the fractured, divided, untotalizable,

polemical, contingent—in a word: political—character of both actants, and the resulting impossibility of dividing them as such into two homogeneous opposing camps. The two mythical characters of our essay merge here into a single-sided figure; humankind is not on the other side of being, is not the world's reverse or negative, just as the world is not the context (the environment) of a subject that counterdefines it as object. It is not this duality that counts, nor is this the negativity that imposes itself.

However, it is exactly for that reason that it is necessary to recognize that we are at war. If the falling apart of the modern constitution was already visible to the naked eye, as is attested by the proposal of an ontological reform of modernity long developed by Latour and finally presented in his *An Inquiry into Modes of Existence*, the climate crisis—a subtle but insistent undercurrent running across that book, brought to the fore in its closing pages—has given this war a character of urgency, placing before us the imperative of practically determining who these all are, against whom exactly the war is being waged, and which side we are on.[21] The path to a desired future universal peace can only be walked, as Latour sees it, if we start by a multiple and combined refusal of the present cosmopolitical assemblage (demos-theos-nomos) instituted by the moderns. Refusal, then, of the precocious cosmopolitical unification of the multiverse (that is, a refusal of the unification of the world, this multinatural space of coexistence for planes of immanence traced by the numberless collectives that traverse and animate it); refusal of the separation of and precedence of fact over value, given over constructed, natural over artificial, nature over culture; refusal of the power of police ascribed to science as the sole authorized intermediary of first nature; refusal of the only true fetishism, to wit, the self-referentiality of the economy as the science of second nature, with its pretension to measuring values that are in fact established by the measuring activity itself. Refusal, finally, of the idea of anthropos as a prematurely unified entity, a figure that eclipses the contradictory and heterogeneous plurality of conditions and interests of the collectives that are faced with Gaia's daunting theophany in the name, once again, of a nature—human nature, this strange amalgam of the first and second natures contrasted in *An Inquiry into Modes of Existence*.

So that we can follow the "political theology" argument developed by Latour in the Gifford Lectures, which are a postface of sorts to *An Inquiry*, we should begin by taking up once more the world pole of our mythical macroscheme. The author entreats us to witness an ongoing historical transition (and to fight for its completion) between two images of the world: the modern Earth of Galilean science, a heavenly body among others that wanders across an isotropic and infinite universe in conformity with the eternal laws of mathematics; and James Lovelock's Gaia (championed by Lynn Margulis and others), an exceptional local region in the universe, a cosmic accident created by life's geomorphic agency, whose physicochemical contribution to the constitution of a far-from-equilibrium system was and is determinant for the continuation of life itself. The macrophysical agency of humans on which Chakrabarty rightly insists is, therefore, only one example, though an admittedly disastrous one for humans and other living beings in the present geological epoch, of this ontological inseparability of ground and form, of the living and its environment. What Isabelle Stengers has aptly named the "intrusion of Gaia" marks a decisive event in this hapax that is Lovelock's Gaia, the advent of a novel historical situation in which it has become definitively impossible to live without taking into account the meaning of this inseparability.[22]

Gaia-Earth thus detaches itself from heavenly body–Earth, the sublunary becomes once more distinct from the superlunary, and the idea of world recovers a radically closed sense, which is also to say that it becomes immanent: terrestrial, local, proximate, secular, nonunified. The expression "this sublunary realm of ours" (or "sublunar oikos of Gaia") is recurrent throughout the Gifford Lectures, always appearing in contexts in which the author differentiates between the situation of universal legality (*quid juris?*) of nature, such as asserted by relativity or quantum mechanics—a legality that Latour does not refuse as such, but only as a mystical emanation of a disembodied model of science as supreme arbiter, mystical oracle supposedly come to dethrone the old deities—and the situation of empirical entanglement that we could name, for once without pejorative connotations, Terran exceptionalism.[23] It is here that we can see the full political significance of the choice presented by Paul Ennis between the cosmocentrism of speculative realists, "deterritorializers" who are firmly reterritorialized in big science (the physico-mathematical knowledge and techno-economic *dispositif* of access to what is farthest from us), and the geocentrism of "continental philosophy," represented in Latour's case by a passion for "small sciences" (Terran sciences in the double sense of being close to home—proximate knowledges concerning the soil, the climate, ecology, the city—and of being secular, that is, engaging nature as an internal, multiple, animate, the perpetually *in fieri* correlate of the concrete activity of scientists).[24] Implications that Isabelle Stengers has perhaps managed to make explicit even more radically than Latour with her notion of "slow science."[25] For the only thing we need to accelerate, in light of the "coming barbarism," is precisely the process of slowing down the sciences and the civilization that instrumentalizes them.[26]

Even though it is essentially animate—as in a fairy tale, where each object can cut itself off the background in order to become an actor in the proscenium—Latour's Gaia is not a superanimate entity, a mysterious all-powerful eminence, a superorganism endowed with a puzzling type of intentionality that would be akin to the balanced result of all the forces acting in its bosom, which would suppose an engineer or governor that would just distribute the roles and functions of previously existing parts, coordinating them through feedback loops.[27] In Latour's reinterpretation (or scientific portrait, we could say with a Deleuzian wink) of Lovelock, Gaia is a gigantic discordant harmony, mutable and contingent, "a mess" of multiple intentionalities distributed among all agents.[28] Each organism manipulates its environment "to render its own survival slightly less improbable."[29] That dissolves the opposition between inside and outside, organism and environment, since the environment of each organism, and therefore of all organisms, is all other organisms (the environment as a society of societies, as in the Amerindian world?); their entangled intentionalities constitute overlapping "waves of action" (as in Tarde's monads?) in perpetual cycles of ebb and flow, expansion and contraction. If Gaia is also a living and plural world, as in the Edenic image of the wilderness, it is not a harmonious or balanced one, let alone dependent, for its existence, on the exclusion of humankind, as if the latter were an extraterrestrial invader come to spoil a pastoral idyll. The Edenic world is a world without history (the latter only beginning, precisely, with the Fall), whereas Gaia is first and foremost made of history, is history materialized, a contingent and tumultuous sequence of events rather than the unfolding of a superlunary causality following timeless laws. In Latour's conception, thus, it is not so much the case that human history comes to an unexpected fusion with geohistory; rather, it is Gaia-Earth that becomes historicized, narrativized as human history—with which it shares, and this caveat is essential, the absence of any intervention from whatever kind of providence.[30]

What we still need to work out is who is the demos of Gaia, the people that this entity gathers and convokes, and who their enemy is. As stated above, we must begin by rejecting any sole candidate for the (in)dignity of being the Anthropocene's eponymous. The Wilsonian notion of species is dismissed less on the grounds of its phenomenological evanescence, as in Chakrabarty, than because it is a tributary of modernity's apolitical, ahistorical conception of nature, as well as of science's absolute power of arbitrage. But neither are the revolutionary masses of the classical left, that other recurring incarnation of the modern universal, up to the task; if the latter-day priests of the philosophy of praxis are to be believed, their liberation continues to depend on a generalization and intensification of the modernization front, on the practical (environmental destruction) as well as theoretical (the cult of nature and reason) levels. What the Anthropocene preempts is precisely the notion of an anthropos, a universal subject (species, but also class or multitude) capable of acting as a single people. The properly ethnopolitical situation of "human" as intensive and extensive multiplicity of peoples must be acknowledged as being directly implicated in the Anthropocene crisis. If there is no positive human interest, it is because there is a diversity of political alignments among the various world peoples or cultures with several other nonhuman actants and peoples (constituting what Latour calls "collectives") against the self-appointed spokespeople of universal human. The multiverse, the antenomic or precosmic background state, remains nonunified, on the human as well as on the world side. All unification lies in the future, under what we could call a multiple hypothetical mode, and will depend on negotiating capacities once the "war of the worlds," as Latour has called it elsewhere, has been declared. In this older text by Latour, "war of the worlds" made reference above all to the relations between the moderns and other peoples along the so-called modernization front.[31] In the Gifford Lectures, Latour redefines the two opposing camps as humans (the moderns who believe it will be possible to go on living in the unified, indifferent nature of the Holocene) and Terrans (the people of Gaia), even though he also sometimes refers to a war between humans and Gaia, which therefore appears the enemy of humans proper.[32]

The Gaia war is a war of the worlds, and not a conflict about the present and future state of the world, because we are not discussing whether there are such things as global warming and an ongoing environmental collapse; these are among the best-documented—"referenced" in Latour's sense—phenomena in the history of sciences.[33] We are not dealing with a matter of fact, since there is hardly any significant controversy among scientists concerning the anthropogenic origin of climate catastrophe. Certainly, that does not stop segments of public opinion, academia included—not to mention governments, big corporations, and their "merchants of doubt"—from questioning that consensus and insisting on business as usual, nor does it dampen green capitalist optimism about "crisis as opportunity."[34] That this is so is because the rationalist theory of action (from establishing facts to discussing the measures to be taken and finally to taking action) does not function in such cases where matters of fact and matters of concern prove themselves to be indissolubly entangled, as the Cold War's nuclear crisis made perfectly obvious. What is at stake in environmental controversy is the positions in which actors are politically implicated, where some have everything to lose while others have a lot to gain, which entails that the distinction between fact and value has, precisely, no value whatsoever.[35] It is a civil war situation, and not a police operation exercised from a point of legitimate authority, in order to bring delinquents back to reason through application of the law. It is, in short, a matter of deciding what world we want to live in.

If the Terrans of the Anthropocene cannot be confused with the human species as a whole, would that entail that the people of Gaia are a part of that species, and that species alone? Terrans are the party toward which Latour seems inclined, the one he seeks to evoke and convoke in his lectures in political theology.[36] Ontologically and politically tied to the Earth's cause, Terrans are today up in arms, although Latour hopes, in a strange repetition of Carl Schmitt, that they "might be the 'artisans of peace'" against the ambiguous and treacherous humans.[37] These are, it is well understood, none other than the moderns, that race—originally northwestern, but increasingly less European and more Chinese, Indian, Brazilian—which twice denied the Earth: first by defining itself as technologically exempt from nature's trials, then by defining itself as the only civilization to have escaped the closed (but dangerous and unpredictable) world of archaic animisms, the only one who opened itself up to the infinite (but saturated with imperturbable necessity) universe of inanimate matter.

But the author of *We Have Never Been Modern* does not seem too sure what to think about his Terrans. At times they are conceived as an emerging network of independent Latourian scientists (as opposed to modernist scientists and their corporate backers), practicing a "fully incarnated," dynamic, politicized science that is oriented toward our sublunary realm;

they represent "the small, the tiny source of hope" that the author is not entirely convinced we should still hold on to ("it is my *duty* to be optimistic").[38] At other times, Terrans appear as the name of a common cause, which concerns all of the planet's collectives, but which can only properly come together if future ex-moderns make their anxiously anticipated vow of humility and open up a space for cosmopolitical dialogue:

> If the multiverse is reintroduced and if the natural sciences are relocated inside it, is it possible to let the other collectives stop being "cultures" and give them full access to reality by letting them compose their cosmos, but by using other keys, other modes of extension than the one allowed by knowledge production? Such a reinterpretation is especially relevant today because, if nature is not universal, climates have always been important to all people. The reintroduction of climates and atmospheres as the new common cosmopolitical concern gives a new urgency to this communality between collectives.[39]

A throw of the dice of the "common world" will therefore never abolish the multiverse. It is less a matter of theoretical universality than of practical interest, a question of subsistence. The climate, that variable and fluctuating thing par excellence, becomes the element of historico-political synchronization of the interest of all the world's peoples. What the weather is like becomes what counts (in) the flow of time.[40] In that respect, Latour's "common world" is the opposite of a "world without us" in the sense of a universe without anyone, a cosmos unified by the absence of experience, by the unreality of everything that is not figure and movement.

However, our author hesitates when it comes to identifying his Terrans.[41] In the fifth conference, he identifies these "people bound to the Earth" with the two human characters in Béla Tarr's *The Turin Horse*, perpetually condemned to survive—one should really say *subvive*—on an Earth that progressively loses its worldy condition.[42] We must confess that this move strikes us as a terribly enigmatic one. It would no doubt be reasonable to take the deadly monotony that crushes the film's protagonists as an eloquent metaphor of the condition of so many indigenous peoples around the world after the modernization front crossed their lives.[43] (Or maybe, as some have argued, as an allegory of the shameful debacle of socialism.) In that case, however, we should not forget to note the fleeting flash of a solitary and incongruous ray of joy in the film, brought and carried away by the gypsy cart that noisily turns up at the farm to ask for water and then travels on, presenting the female protagonist (who, invited to come with them, declines) with a mysterious book that talks about the closing and demolition of churches.[44] Maybe those gypsies (one should pause to think what it means to be a gypsy in Hungary these days) are the true anticipatory image of the Terran vanguard, capable of leading the war against humans all the way to its decisive moments. For it is difficult to conceive the people of Gaia as a majority, as the universalization of European good conscience; Terrans cannot but be an "irremediably minor" people, however numerous they may come to be, a people that would never mistake the territory for the Earth.[45] In that regard, they probably resemble less the "phantom public" of Western democracies than the people that is missing which Deleuze and Guattari speak of: Kafka and Melville's minor people, Arthur Rimbaud's inferior race, the Indian that the philosopher becomes ("perhaps 'so that' the Indian who is himself Indian becomes something else and tears himself away from his own agony")—the people, that is, to come; capable of launching a "resistance to the present" and thus of creating "a new earth," the world to come.[46]

The End of the World as a Fractal Event

I do not want to die again.
—DAVI KOPENAWA

Further into his account, Latour wonders whether it would not be possible to "accept the candidacy of those people who claim to be assembled, for instance, by Pachamama, the Earth goddess."[47] He is obviously referring to Amerindian peoples and their fellow nonmoderns, who have increasingly adapted Western environmental rhetoric to their cosmologies, conceptual vocabularies, and existential projects, and retranslated the latter into a modernized language whose political intent is unequivocal and has started to make itself heard by the citizens of privileged societies in the global North—at least by those who have realized that, this time, things will turn out badly for everyone, everywhere. Latour, however, does not think that these "people of Pachamama" are really up to the task: "Maybe, if only we could be sure that what passes for a respect for the Earth is not due to their small numbers and to the relative weakness of their technology. None of those so called 'traditional' people, the wisdom of which we often admire, is prepared to scale up their ways of life to the size of the giant technical metropolises in which are now corralled more than half of the human race."[48]

It seems to us that Latour fails to consider the possibility that the generally small populations and relatively weak technologies of indigenous peoples and so many other sociopolitical minorities of the Earth could become a crucial advantage and resource in a postcatastrophic time, or, if one wishes, in a permanently diminished human world. Our author does not seem prepared, himself, to accept the highly likely possibility that we—the people of the (capitalist) core, the overweight, media-controlled, psychopharmacologically stabilized automata of technologically advanced societies that are highly dependent on a monumental consumption (or rather, waste) of energy—that we, when the chips are down, might be the ones who will have to scale down our precious ways of living.[49] As a matter of fact, if someone needs to be prepared for something, that someone is us, the ones who are crowded together in "giant technical metropolises."

The opposition between moderns and nonmoderns, developed in Latour's seminal *We Have Never Been Modern*, largely depended on the idea of a difference of scale, that is, the difference in length of sociotechnical networks in these two regimes of collectives. In his proposal for a new constitution, Latour's concern was precisely with how to retain the "long networks" of modern collectives, considered as an undeniable historical step forward. But given that the Anthropocene consists in the collapse of scalar magnitudes, when the species as biological agent becomes species as geophysical force (through the historical mediation of the species as thaumaturgical engineer), when political economy meets cosmic entropy, it is the very ideas of scale and dimension that seem out of scale. After all, is it not Latour himself who observes, in the same conferences, that "nothing [is] at the right scale"? What do we know about the expansion and reduction of scales we will have to undergo in the course of this century? Not much. The future is ever less certain; better (or worse) still, what can be known about it is only that, as the song goes, "nothing will be like before."[50]

As for the small population of "so called 'traditional'" peoples, there are in fact around 370 million indigenous people—members of collectives that are not recognized nor recognize themselves as standard citizens of the nation-states that encompass and often divide them—spread over seventy countries in the world, according to a United Nations Permanent Forum on Indigenous Issues estimate.[51] This is certainly nowhere near the roughly 3.5 billion of people (read half the human species) crowding our "technical metropolises," around a billion of which, it should be noted, live in not particularly technical slums.[52] Still, it is more than the population of the United States (314 million) and Canada (35 million) put together, which surely must be worth something. Above all, however, who knows what demographic transitions await humankind before the end of this century, or even earlier, if we consider that we could arrive at a 4 degrees Celsius increase in temperature already by 2060 or 2070?[53] Not to mention the well-known argument according to which five Earths would be required if all the seven billion human inhabitants of the planet adopted that bizarre modern version of *vivir bien* that is the American way of life.[54] That means that the country to the north of Mexico owes the rest of the world at least four worlds, in an unexpected transformation of the mythical humans without world theme. Apart from there being too many people in the world (unfortunately, no amount of rationalization can unmake that evidence), the problem above all is that there are too few people with too much world, and too many people with way too little.

Plus intra is Latour's plea against this danger, a correction to and necessary update of the *plus ultra* that was the motto of the Age of Discovery—which, let us not forget, instituted the modern nomos of the Earth, which required the American genocide and, more generally, the extermination of several millions of human beings that lay outside the jus gentium of Europe, and thus in the legitimately appropriable, up-for-grabs free zones of the globe.[55] According to Latour, it is now imperative that we recognize the existence of limits ("Terrans must explore the question of their limits"); that we let the idea sink in that every action in this sublunary realm of ours has a cost, that is, consequences that inevitably act back on the agent.[56] Latour's motto evidently strikes us as most sensible. We interpret it nonetheless as a plea for us to prepare for a nonmaterial intensification of our way of life, which is to say, a total transformation thereof, in a process that should definitely steer clear of any fantasy of Promethean mastery or managerial control over the world understood as humankind's Other.[57] The time has come to transform *enkrateia*, the mastery of oneself, into a collective project of recivilization—"civilizing modern practices," writes Stengers—or maybe a more "molecular," less titanic project, of uncivilization.[58] Plus intra must mean, in that sense, a technology of slowing down, a diseconomy no longer mesmerized by the hallucination of continuous growth, a cultural insurrection (if the expression may be pardoned) against the zombification of the citizen-consumer.

One word on technology. We believe it is necessary to do the same in relation to technology and technologies that Latour has done in relation to the fateful amalgam of science and sciences: rejecting the unidirectional, modernist understanding of technology that regards it as an onto-anthropological essence whose triumphant deployment blossoms across history. (Breakthough Institute–style technophiles are as essentialist as their retro-Heideggerean enemies.) For there are human and Terran technologies, a difference that we do not think is reducible to the mere issue of network length. The war between humans and Terrans will essentially take place at this level, especially when we bring under an enlarged and pluralized category of technology a whole series of recent sociotechnical detours and institutional inventions, some very ancient, others quite recent, from the kinship systems and totemic maps of Australian Aboriginals to the horizontal organization and the defensive black bloc tactics of alter-globalist movements, from the forms of production, circulation, mobilization, and communication created by the internet to the organizations who protect and exchange traditional seeds and plants in zones of peasant resistance all over the world, from efficient extrabanking financial transfer systems such as *hawala* to the differential arboriculture of the Amazonian indigenous and to Polynesian stellar navigation, from the "experimental agriculturalists" of the Brazilian semiarid to hypercontemporaneous innovations such as ecovillages, from the psychopolitics of technoshamanism to the decentralized economies of social currencies, bitcoin, and crowdsourcing.[59] Not every technical innovation key to the resilience of the species needs to go through the corporate channels of big science or the very long human and nonhuman networks mobilized by cutting-edge technologies.

To Terran technologies we should add, finally, the vast repertoire of technical detours mobilized by Darwinian evolution in organisms. Pace Latour, we think technologies do not historically and ontologically precede the human only because they have made him, and made him as *Homo faber*.[60] Bricolage, tinkering, the hack, the crack, the exploit—all of these are anthropogenetic to the extent that they are inherent to the living.

Once we accept this enlarged definition of "technique" or "technology," it is possible to see with greater clarity that the division between humans and Terrans is not only internal to our species. (That, we suppose, is something Latour would easily agree with.) The Gaia war opposes two camps or sides populated by humans and nonhumans—microorganisms, animals, plants, machines, rivers, glaciers, oceans, chemical elements, and compounds.

In short, this is the whole range of existents that find themselves implicated in the advent of the Anthropocene, and whose persistence is virtually or actually posed as the negation of the opposing camp, or is negated by it—in short, in the Schmittian position of the political enemy. The lethal viruses propagated by equally damaging intercontinental tourism; the vast symbiotic fauna of bacteria that have coevolved with humans; the lethal bacteria that have become definitively resistant to antibiotics;[61] the atomic weapons silently awaiting their hour in underground silos and perpetually mobile submarines; the uncountable legion of confined and mistreated animals in extermination camps for the extraction of protein;[62] the powerful methane factories located in the stomachs of billions of human-raised ruminants in industrial farms; the floods and devastating droughts caused by global warming; the Aral Sea that is no more; the tens of thousands of species becoming extinct every year (at a rate perhaps one thousand times higher than the average rate of extinction on the evolutionary scale[63]); the accelerated deforestation of the Amazon and of Indonesia; the damming of the Amazonian basin to produce hydroelectric energy, with very likely nefarious, if not catastrophic, effects for the macroregion; the saturation of arable soils by pesticides; the brave *Amaranthus palmeri*, the Inca amaranth that resists Monsanto's Roundup herbicide and spreads into transgenic soya plantations; the Terminator seeds produced by that same detestable corporation, which invade traditional corn, manioc, rice, or millet plantations carefully preserved by peasants in zones that resist the encroachment of agribusiness; the many mysterious chemical additives in our food; pets and police dogs; the grizzlies that lose their patience with humans who cannot respect the difference between species; the irreplaceable bee people at risk of disappearing by virtue of a synergy of anthropogenic factors; killer drones, the melting permafrost, the internet, GPS satellites, the paraphernalia of scientific instruments, models, and experiments that allow us to evaluate the progress of planetary boundaries—in short, all these countless agents, agencies, actants, actors, acts, phenomena, or however else one may wish to call them are automatically enlisted in the Gaia war, some or maybe many of which may change camps (function, effects) in the most unexpected ways, and which enter into articulations with different peoples, collectives, and organizations of individuals of the *Homo sapiens* species, which oppose each other precisely by dint of the alliances that they establish and maintain with this nonhuman multitude, that is, of the vital interests that connect them to their others.

While it is not too difficult to list the nonhumans that are involved in this war, we have seen that it is not as easy to identify within the human species who the Terrans are and who are their human enemies. We have seen that the latter are rather generically associated by Latour with the "Moderns," that is, all those agents, from corporations to countries and individuals, which are implicated in some way or another (and the difference among modes of implication is, it bears repeating, essential) in the implacable advance of the modernization front. Yet it is neither impossible nor useless to name at least some of those on the frontlines of the human army, those who are most immediately responsible for the accelerating worsening of anthropogenic catastrophe and more directly interested (or uninterested?) in the defeat of the Terrans. After all, just for starters, only ninety big companies are responsible for two-thirds of greenhouse gas emissions into the Earth's atmosphere: Chevron, Exxon, BP, Shell, Saudi Aramco, Russian Gazprom, Norway's Statoil, Brazil's Petrobras, and the coal and mining state companies of countries such as China, Russia, and Poland.[64] Right after those, names like Monsanto, DuPont, Syngenta, Bayer, Cargill, Bunge, Dow, Rio Tinto, Nestlé, "our very own" Brazilian Vale, the companies belonging to the sinister Koch brothers, and several others also deserve a mention for their various contributions to the conversion of the moderns' cosmological mononaturalism into a large-scale agricultural economy of monocultures, to the lasting perturbation of the geochemical cycles of soil and water, to massive environmental pollution, to the dissemination of food that is harmful to human health.[65] We should not forget the 147 banks and other corporations, the tentacles of whose supernetwork involve the planet in a deadly embrace.[66] Nor the governments of countries such as Canada, Australia, the United States, Brazil, and several others that have stimulated deforestation and the extraction of fuels and minerals with high contaminating potentials, as well as created obstacles to negotiations around the climate catastrophe. It is a long list, to be sure, but certainly not an infinite one. It is not against civilization, progress, history, destiny, or humankind that Terrans are fighting, but against these entities acting on behalf of humans.

Yet let us go back to our elusive Terrans, considering again for an instant the Amerindian cosmogonies and eschatologies evoked earlier on, when we spoke of their aesthetic anthropomorphism and metaphysical panpsychism. In a world where everything is alive, it is necessary to account for death. Indigenous myths see the origin of culture and society as being intrinsically bound with the origin of humans' short life span, that is, of their mortality as existential condition. The latter is commonly imagined as the result, not of a crime or a sin against divinity, but of a blunder, a mistake, some careless act of unexplainable stupidity on the part of our ancestors. Archaic humans made the wrong choice when confronted with certain alternatives offered by the demiurge, the consequence of which is aging and dying quickly, as opposed to living forever like other beings (rocks, hardwood trees) or remaining forever young through periodic changes of skin, like reptiles and various invertebrates. On top of that, postmythical speciation being derived from an originary intensive continuum of human consistency, inter- and intracultural distinctions among presently existing humans are usually explained as resulting from demographic impoverishment—in other words, from the high death rate inflicted on an excessively large and homogeneous population (extinction by catastrophe, extermination by a divinity), which produced holes and distances that allowed for the diversification of humankind into categorially discrete peoples, tribes, and clans.[67]

Yet none of this is seen as entirely negative, even if we might lament our ancestors' foolishness. After all, if people did not die, there would not be enough space in which to raise and feed future generations. "How could we have children if we lived forever and the world were saturated with people? Where would they live, what would they eat?" are the kinds of comments that the narrators of these myths normally make. Now, if Amerindians, like so many other nonmodern peoples, share some sort of fundamental cultural goal, it is that of having children, constituting groups of relatives, allying themselves through marriage to other groups of relatives, distributing and disseminating themselves through their descendants, for people live in other people, with other people, for other people.[68] Ultimately, Amerindians prefer to maintain a relatively stable population instead of increasing productivity and improving technology in order to create conditions (surplus) so that there can always be more people, more needs, more concerns. The ethnographic present of slow societies contains an image of their future. Indians are Malthusians in their own way.

It is not possible to know for sure whether these myths precede the Conquest, but that is in all likelihood the case. Indigenous imagination had already started to think the reduction or slowing down of their Anthropocene, except they placed the process at the origin rather than the end of the world. Little could they imagine then, perhaps, that their world would soon be taken away from them by those world-forming, world-destroying aliens, the Europeans. Be that as it may, what we hinted above, that indigenous people have something to teach us when it comes to apocalypses, losses of world, demographic catastrophes, and ends of history, means simply this: for the native people of the Americas, the end of the world already happened—five centuries ago. To be exact, it began on October 12, 1492. (As someone once said on Twitter, "The first Indian to find Columbus made a horrible discovery.") The indigenous population of the continent, larger than that of Europe at the time, may have lost—by means of the combined action of viruses (smallpox in particular being spectacularly lethal), iron, gunpowder, and paper (treaties, papal bulls, royal *encomienda* concessions, and of course the Bible)—something on the order of 95 percent of its bulk throughout the first one and a half centuries of the Conquest. That would correspond, according to some demographers, to one-fifth of the planet's population.[69] We could therefore call this American event the first great modern extinction, when the New World was hit by the Old one as if by a giant celestial body that we could call, by analogy with Lars von Trier's Melancholia, planet Commodity.[70] If it comes to comparing apocalypses, we can safely say that the American genocide of the sixteenth and seventeenth centuries—the biggest demographic catastrophe in history until now, with the possible exception of the Black Death—will always be among the very top ones, at least as far as the human species is concerned, even if we take into account the portentous future possibilities of nuclear war or rampant global warming.

Naturally, these ends of the world occasioned by the advance of the modernization front, which began precisely with the plus ultra! of European expansion in the sixteenth century, continue to take place at different scales, in several more or less remote parts of the planet, to this day. It is not necessary to insist on what goes on today in Africa, New Guinea, or the Amazon—or, to pick our examples from further up north, in those indigenous territories in the United States and Canada suffering the impacts of hydraulic fracturing or fracking. "Fracturing" is in fact a most appropriate word; for it is as if the end of the world were a truly fractal event, indefinitely reproduced at different scales, from ethnocidal wars in parts of Africa to the systematic assassination of indigenous leaders or environmental activists in the Amazon, from the purchase of vast portions of poor countries by hyperindustrial powers to the squatting on and deforestation of indigenous land by mining and agribusiness to the forcible exodus of peasant families only to give way to the expansion of transgenic soya—not to mention the fractalization of the end that runs across the great chain of being from top to bottom with the disappearance of countless *Umwelten* of living things.[71] Gaia is just the name of the final reckoning of these figures of the end; Gaia is, in short, the maximal scale that we can reach.

If the humans who invaded it represented the indigenous America of the sixteenth and seventeenth centuries as a world without humans—be it because they objectively depopulated it or be it because the humans they found there did not fit the category of "humans"—the surviving Indians, fully entitled Terrans from that New World, reciprocally found themselves as humans without world: castaways, refugees, precarious lodgers in a world in which they no longer belonged, because it could not belong to them. And yet, it just so happens that many of them survived. They carried on in another world, a world of others, their invaders and overlords. Some adapted and became modernized, but in ways that bear little relation to what moderns understand by that word. Others still struggle to hold on to whatever little world is left to them, and hope that, in the meantime, the whites will not manage to destroy their own white world, now become for all living beings the common world—in a rather non-Latourian sense.

It strikes us as powerfully symbolic that one of the more recent versions of the end of the world that captured the attention and excitement of this new generation of planetary gawkers that is the vast globalized audience of the web should be the so-called Mayan apocalypse due to take place on December 21, 2012. As we can obviously notice, the world did not end, which was something that in any case had never been foretold by any written or oral Mayan indigenous tradition. The mistake notwithstanding, it is not unreasonable to connect the name of the Maya to the idea of the end of the world, nor should we overlook the significance of the fact that the only date from a supposedly Amerindian calendar to be incorporated into world pop culture refers to an apocalypse.

As a matter of fact, Mayan history has known several ends. First of all, the great Mesoamerican civilization that left us monuments such as Chichen Itzá, Tikal, and Copán went through a slow decadence between the seventh and the tenth centuries, in all likelihood due to a combination of sociopolitical conflicts (revolts and wars) and prolonged environmental stress (droughts linked to El Niño events, depletion of cultivable soils), ultimately leading to the collapse of their society and the abandonment of those majestic pyramids and temples and, very probably, of the scientific and artistic culture that flourished in those jungle cities. A first, pre-Columbian end of the world, then, which can serve us as example and warning regarding contemporary processes in which economy and ecology are entering collapse-inducing feedback loops at the same time as insurrectional events sprout here and there all over the planet. Following that, with the invasion of the Americas in the sixteenth century, the Maya were, like the other native peoples of the continent, subjected and enslaved, as well as ravaged by epidemics brought by the invaders. The genocide of Amerindian peoples—the end of the world for them—was the beginning of the modern world for Europe: without the despoiling of the Americas, Europe would have never become more than the backyard of Eurasia, the home continent of civilizations that were much richer than the Europeans during our Middle Ages (Byzantium, China, India, the Arab polities). No pillage of the Americas, no capitalism, no Industrial Revolution, thus perhaps no Anthropocene either. This second end of the world that hit the Maya is even more emblematic if we consider that the first tirade against that genocide came from the bishop of Chiapas, Bartolomé de las Casas, a champion of human rights who early on regretted the brutal treatment dealt by the very Catholic Europeans to the Indians in his bishopric.

All that considered, even though they have gone through successive ends of the world, even though they have been reduced to a poor and oppressed peasantry, have had their territory broken up and handed over to different nation-states (Mexico, Guatemala, Belize, Honduras, El Salvador), the Maya continue to exist, their population grows, their world resists: diminished but defiant.

And it is indeed the Maya who offer us today what may be the best example of a successful popular insurrection against the two-headed state-market monster that oppresses the world's minorities (namely, successful in that it did not eventually turn into something else). It was the only revolt of an indigenous people in Latin America that managed to sustain itself without degenerating into a national state project, most importantly, the only one to have chosen its own cosmopolitical path, quickly abandoning the so-called Marxist revolutionary eschatology (profoundly Christian, in actual fact) with which Europe, through the mediation of its caste of clergymen/intellectuals, continues to try to control struggles for emancipation. We speak, of course, of the Zapatista uprising in Chiapas, that rare revolt that is a model of sustainability—political sustainability, also and above all. The Maya, who lived through their various ends of the world, show us today how it is possible to live after the end of the world. How, in short, it is possible to challenge the state and the market, and to enact the right to self-determination.

Veritable end-of-the-world experts, the Maya and all other indigenous peoples of the Americas have a lot to teach us now that we are on the verge of a process in which the planet as a whole will become something like sixteenth-century America: a world invaded, wrecked, and razed by barbarian foreigners. Let the reader imagine herself watching—or rather, acting in—a sci-fi B movie in which the Earth is taken over by an alien race pretending to be humans, whose goal is to dominate the planet and to extract all its resources, after having used up their own home planet to the full. Usually, the aliens in such films feed on humans themselves: their blood, mental energy, and so forth. And now let the reader imagine that this has already happened, and that the alien race is, in fact, we ourselves. We were taken over by a species disguised as human, and they have won: we are them. Or are there in fact two different species of human, as Latour suggests—an indigenous and an alien one? Maybe it is the species as a whole and each one of us individually that is split in two, the alien and the indigenous living side by side in the same body: suppose a small shift in sensibility has suddenly made that self-colonization visible to us. We would thus all be indigenous, that is, Terrans, invaded by Europeans, that is, humans; all of us, of course, including Europeans, who were after all the first Terrans to be invaded. A perfect intensive doubling (plus intra!), the end of extensive partitions: the invaders are the invaded, the colonized are the colonizers. We have woken up to an incomprehensible nightmare. And as Oswald de Andrade put it, only the naked man shall understand.

NOTES

A slightly different version of this chapter appears in the final part of the authors' book *The Ends of the World*, published by Polity Press. Déborah Danowski and Eduardo Viveiros de Castro, *The Ends of the World*, trans. Rodrigo Nunes (Cambridge, MA: Polity, 2017).

1. Bruno Latour, "War and Peace in an Age of Ecological Conflicts," lecture at the Peter Wall Institute, Vancouver, September 23, 2013.

2. See Andrew Shryock and Daniel Lord Smail, *Deep History: The Architecture of Past and Present* (Berkeley: University of California Press, 2011); John Brooke, *Climate Change and the Course of Global History* (Cambridge: Cambridge University Press, 2014).

3. Dipesh Chakrabarty, "The Climate of History: Four Theses." *Critical Inquiry* 35 (2009): 218.

4. Even though the American way of life remains the undisputed champion when it comes to per capita greenhouse gas emissions, China has overtaken the United States in becoming the world's greatest producer of carbon dioxide in absolute terms. See Anderson and Bows for a desolating projection of the increase in global temperatures in a scenario taking into account the rapid growth of emissions in countries such as China and India. The two authors show that, taking these into account, reduction goals set for so-called Annex I countries (notionally the most developed) in United Nations climate negotiations are irrisory and unable to prevent a rise in temperature well above 2 degrees Celsius—a limit that, incidentally, is far from being safe, as was once thought. In the world scene, Brazil still reaps the credit acquired with the reduction of emissions caused by deforestation in the period between 2004 and 2012; however, apart from deforestation having started to climb up again since 2013, emissions coming from the energy sector have been growing in relative importance. Note to the English edition: The Paris Agreement does not mention Annex I and Annex II countries, referring to developing and least developed countries. Kevin Anderson and Alice Bows, "Beyond 'Dangerous' Climate Change: Emission Scenarios for a New World," *Philosophical Transactions of the Royal Society A* 369, no. 1934 (2011): 20–44.

5. Chakrabarty, "The Climate of History," 212.

6. Chakrabarty, "The Climate of History," 215. Edmund Wilson, the famous entomologist, father of sociobiology, and today an activist in the struggle against global warming, might be considered one of the high priests of the cult, discussed by Latour in the first of his Gifford Lectures, of an "epistemological Nature" defined by the attributes of exteriority, unicity, de-animation, and indisputability. Bruno Latour, "Facing Gaia: Six Lectures on the Political Theology of Nature. Being the Gifford Lectures on Natural Religion" (lectures at Edinburgh University, February 18–28, 2013).

7. Chakrabarty, "The Climate of History," 220.

8. Of great pertinence to this discussion is a piece by Idelber Avelar, in which the author sets up a dialogue between the cosmopolitical aporias of the Anthropocene (following Chakrabarty) and Amerindian perspectives. Idelbar Avelar, "Amerindian Perspectivism and Non-human Rights," *Alter/nativas* 1 (2013): 1–21.

9. Translator's note: "humankind of reference" and "ethnos of reference" should be understood in the context of Viveiros de Castro's proposed solution to the apparent antinomy between the so-called animism of indigenous peoples (which extends humanity to all beings) and their ethnocentrism (which denies humanity to all outside the group): Amerindian perspectivism entails that each being/collective conceives itself as human from its own perspective—thus constituting a "humankind of reference" that establishes the criteria according to which humanity can be extended or denied to others. For the classic statement of that thesis, see Eduardo Viveiros de Castro, "Cosmological Deixis and Amerindian Perspectivism," *Journal of the Royal Anthropological Society* 4, no. 3 (1998): 469–88.

10. Taking note of the insufficiency of critical sociology in no way entails, for Chakrabarty, that the latter is superfluous, let alone wrong-headed. It cannot be argued, however, that such a diagnosis implies an ideological jolt, not to say a narcissistic wound, to the several strains of the left that claim faithfulness to historical

materialism, since the problem with the sociology of globalization would ultimately be precisely its lack of materialism and its narrow historical provincialism. For a stimulating critique of the recent use of the notion of human species or humankind as agent of environmental collapse that seeks to circumvent economistic simplism, see Christophe Bonneuil and Jean-Baptiste Fressoz, *The Shock of the Anthropocene: Earth, History and Us* (London: Verso, 2016).

11. Chakrabarty, "The Climate of History," 221.

12. Chakrabarty, "The Climate of History," 222; Günther Anders, *Le Temps de la Fin* (Paris: L'Herne, 2007), 92. "From the present perspective of total catastrophe, Marx and Paul seem to have become contemporaries" (Anders, *Le Temps de la Fin*).

13. Chakrabarty, "The Climate of History," 221–22, emphasis added.

14. Anders, *Le Temps de la Fin*.

15. Anders, *Le Temps de la Fin*, 79.

16. As in the vast majority of antinuclear discourse from the Cold War period, Anders's text proceeds as if humans were the only species whose extinction was at stake in the prospect of nuclear holocaust. See Déborah Danowski, "O Hiperrealismo das Mudancas Climáticas e as Várias Faces do Negacionismo," *Sopro* 70 (2012): 2–11.

17. On top of having forced cattle into cannibalism—see Claude Lévi-Strauss, "La Leçon de Sagesse des Vaches Folles," *Études Rurales* 157–58 (2001): 9–14.

18. Anders, *Le Temps de la Fin*, 33.

19. Latour, "Facing Gaia."

20. The triad demos, theos, and nomos structures the exposition of the "political theology of nature" advanced in Latour, "Facing Gaia."

21. Bruno Latour, *An Inquiry into Modes of Existence: An Anthropology of the Moderns*, trans. Catherine Porter (Cambridge, MA: Harvard University Press, 2013).

22. Isabelle Stengers, *In Catastrophic Times: Resisting the Coming Barbarism*, trans. Andrew Goffey (London: Open Humanities, 2015).

23. But we should also bear in mind that the atemporality and universality of these laws are equally open to discussion nowadays; see, for example, the work of Lee Smolin, who partially takes up Peircean ideas (which are also, even if the author might not realize it, Tardean and Nietzschean) on the historicity of cosmic forces. See Elizabeth Povinelli, "Geontologies: Indigenous Worlds in the New Media and Late Liberalism" (lecture at the Colloquium Métaphysiques Comparées, Centre Culturel International de Cérisy, July–August 2013). See also Bruno Latour, "Waiting for Gaia: Composing the Common World through Arts and Politics" (lecture at the Institut Français, London, November 21, 2011), where the sublunary/supralunary distinction makes its first appearance, derived perhaps from Peter Sloterdjik's *Spheres* series.

24. Paul Ennis, "The Claim That We Are Already Dead" (unpublished manuscript, May 14, 2013), PDF file.

25. Isabelle Stengers, "Matters of Cosmopolitics: Isabelle Stengers in Conversation with Heather Davis and Etienne Turpin on the Provocations of Gaïa," in *Architecture in the Anthropocene: Encounters among Design, Deep Time, Science, and Philosophy*, ed. Etienne Turpin, 171–82 (Ann Arbor, MI: Open Humanities, 2013).

26. Isabelle Stengers, *Une Autre Science Est Possible! Manifeste pour un Ralentissement des Sciences* (Paris: La Découverte, 2013); Stengers, *In Catastrophic Times*.

27. It is precisely because it is not a work of architecture or engineering that Gaia cannot be reengineered either, which suggests that the author does not harbor great hopes in relation to climate geoengineering projects. Latour, "Facing Gaia," 66.

28. Latour, "Facing Gaia," 68.

29. Latour, "Facing Gaia," 67.

30. Gaia would be, so to speak, the agent of a geostory rather than the patient of a geohistory.

31. Bruno Latour, *War of the Worlds: What about Peace?* (Chicago: Prickly Paradigm, 2002).

32. Latour, "Facing Gaia," 121–22.

33. Latour, *An Inquiry into Modes of Existence*.

34. Naomi Oreskes and Erik M. Conway, *Merchants of Doubt: How a Handful of Scientists Obscured the Truth on Issues from Tobacco Smoke to Global Warming* (New York: Bloomsbury, 2010). Even people who accept this consensus, Latour points out, often do not feel capable of doing anything immediate and concrete that could help us escape the catastrophe. We are practical denialists in our comfortable or fatalistic quietism, he concludes in consternation, speaking for many though not, it should be said, for all. Latour, "Facing Gaia."

35. See Shapin on the perennial debate surrounding Thomas Robert Malthus's thesis: "Malthusian debates belong to scientific inquiry, but it's an inquiry that is itself embedded within ongoing moral conversations—and we rarely expect consensus to emerge from those." Steven Shapin, "Libel on the Human Race," *London Review of Books* 36, no. 11 (2014): 29.

36. The above passage is, if memory does not fail us, the most trenchant expression of radicality and engagement on the part of Latour, who remains somewhat ambivalent as regards his own position in this war between two worlds. Although he has declared (or confessed) himself several times as a diplomat representing the moderns, it is not hard to see that the author has tended more and more in the opposite direction, seemingly wishing to act, as Alyne Costa has remarked, "as a Terran infiltrated among Humans," whose mission would be to convert them and eventually help them to come around to the side of the people of Gaia. Alyne de Castro Costa, "Guerra e Paz no Antropoceno: Uma Análise da Crise Ecológica segundo a Obra de Bruno Latour" (master's thesis, Pontifical Catholic University of Rio, Rio de Janeiro, 2014).

37. Latour, "Facing Gaia," 118ff.

38. Latour, "Facing Gaia," 120, 121.

39. The terms "key" and "mode of extension" make reference here to the vocabulary of *An Inquiry into Modes of Existence*. Latour, "Facing Gaia," 50.

40. Translator's note: an untranslatable play on the fact that, in Latinate languages, the same word (*tempo, tiempo, temps*) can be used to say both "time" and "weather."

41. We refer the reader back to the prefatory note, in which we discuss our choice of "Terrans" (rather than "Earthlings" or "Earthbound people," the terms that Latour himself employs in his Gifford Lectures) to translate the French "Terriens."

42. The horse in the title, a key character, disappears as Terran from Latour's analysis, as Juliana Fausto points out. Juliana Fausto, "Terranos e Poetas: o 'Povo de Gaia' como 'Povo que Falta,'" *Landa* 2, no. 1 (2013): 165–81.

43. See Wagner on the "dullness that we find in mission schools, refugee camps, and sometimes in 'acculturated' villages." Roy Wagner, *The Invention of Culture*, 2nd ed. (Chicago: University of Chicago Press, 1981), 89.

44. The book is a Nietzschean "anti-Bible," the director explains. Vladan Petkovic, "Béla Tarr, Director: Simple and Pure," *Cineuropa*, March 4, 2011, http://cineuropa.org /it.aspx?t=interview&lang=en&documentID=198131.

45. "The territory is German, the Earth Greek." Gilles Deleuze and Félix Guattari, *A Thousand Plateaus*, trans. Brian Massumi (Minneapolis: University of Minnesota Press, 1987), 339.

46. On the "phantom public" of Western democracies, see Bruno Latour, "Le Fantôme de l'Esprit Public: Des Illusions de la Démocratie aux Réalités de Ses Apparitions," introduction to *Le Public Fantôme*, by Walter Lippmann, 3–49 (Paris: Editions Demopolis, 2008). Gilles Deleuze and Félix Guattari, *What Is Philosophy?*, trans. Hugh Tomlinson and Graham Burchell (New York: Columbia University Press, 1994), 108–9. The approximation between Terrans and Deleuze and Guattari's "people that is missing" was suggested to us by Fausto, "Terranos e Poetas." Alexandre Nodari, on the other hand, has reminded us of the passage in Clarice Lispector's *The Hour of the Star* in which the main character, Macabéa, is described as belonging to "a stubborn race of dwarves that one day might reclaim the right to scream." Clarice Lispector, *The Hour of the Star*, trans. Benjamin Moser (New York: New Directions, 2011), 102.

47. Latour, "Facing Gaia," 126.

48. Latour, "Facing Gaia," 128.

49. "This 'anthropos' whose civilization is already powered by around 12 terawatts (each being 10^{12} watts), and which is heading toward 100 terawatts if the rest of the world develops at the level of the US, a stunning figure if one considers that plate tectonic forces are said to develop no more than 40 terawatts of energy." Latour, "Facing Gaia," 76. In fact, several sources indicate an even higher global consumption than that (around 15 terawatts), and the United States of America, where only 5 percent of the global population lives, is responsible for 26 percent of that total amount.

50. We can do no better here than recommend the sharp critique to which Marilyn Strathern has subjected the Latourian notion of the moderns' "long networks," as well as the same author's reflection on scalarity as an instrument (and/or effect) of anthropological theory rather than as a property of phenomena observable, so to speak, to the naked eye. Marilyn Strathern, *Partial Connections* (Walnut Creek, CA: AltaMira, 2004).

51. United Nations Permanent Forum on Indigenous Issues, "Who Are Indigenous Peoples?," 2009, http://www.un.org/esa/socdev/unpfii/documents/5session_factsheet1.pdf.

52. Mike Davis, *Planet of Slums* (London: Verso, 2005). See also John Vidal, "Every Third Person Will Be a Slum Dweller within 30 years, UN Agency Warns," *The Guardian*, October 4, 2003, https://www.theguardian.com/world/2003/oct/04/population .johnvidal.

53. Richard Betts et al., "When Could Global Warming Reach 4°C?," *Philosophical Transactions of the Royal Society A* 369, no. 1934 (2011): 67–84.

54. Translator's note: Spanish in the original. "Good living" (*vivir bien*, in Spanish; *suma qamaña*, in Aymara; *sumak kawsay*, in Quechua; *teko porã*, in Guarani) is a concept common to various indigenous peoples of South America that gained political and international currency over a decade ago as a consequence of the rise of left-leaning, indigenous-supported governments in the region.

55. Latour, "Facing Gaia," 129–30. We thank Alexandre Nodari for his clarifications regarding the Schmittian notion of the modern nomos or partition of the Earth, inaugurated with the invasion of America and India, then terminated (always according to Schmitt) with the rise of the United States and the creation of the League of Nations. Nodari suggests that the contemporary nomos would be something like the division between legitimate nation-states and rogue states or the axis of evil (to which we could add vandals, *casseurs*, black blocs, Zapatistas, the people up in arms, etc.), and that a future nomos would emerge from the catastrophic scenario imagined by Isabelle Stengers, in which a world state would exercise its universal domination authorized to intervene wherever, whenever, and however by the urgency (exception) of environmental collapse.

56. The "question of limits," we dare say, marks a veritable tipping point in Latour's worldview. See Latour's statement about the idea of a loop being constitutive of "what it means to be 'of this Earth.'" Latour, "Facing Gaia," 95.

57. This project has also been given the name of "intensive sufficiency." Eduardo Viveiros de Castro, "Transformação na Antropologia, Transformação da Antropologia," *Mana* 18, no. 1 (2012): 151–71.

58. Stengers, *Une Autre Science Est Possible!*, 113. For the idea of "uncivilization," see the Dark Mountain Project's manifesto. Dougald Hine and Paul Kingsnorth, "Uncivilisation: The Dark Mountain Manifesto," Dark Mountain Project, 2009, http://dark-mountain.net/about/manifesto/.

59. McKenzie Wark, *A Hacker Manifesto* (Cambridge, MA: Harvard University Press, 2004). See ASPTA, "Encontro Nacional de Agricultoras e Agricultores Experimentadores termina celebrando a partilha e a união," November 1, 2013, http://aspta.org.br/2013/11/30-encontro-nacional-de-agricultoras-e-agricultores-experimentadores-termina-celebrando-a-partilha-e-a-uniao/.

60. See Latour, *An Inquiry into Modes of Existence*, chapter 3.

61. Who says history does not go back? See Fergus Walsh, "'Golden Age' of Antibiotics 'Set to End,'" BBC News, January 8, 2014, http://www.bbc.com/news/health-25654112; and the equally, if not even more, troubling article by Lynn Peeples, "The Stomach Bacteria That Could Prolong Your Life," *Huffington Post*, May 21, 2014, https://www.huffingtonpost.com/2014/05/21/microbes-children-health_n_5366066.html.

62. Jonathan Safran Foer, *Eating Animals* (London: Penguin, 2010).

63. See Elizabeth Kolbert, *The Sixth Extinction: An Unnatural History* (New York: Henry Holt, 2014).

64. See Duncan Clark and KILN, "Which Fossil Fuel Companies Are Most Responsible for Climate Change?—Interactive," *The Guardian*, November 20, 2013, http://www

.theguardian.com/environment/interactive/ 2013/nov/20/which-fossil-fuel-companies-responsible-climate-change-interactive. See also the Carbon Tracker Initiative website, https://www.carbontracker.org/.

65. See ETC Group, "Who Owns Nature? Corporate Power and the Final Frontier in the Commodification of Life," November 12, 2008, http://www.etcgroup.org/content/who-owns-nature; Food Processing, "Food Processing's Top 100," 2017, https://www.foodprocessing.com/top100/top-100-2017/.

66. See Andy Coghlan and Debora MacKenzie, "Revealed: The Capitalist Network That Runs the World," *New Scientist*, October 19, 2011, https://www.newscientist.com/article/mg21228354-500-revealed-the-capitalist-network-that-runs-the-world/.

67. Lévi-Strauss, "La Leçon de Sagesse des Vaches Folles."

68. Marshall Sahlins, *What Kinship Is—and Is Not* (Chicago: University of Chicago Press, 2013).

69. An overview of the still-heated debate concerning the extent of the invasion of the Americas' demographic can be found in Mann's well-documented book. Charles Mann, *1491: New Revelations of the Americas before Columbus* (New York: Vintage, 2005).

70. Translator's note: The authors make an untranslatable play here on the sound of the words *melancolia* (melancholia) and *mercadoria* (commodity) in Portuguese.

71. See the International Union for Conservation of Nature, as well as the previously mentioned Elizabeth Kolbert, and David Ulansey's staggering Current Mass Extinction website (http://www.mysterium.com/extinction.html), which accumulates news on the current mass extinction since 1998. International Union for Conservation of Nature, "Extinction Crisis Continues Apace," November 3, 2009, https://www.iucn.org/content/extinction-crisis-continues-apace; Kolbert, *The Sixth Extinction*.

BIBLIOGRAPHY

Anders, Günther. *Le Temps de la Fin.* Paris: L'Herne, 2007.

Anderson, Kevin, and Alice Bows. "Beyond 'Dangerous' Climate Change: Emission Scenarios for a New World." *Philosophical Transactions of the Royal Society A* 369, no. 1934 (2011): 20–44.

ASPTA. "Encontro Nacional de Agricultoras e Agricultores Experimentadores termina celebrando a partilha e a união." November 1, 2013. http://aspta.org.br/2013/11/30-encontro-nacional-de-agricultoras-e-agricultores-experimentadores-termina-celebrando-a-partilha-e-a-uniao/.

Avelar, Idelber. "Amerindian Perspectivism and Non-human Rights." *Alter/nativas* 1 (2013): 1–21.

Betts, Richard A., Matthew Collins, Deborah L. Hemming, Chris D. Jones, Jason A. Lowe, and Michael G. Sanderson. "When Could Global Warming Reach 4°C?" *Philosophical Transactions of the Royal Society A* 369, no. 1934 (2011): 67–84.

Bonneuil, Christophe, and Jean-Baptiste Fressoz. *The Shock of the Anthropocene: Earth, History and Us.* London: Verso, 2016.

Brooke, John. *Climate Change and the Course of Global History*. Cambridge: Cambridge University Press, 2014.

Catraca Livre. "A Desigualdade Social no Mundo Captada em 6 Imagens Aéreas." June 18, 2014. https://catracalivre.com.br/geral/arquitetura/indicacao/a-desigualdade-social-pelo-mundo-captada-em-6-imagens-aereas/.

Chakrabarty, Dipesh. "The Climate of History: Four Theses." *Critical Inquiry* 35 (2009): 197–222.

Clark, Duncan, and KILN. "Which Fossil Fuel Companies Are Most Responsible for Climate Change?—Interactive." *The Guardian*, November 20, 2013. http://www.theguardian.com/environment/interactive/2013/nov/20/which-fossil-fuel-companies-responsible-climate-change-interactive.

Coghlan, Andy, and Debora MacKenzie. "Revealed: The Capitalist Network That Runs the World." *New Scientist*, October 19, 2011. https://www.newscientist.com/article/mg21228354-500-revealed-the-capitalist-network-that-runs-the-world/.

Costa, Alyne de Castro. "Guerra e Paz no Antropoceno: Uma Análise da Crise Ecológica segundo a Obra de Bruno Latour." Master's thesis, Pontifical Catholic University of Rio (PUC-Rio), Rio de Janeiro, 2014.

Danowski, Déborah. "O Hiperrealismo das Mudancas Climáticas e as Várias Faces do Negacionismo." *Sopro* 70 (2012): 2–11.

Danowski, Déborah, and Eduardo Viveiros de Castro. *The Ends of the World*. Translated by Rodrigo Nunes. Cambridge, MA: Polity, 2017.

Davis, Mike. *Planet of Slums*. London: Verso, 2005.

Deleuze, Gilles, and Félix Guattari. *A Thousand Plateaus*. Translated by Brian Massumi. Minneapolis: University of Minnesota Press, 1987.

Deleuze, Gilles, and Félix Guattari. *What Is Philosophy?* Translated by Hugh Tomlinson and Graham Burchell. New York: Columbia University Press, 1994.

Ennis, Paul. "The Claim That We Are Already Dead." Unpublished manuscript, May 14, 2013. PDF file.

ETC Group. "Who Owns Nature? Corporate Power and the Final Frontier in the Commodification of Life." November 12, 2008. http://www.etcgroup.org/content/who-owns-nature.

Fausto, Juliana. "Terranos e Poetas: o 'Povo de Gaia' como 'Povo que Falta.'" *Landa* 2, no. 1 (2013): 165–81.

Foer, Jonathan Safran. *Eating Animals*. London: Penguin, 2010.

Food Processing. "Food Processing's Top 100." 2017. https://www.foodprocessing.com/top100/top-100-2017/.

Hine, Dougald, and Paul Kingsnorth. "Uncivilisation: The Dark Mountain Manifesto." Dark Mountain Project, 2009. http://dark-mountain.net/about/manifesto/.

International Union for Conservation of Nature. "Extinction Crisis Continues Apace." November 3, 2009. https://www.iucn.org/content/extinction-crisis-continues-apace.

Kolbert, Elizabeth. *The Sixth Extinction: An Unnatural History*. New York: Henry Holt, 2014.

Latour, Bruno. "Facing Gaia: Six Lectures on the Political Theology of Nature. Being the Gifford Lectures on Natural Religion." Lectures at Edinburgh University, February 18–28, 2013.

Latour, Bruno. *An Inquiry into Modes of Existence: An Anthropology of the Moderns.* Translated by Catherine Porter. Cambridge, MA: Harvard University Press, 2013.

Latour, Bruno. "Le Fantôme de l'Esprit Public: Des Illusions de la Démocratie aux Réalités de Ses Apparitions." Introduction to *Le Public Fantôme*, by Walter Lippmann, 3–49. Paris: Editions Demopolis, 2008.

Latour, Bruno. "Waiting for Gaia: Composing the Common World through Arts and Politics." Lecture at the Institut Français, London, November 21, 2011.

Latour, Bruno. "War and Peace in an Age of Ecological Conflicts." Lecture at the Peter Wall Institute, Vancouver, September 23, 2013.

Latour, Bruno. *War of the Worlds: What about Peace?* Chicago: Prickly Paradigm, 2002.

Lévi-Strauss, Claude. "La Leçon de Sagesse des Vaches Folles." *Études Rurales* 157–58 (2001): 9–14.

Lispector, Clarice. *The Hour of the Star.* Translated by Benjamin Moser. New York: New Directions, 2011.

Mann, Charles. *1491: New Revelations of the Americas before Columbus.* New York: Vintage, 2005.

Oreskes, Naomi, and Erik M. Conway. *Merchants of Doubt: How a Handful of Scientists Obscured the Truth on Issues from Tobacco Smoke to Global Warming.* New York: Bloomsbury, 2010.

Peeples, Lynn. "The Stomach Bacteria That Could Prolong Your Life." *Huffington Post*, May 21, 2014. https://www.huffingtonpost.com/2014/05/21/microbes-children -health_n_5366066.html.

Petkovic, Vladan. "Béla Tarr, Director: Simple and Pure." *Cineuropa*, March 4, 2011. http://cineuropa.org/it.aspx?t=interview&lang=en&documentID=198131.

Povinelli, Elizabeth. "Geontologies: Indigenous Worlds in the New Media and Late Liberalism." Lecture at the Colloquium Métaphysiques Comparées, Centre Culturel International de Cérisy, July–August 2013.

Sahlins, Marshall. *What Kinship Is—and Is Not.* Chicago: University of Chicago Press, 2013.

Shapin, Steven. "Libel on the Human Race." *London Review of Books* 36, no. 11 (2014): 26–29.

Shryock, Andrew, and Daniel Lord Smail. *Deep History: The Architecture of Past and Present.* Berkeley: University of California Press, 2011.

Stengers, Isabelle. *In Catastrophic Times: Resisting the Coming Barbarism.* Translated by Andrew Goffey. London: Open Humanities, 2015.

Stengers, Isabelle. "Matters of Cosmopolitics: Isabelle Stengers in Conversation with Heather Davis and Etienne Turpin on the Provocations of Gaïa." In *Architecture in the Anthropocene: Encounters among Design, Deep Time, Science, and Philosophy*, edited by Etienne Turpin, 171–82. Ann Arbor, MI: Open Humanities, 2013.

Stengers, Isabelle. *Une Autre Science Est Possible! Manifeste pour un Ralentissement des Sciences.* Paris: La Découverte, 2013.

Strathern, Marilyn. *Partial Connections.* Walnut Creek, CA: AltaMira, 2004.

United Nations Permanent Forum on Indigenous Issues. "Who Are Indigenous Peoples?" 2009. http://www.un.org/esa/socdev/unpfii/documents/5session_factsheet1.pdf.

Vidal, John. "Every Third Person Will Be a Slum Dweller within 30 years, UN Agency Warns." *The Guardian*, October 4, 2003. https://www.theguardian.com/world/2003/oct/04/population.johnvidal.

Viveiros de Castro, Eduardo. "Cosmological Deixis and Amerindian Perspectivism." *Journal of the Royal Anthropological Society* 4, no. 3 (1998): 469–88.

Viveiros de Castro, Eduardo. "Transformação na Antropologia, Transformação da Antropologia." *Mana* 18, no. 1 (2012): 151–71.

Wagner, Roy. *The Invention of Culture.* 2nd ed. Chicago: University of Chicago Press, 1981.

Walsh, Fergus. "'Golden Age' of Antibiotics 'Set to End.'" BBC News, January 8, 2014. http://www.bbc.com/news/health-25654112.

Wark, McKenzie. *A Hacker Manifesto.* Cambridge, MA: Harvard University Press, 2004.

MARIO BLASER is the Canada Research Chair in Aboriginal studies at Memorial University of Newfoundland and Labrador. He is the author of *Storytelling Globalization from the Chaco and Beyond* (Duke University Press, 2010) and coeditor of *Indigenous Peoples and Autonomy: Insights for the Global Age* (2010) and *In the Way of Development: Indigenous Peoples, Life Projects and Globalization* (2004). His recent work examines the political ontology of heterogeneous life projects under the shadow of the Anthropocene.

ALBERTO CORSÍN JIMÉNEZ is associate professor in social anthropology at the Spanish National Research Council in Madrid. His interest in the organization of ethnography and anthropological knowledge as descriptive and theoretical forms led to the publication of *An Anthropological Trompe L'Oeil for a Common World* (2013). He is currently working with guerrilla architectural collectives and open-source urban activists on the intersections between informal, autoconstructed, and free urbanism.

DÉBORAH DANOWSKI has been professor of philosophy at Pontícia Universidade Católica do Rio de Janeiro since 1987 and a researcher of the Brazilian National Council for Scientific and Technological Development since 2007. Her main lines of interest are in modern philosophy, new ontologies, and ecological thought. Among her recent publications are "Ordem e desordem na *Teodiceia* de Leibniz," "David Hume, o começo e o fim," "O hiperrealismo das mudanças climáticas e as várias faces do negacionismo,"

"Predicados como acontecimentos em Leibniz," "Um mundo vivo: Sobre a *Encíclica Laudato Si'*" (in print), and, with Eduardo Viveiros de Castro, *The Ends of the World*.

MARISOL DE LA CADENA teaches at UC Davis; she was trained as an anthropologist in Peru, England, France, and the US. The Andes of Peru have been her field site, and recently she has been working in Colombia. Thinking through ethnographic concepts, she has published extensively on race and indigeneity; her current work is on multispecies political economies.

JOHN LAW is emeritus professor in sociology at the Open University, UK, and holds visiting and honorary appointments at the Sámi University of Applied Sciences and in science studies at Lancaster University. He has worked on actor-network theory and its successor projects, on methods in practice, and on human-animal relations. He now works primarily on the power-saturated (post)colonial intersections between Euro-American technoscience and non-Western practices, knowledges, and realities.

MARIANNE LIEN is professor of social anthropology at the University of Oslo. She has done research in Norway and Australia on topics including food production and consumption, nature, and domestication practices. She leads a research team at Center for Advanced Study (CAS) on Arctic Domestication in the Era of the Anthropocene (2015–16). Her most recent book is *Becoming Salmon: Aquaculture and the Domestication of a Fish* (2015).

ISABELLE STENGERS, professor at the Université Libre de Bruxelles, has written numerous books, among which have been published in English, *Order out of Chaos* with Ilya Prigogine, *A Critique of Psychoanalytical Reason* with Léon Chertok, *A History of Chemistry* with Bernadette Bensaude-Vincent, *Power and Invention: Situating Science*, *The Invention of Modern Science*, *Capitalist Sorcery: Breaking the Spell* with Philippe Pignarre, *Women Who Make a Fuss* with Vinciane Despret, *Thinking with Whitehead*, *Cosmopolitics I* and *II*, and *Catastrophic Times*. Starting with the defense of the passionate adventure of physics against its enrollment as model of rationality and objectivity, she has developed the concept of an ecology of practices affirming a speculative constructivism in relation with the philosophy of Gilles Deleuze, Alfred North Whitehead, and William James and the anthropology of Bruno Latour.

MARILYN STRATHERN is emeritus professor of social anthropology at the University of Cambridge and (honorary) life president of the Association of Social Anthropologists (of the UK and Commonwealth).

HELEN VERRAN is professor on the Contemporary Indigenous Knowledge and Governance team at Charles Darwin University's Northern Institute in Australia. Previously she taught history and philosophy of science at University of Melbourne for twenty-five years. Her best-known publication is *Science and an African Logic*.

EDUARDO VIVEIROS DE CASTRO is professor of social anthropology at the Museu Nacional (Universidade Federal do Rio de Janeiro), where he has taught since 1978. He was Simon Bolívar Professor of Latin American Studies at Cambridge University (1997–98) and directeur de recherches at the CNRS (1999–2001). He has been doing ethnographic research in indigenous Amazonia since 1975. His main publications are *From the Enemy's Point of View*, *A Inconstância da Alma Selvagem*, *Cannibal Metaphysics*, and *The Relative Native*.

INDEX

nature and culture and, 141–42; nature and
politics and, 177–78; nonmoderns and, 184;
Pacific Island academics and, 26; pluriverse
and, 2–4; politics and, 188; scholarly versus
political recognition of, 2–3; science and, 177,
182; universal interests and, 183; victims and
culprits and, 176; world state and, 199n55.
See also acidification; emissions; environmentalism; resistance
"The Climate of History" (Chakrabarty), 172–74,
176
cod, 159n13, 160n15, 161n28
coercion/persuasion axis, 115
coevolution, 91
Cold War nuclear crisis, 182, 196n16
collective and individual, 24
colonialism, 3, 16, 18, 95, 99, 143, 158, 194.
See also decolonial practice
Columbus, Christopher, 191, 200n69
coming together of heterogeneous components,
105
commitments, 99
commoditization, 152
common good, 2, 4, 18–19
common interests: Amerindians and, 190; survival proposals and, 3; symbiosis and, 50n66;
that are not the same interest, 6, 9–10, 12–14,
20n17, 50n66. *See also* climate crisis; common
world; cosmopolitics; divergence; end of the
world as we know it; interests; uncommons
commons. *See* uncommons
common world, 3, 177, 183, 192
communities, 7, 96
community garden stand, 70–72, 71f, 73, 74
concept duplication that is not quite duplication,
24, 25
concepts: crisis of, 17–18; difference between
knowers and, 10–11; effects and, 41–42;
ethnography and, 5; math curriculum and, 115,
118, 124–25; multiverse and, 112; as worlding
tools, 5. *See also* Anthropocene; knowledge;
knowledge, concept of *and other concepts*;
modern knowledge
concepts of concepts, 6–12, 46n8. *See also* culture:
concept of; knowledge, concept of; relations,
concept of; "what concepts think concepts"
conceptual furniture, 69–75
conflicts of opinion: cosmological, 5; diplomacy
and, 83; European philosophers and, 84; Greek
politics and, 93; knowledge exchange and,

44; perspectivism and, 5; relations and, 33;
"ritual," 36–38, 49n47. *See also* culprits and
victims; human remains in museums; interests; perspectivalism; polarization; Science
Wars; war
conservationists, 95–96, 143, 148
contrapuntal likeness, 64
Cook, Captain, 162n43
copresent states of affairs, 41
corporations, 2, 70, 73–74, 176, 182, 188, 189.
See also extractivism
Corsín Jiménez, Alberto, 7–8, 41, 42. *See also*
spiderweb trap metaphor
cosmocentrism, 179
cosmologies, 112–13, 119. *See also* cosmopolitics;
worlding practices
cosmonauts, 80n61
Cosmopolis (Toulmin), 110n13
cosmopolitanism, 85, 127
cosmopolitics: agency of concepts of relations
and, 28; characterized, 12, 16–17, 120; civilized
practitioners and, 90–95, 96, 97, 99–100;
difference between knowers and, 12, 115; end
of the world and, 16–17; ethos and, 114–15,
120; Gaia war and, 178; ontological politics
and, 12–14, 93–98; other-than-humans and,
99–100; relations and, 28, 114; supplanting
and, 24; Terrans and, 183. *See also* civilized
practitioners; common interests; diplomacy;
divergence; epistemic practices and demeanor;
indigenous cosmopolitics; relations, opening
up; speculative openings
Costa, Alyne, 197n36
Cranach the Elder, Lucas, 142, 143f
crises of destruction of Earth, 4
critical sociology, 175, 195n10
Cronon, William, 134, 151, 153
Crook, Tony, 26, 45n7
crossroads, 5, 19n6
Crutzen, Paul J., 1, 3
Cuban divination, 37
culprits and victims, 16, 94–95, 99–100, 176, 177,
196n17
culture: concept of, 7, 17–18, 35–36, 48n42; difference and, 20n10; divergence compared, 10; history and, 7; nature and, 2, 14–15, 17–18, 24–25,
133–58; as object, 25; relative ontologies and, 84;
Romanticism and, 153; worldings and, 9. *See also*
culture: concept of; history; indigenous people;
ontological politics

interface: spiderweb trap metaphor and and, 63–64, 64–65, 66

intersections, 42, 43

intolerance, 13

invaded invaders, 194

The Invention of Modern Science (Stengers), 88

isonomia, 83

James, William, 103, 106, 112, 166n81

Jeremijenko, Natalie, 67

Jotunheim massif, 153

Kafka, Franz, 184

Katzschner, Tania, 95–96

Kelly, Ann, 61

"key," 183, 197n39

kinship, 29–32, 48n32, 117, 118, 124–25, 187

Kinship, Law and the Unexpected: Relatives Are Always a Surprise (Strathern), 46n8

knowers, 12, 13–14, 34, 120, 121–27, 128. *See also* difference between knowers; encounters and engagement; Europeans; indigenous people; relations; subject/object relation

knowledge: detachment and, 34; differences and, 33; indigenous, 46n10; kinship and, 29–32; land shamanism and, 55; as means to knowledge, 23, 25; modern, 6–12, 14, 56–57, 119; nonrelational forms of, 41–45; objects as actors and, 27–28; relations and, 23–35, 40–41, 44, 47n28, 48n36; relations through relations and, 44–45; representation and, 87; Romanticism and, 153; situation, 27–28; subject-object mode of relationality and, 24–25; traps and, 75; what counts as, 47n26; worlding and, 6–7. *See also* Anthropocene; anthropology; concepts; domains; epistemic practices and demeanor; knowers; knowledge, concept of; knowledge exchange/sharing; not-knowing; scholarly knowledge and academics; science; storytelling (*torías*)

knowledge, concept of: domains and, 23–24; as means to knowledge, 23, 25, 28, 34–35; relations and, 31–35; science wars and, 85

knowledge exchange/sharing (knowledge economy): actors (agency) and, 28; attachment and detachment and, 33–35; difference and divergence and, 44; dissent and, 92; ethos and, 114; indigenous knowledge and, 46n10; other people's unknowns and, 35–41; relations and, 27, 48n32; subject/object relation and,

26. *See also* cosmopolitics; encounters and engagements; human remains in museums; mathematics curriculum

Kuma people, 36–38, 40–41, 49n47

laboratory things, 13

La Mesa (citizen's round table), 70–72, 71f, 73, 75

landscape, 33, 154–55, 165n79. *See also* place; space

land shamanism, 55, 69

Langåker, R. M., 150f, 151, 152

language, 59, 66, 84, 116, 121–22, 184

Latin America, 1–2, 193–94

Latour, Bruno: on actor-network theory, 160n17; on climate change denial, 182; demos, theos, nomos and, 196n20; fright and, 100; Gaia war and, 176, 177–94, 197n36; humans ↓ nonhumans and, 194; limits and, 199n56; nature and politics and, 177–78; on pacification of modernization, 86; "Parliament of Things" of, 93, 94; on pluriverse, 166n81; Wilson and, 195n6. *See also Inquiry into Modes of Existence*

Law, John, 15, 32, 47n23. *See also* salmon in Norway

laws, atemporal and universal, 179, 196n23

Leach, James, 33–35, 36

"learning from," 90–91

learning roundtable (*mesa de aprendizaje*), 72–73

leppefisk (lip fish), 139

"Libel on the Human Race" (Shapin), 197n35

Lien, Marianne, 15. *See also* salmon in Norway

limits, 186, 199n56

Lispector, Clarice, 198n46

the living, 31, 179, 180, 187, 192. *See also* other-than-humans

living in the ruins, 108, 109

"long networks," 185, 198n50

loops, 186, 199n56

Lovelock, James, 179, 180

Luhmann, Niklas, 24, 43, 45n4, 50n64

Luhrmann, Tanya, 110n22

machine, hegemonic, 50n63, 86–87, 91–92, 97, 109. *See also* extractivism

Madrid Occupy (May 15, 15M movement), 69

Madrid's City Hall, 69–70, 70–73, 71f, 73–74

magic, 104, 106–7, 109

magnetism, 100–101, 110n13

Malthus, Thomas Robert, 197n35

Mann, Charles, 200n69

"many worlds are walked in one world," 1

Paraguayan shamans, 48n38

Parikka, Jussi, 66

Paris Agreement, 195n4

partial connections (↓): divergence of practices and, 5, 91; encounters and, 9, 10; living in ruins and, 108, 109; ontological politics and, 146–49; practices and, 127–28, 132; science and, 90, 91; Yolngu Aboriginal "mathematics" and, 113–15, 119. *See also* both/and natures; common interests: that are not the same interest; concept duplication that is not quite duplication; cosmopolitics; divergence; entanglements; mutual inclusion; together while separate

participation in assemblages, 59, 105–6, 107, 128. *See also* dialogue; resistance

particulars, 132–33

parts and wholes, 16, 23–24, 25, 27, 43, 113, 118, 124. *See also* environments; singularity and multiplicity

Peeples, Lynn, 199n61

Peircean ideas, 196n23

"people that is missing," 198n46

persons: environments and, 69; landscapes and, 33; relations and, 27, 28, 31, 39; ↓ resources, 5. *See also* other-than-humans; perspectives; relations

perspectivalism, 61; Amerindian, 195n9; Euro-American, 47n23, 132, 166n83. *See also* relativism

perspectives (viewpoints), 30–32, 34

persuasion/coercion axis, 115

Peru, 2

phantom public, 184, 198n46

philosophy, Western, 83–85, 179

physics, 84, 87–88

Pig Ceremonial, 36–38, 49n49

place, 5, 33, 122–23, 124. *See also* landscape; space

place-soul, 55

planet Commodity, 191

Plato, 104, 110n21

pluriversal worlding (world of many worlds): academics and, 2, 108; Anthropocene and, 1–3, 14–17; ecological crisis and, 2–4; extractivism and, 5–6; fieldwork and, 4–5; Gaia and, 180; James and, 166n81; Romanticism and, 155–56. *See also* anthropology; cosmopolitics; Gaia; multiverse; one-world world; ontological politics; speculative openings; spiderweb trap metaphor

plurivocality, 129n6

Plus intra, 186

plus ultra!, 191, 194

polarization, 46n19, 46n19

police operations, 86, 178

"political animals," 84

political ecology, 5, 12–14

political economy, 5

political gatherings. *See* uncommons

political ontology. *See* ontological politics

political theology of nature, 177–78, 182, 196n20

politics: Anthropocene and, 188; Australian, 115–16; baroque art and, 59; disconnected from equality, 83; ethical, 10–11, 114–15; math curriculum and, 129n6; modern cosmology and, 119; modern multiverse and, 158; naturalization and, 132; nature and, 177–78; nonmoderns and, 184; postcolonial, 148–49; psycho, 187; relational or nonrelational phenomena and, 45; salmon farming and, 160n16; scholarship's recognition of ecological crisis and, 2–3; science and, 182; technology and, 43–44; Terrans and, 182; truth and, 163n58. *See also* Australians; nationalism

Polynesians, 187

polytheism, 153

Popper, Karl, 164n66

porridge feud, 166n80

possibilities. *See* speculative openings

postcolonialism, 158n1

postcolonial politics, 148

power: benevolence and, 17–18; the modern and, 131; of other-than-humans, 13, 100; of police, 86, 178; of scholarly knowledge, 108–9. *See also* colonialism; energy consumption; machine, hegemonic; one-world world; ontological politics

"practice of realization," 14. *See also* reality, existence, and objectivity

practices: concepts and, 112; constituitiveness versus divergence and, 28–29; cosmopolitics and, 127–28; crossroads of, 19n6; ecologies of, 29, 91, 92; existence and, 132; fly-fishing, 136–37; knowers and, 126–27; modern, scientific, 86, 87–92, 100–101; the modern and, 132–33; nature and, 131–32, 147; as objects of knowledge, 27–28; ontological politics and, 146–49, 156–57; partial connections (↓) and, 127–28, 132; persons ↓ resources, 5; possibilities and, 4–5, 157–58; relations and, 134–35,

relevance, 90

religion, 184. *See also* Christianity; Evangelicals; God; gods; myths; political theology of nature; polytheism; shamans

Rembrandt, 59

Renaissance, 110n13

repatriation, 46n10. *See also* human remains in museums

The Report of the Working Group on Human Remains (dcms), 30, 46nn18–19, 47n27

representation, symbolic, 59, 66, 87, 89, 160n16. *See also* nonrepresentational activity; symbolic infrastructure

resefisk (cleaning fish), 139

resistance (activism) (dissent) (protests): to extractivism, 3–4; Gaia War and, 187; knowledge and, 30–31; knowledge economy and, 92; Mayan, 193–94; the modern and, 131, 132; negotiation/cosmopolitics and, 93–96; ontological politics and, 149; political ontology and, 6; Terrans and, 184. *See also* dissensus; environmentalism; participation in assemblages

resources, 70. *See also* extractivism; salmon in Norway

resources ↓ persons, 5

respect, 84–85

restitution, 29

The Reverse of a Framed Painting (Gijsbrechts), 57–61, 58f

reversibility, 59. *See also* doubling

Rheinberger, Jans-Jörg, 62

Rimbaud, Arthur, 184

"ritual" conflict, 36–38

Romanticism, 134, 136–37, 147, 148f, 152–56, 154f, 163n53, 165n73

Roundup herbicide, 188

ruins, living in, 108, 109

Saenredam, Pieter, 59

Sahlins, Marshall, 78n38

salmon in Norway: acidification and, 149–51, 150f; domestication of, 159n13; escaped, 137, 137–38f, 145–46, 160n15, 161n19, 161n28, 161n30; farmed, 134, 137–38f, 148f, 159n13, 160n16, 161n28, 162n32, 162n35, 162n42; fieldwork methods, 159n4, 159n13; hatchery experiments and, 137, 161n26; nature and culture and, 15, 133–58, 160n16, 162n43, 164n59, 178; ontological politics and, 135; practices and, 132, 147–48; prelapsarian world filled with, 142–44; sea lice and, 139–40; statistics, 140–43f, 150f, 161n30, 162n32, 162n40; wild, 136–38f, 140–42, 141, 144–46, 159n13, 161n28, 162n40, 162n42, 164n59; worldings and, 134–46; world without domesticated, 134–36; wrasse and, 139, 162n32. *See also* fly-fishing; selective breeding

Sandøy, Steinar, 150f, 151, 152

scales, 16, 185, 191, 192, 198n50

Schmitt, Carl, 176–77, 182, 188, 199n55

scholarly knowledge and academics, 2–3, 6–7, 26, 97–102, 106, 108–9, 182. *See also* concepts

science: climate change deniers and, 163n58; climate disorder and, 177, 182; deconstruction of, 88–89; entrepreneurs who might be civilized and, 97; fright and, 98; Gaia war and, 178, 179, 181; imperialism and, 86; indigenous people and, 46n19, 47n20; mutual inclusion and, 164n59; nature and, 179–80; ontological politics and, 87–91; plurivocality and, 129n6; politics and, 182; practices of, 86, 87–92, 100–101; "real" existence and, 101; reality and, 87–90, 100–101, 151–52, 165nn68–69; singular nature and, 149–50; slow, 180; small, 179–80; unity of, 89, 90. *See also* civilized practitioners; genetically modified organisms (gmos); human remains in museums; knowledge; mapping; modern knowledge; mosquito experiment; observation versus theory; physics; rationality; technology

science and technology studies (sts), 131–32, 134–35, 156, 160n16, 160n18

Science Wars, 85, 87–88, 93–94

sea lice, 139–40, 141

seduction, 73–74, 76

seeds, 187, 188

selective breeding, 144–46, 163n54

self-description, 45n4

self-reference, 43, 50n64. *See also* doubling

senses, 103–4

servants of the machine. *See* machine, hegemonic

shamans, 8, 48n38, 103–4. *See also* land shamanism; technoshamanism

Shapin, Steven, 197n35

Shepard, Mark, 67

Siberian Yukaghir hunters, 41–43, 44

silver-covered nomads, 137

singularity and multiplicity, 131–32, 134, 146–52, 153, 155–58, 177–78. *See also* essentialism; parts and wholes

Situationists, 68

39351924R00144

Made in the USA
San Bernardino, CA
19 June 2019